Deleuze and the Social

Deleuze Connections

'It is not the elements or the sets which define the multiplicity. What defines it is the AND, as something which has its place between the elements or between the sets. AND, AND, AND – stammering.'

Gilles Deleuze and Claire Parnet, *Dialogues*

General Editor
Ian Buchanan

Editorial Advisory Board
Keith Ansell-Pearson
Rosi Braidotti
Claire Colebrook
Tom Conley
Gregg Lambert
Adrian Parr
Paul Patton
Patricia Pisters

Titles in the Series
Ian Buchanan and Claire Colebrook (eds), *Deleuze and Feminist Theory*
Ian Buchanan and John Marks (eds), *Deleuze and Literature*
Mark Bonta and John Protevi (eds), *Deleuze and Geophilosophy*
Ian Buchanan and Marcel Swiboda (eds), *Deleuze and Music*
Ian Buchanan and Gregg Lambert (eds), *Deleuze and Space*
Ian Buchanan and Adrian Parr (eds), *Deleuze and the Contemporary World*

Forthcoming
Constantin V. Boundas (ed.), *Deleuze and Philosophy*

Deleuze and the Social

Edited by Martin Fuglsang
and Bent Meier Sørensen

Edinburgh University Press

© in the edition, Edinburgh University Press, 2006
© in the individual contributions is retained by the authors

Edinburgh University Press Ltd
22 George Square, Edinburgh

Typeset in 10.5/13 Sabon
by Servis Filmsetting Ltd, Manchester, and
printed and bound in Great Britain by
The Cromwell Press, Trowbridge, Wilts

A CIP record for this book is available from the British Library

ISBN-10 0 7486 2092 3 (hardback)
ISBN-13 978 0 7486 2092 0 (hardback)
ISBN-10 0 7486 2093 1 (paperback)
ISBN-13 978 0 7486 2093 7 (paperback)

The right of the contributors
to be identified as authors of this work
has been asserted in accordance with
the Copyright, Designs and Patents Act 1988.

Contents

Acknowledgements

The editors would like to thank Edinburgh University Press for its support for the making of this book, a support which was steadfastly personified in Jackie Jones. We are also grateful for the enthusiastic efforts of the anonymous reviewers at EUP, which moved us to enlarge the group of contributors. Ian Buchanan's invaluable advice as series editor throughout the process proves that Deleuzism is not a concept, but a practice, indeed, a set of practices always pertaining to the body without organs.

In a book such as this one, the texture of the language itself is of course of enormous importance. In this regard we would like to thank Alberto Toscana for his precise translation, Thomas Basbøll for his detailed line-editing, and Henrik Bjelke Hansen for his meticulous efforts at checking the accuracy of references and copy-editing the final drafts.

The Copenhagen Business School has contributed financially to this edition, allowing us to let more non-native English speakers into the book. For this we are very grateful.

As editors, we could, of course, take responsibility for the textual obscurities that might remain throughout the book. Humility, however, prevents us from doing so. We fully expect that it is from these very zones of indiscernability that this book's most substantial lines of flight will depart. In many ways, they are the reason we wanted to make this book and, in the end, they belong to no one. They are what is to come.

Deleuze and the Social: Is there a D-function?

Martin Fuglsang and Bent Meier Sørensen

In the midst of the delirium of *Anti-Oedipus*, Gilles Deleuze and Félix Guattari calmly inform us that we 'always make love with worlds' (1984: 294). This marks their final transgression of the repressive segmentation of contemporary critique: the segmentation of the libidinal economy and the political economy, desire production and social production, Freud and Marx. In the Oedipal triangle and its double bind, desire was forever betrayed and political critique was forever kept from connecting with the real processes of production. This impasse is still with us: contemporary sociology makes love with no worlds we are aware of; social and economic analysis in general is paralysed before the problem of liberating desire, criticising its capture and expressing its abundance.

But is it feasible to put together a book that makes love with worlds? It will, in any case, put us in the volatile position of the alcoholic engaged in the experiment of drinking, always searching for the penultimate rather than the ultimate drink. The penultimate drink is a limit of relative deterritorialisation (you change, but you don't leave), whereas the threshold is the ultimate drink that will make the alcoholic change assemblage altogether, progressing into a hospital assemblage or a suicide assemblage. The penultimate drink will enable him to keep on drinking, living, moving, loving, while the ultimate drink is the end (Deleuze and Guattari 1987: 438).

A book such as this should be penultimate, not only because it is in its actualisation in the life of the reader that the experiment should prove its worth, but also because 'the social' in the works of Deleuze and Guattari can only be approached as a liminal experience, that is, as the penultimate task in an infinite experiment, an event of counter-actualisation (Deleuze 1990: 150). The social certainly has an absolute limit: the plane of immanence or the body without organs. But we can't stay there, for it is here that the fatal breakdown of the schizophrenic occurs; it is here that we find cases to fill the textbooks on the clinically insane. If Deleuze and Guattari can report that they have never seen such a schizophrenic, we are less certain, perhaps more afraid. On these pages we can only try to construct a body without organs as the relative limit of a specific and concrete social situation. To construct this body, to edit this book, is to make love with worlds.

The body without organs is unquestionably a dangerous 'set of practices', but so are the strata from which desire constantly escapes and to which it returns through processes of deterritorialisation and reterritorialisation (Deleuze and Guattari 1987: 149–50). The strata are the habitual and 'striated' orderings of all productive processes as they become actualised in the world. Even if the strata are necessary, even if they cannot be judged good or bad, they systematically suffer from a lack of consistency. They can afford this because there are strong forces to support them: everyday practice, habit, stupidity, capital. The primary stratifications are, as Foucault taught us, knowledge and power, and to this *A Thousand Plateaus* adds the three stratifications of the Organism, Signification and Subjectivation as specifically modern maladies. These establish the dominant strata: Organism and Discipline, Sign and Interpretation, Subject and Subjectivation:[1]

> [1.] You will be organised, you will be an organism, you will articulate your body – otherwise you're just depraved.
> [2.] You will be signifier and signified, interpreter and interpreted – otherwise you are just a deviant.
> [3.] You will be a subject, nailed down as one, a subject of the enunciation recoiled into a subject of the statement – otherwise you are just a tramp. (Deleuze and Guattari 1987: 159)

'The social' is only grasped in the dynamic relation between the strata and the plane, and it is to be construed as an actualisation of the 'machinic assemblage', which is situated between the strata and the plane of immanence (cf. ibid.: 506ff.). It is with the concept of the assemblage that Deleuze and Guattari manage to replace and reconfigure the staple sociological and philosophical issue of the relationship between the human and its world (Buchanan 2000: 120).

It also changes the status of the body. The diagrammatic relationship between desiring machines and the body without organs sets the conceptualisation of the body against a remarkably new horizon of sense. The body is of course corporeal, tattooed and scarified by common sense and embedded in the informational and communicative arrangement we call our everyday life. But at the same time the body is incorporeal, that is, transformed by the incorporeality of sense itself, announcing the order-word (*mot d'ordre*) as a unique kind of 'action' constituted by the incision of the event. 'Nothing happens, and yet everything changes, because becoming continues to pass through its components again and to restore the event that is actualised elsewhere, at a different moment' (Deleuze and Guattari 1994: 158). This logic of sense coincides with the biopolitical production of affective effects and sets new standards for social analysis. It has to transgress the idea of action as a marriage between causality and human intention and establish *another awareness*, adding to the notion of action which effects the body as an actualised entity in the social organisation. This affords us a notion of action that transforms the body's incorporeal attributes through statements, that is, pure sense-events that change the sensible arrangement and compositional architecture of the body and thereby actualising it in a new affective state organised by a new socio-machinic production, new abstract machines.

This particular connection between production and sense, that is, the corporeal differenciation of the actual and the incorporeal differentiation of the virtual (cf. Deleuze 1994: 209), is the prime organiser of the *socius*. This opens the horizontal axis of the collective assemblages of enunciation and the forms of content to analysis and enables a diagnosis of the vertical diagrammatic axis of the processes of de- and reterritorialisation on the strata.

The strata, too, are children of love.

> [T]here are no revolutionary or reactionary loves . . . [but] . . . there are forms of love that are the indices of the reactive or the revolutionary character of the investment made by the libido of a sociohistorical or geographic field, from which the loved and desired beings receive their definition. (Deleuze and Guattari 1984: 365–6; see also Patton 2000: 77)

The various forms of love correspond to the predicament of any machinic assemblage as it finds itself situated between the strata (the plane of organisation: organisms, signs and subjects) and the plane of immanence (where everything is in a state of transformation). Love as a method experiments with bringing any given assemblage out of joint, unbalancing what seems to be balanced, disorganising what appears organised: 'This is the model of the pendulum or balance wheel, the *Unruhe*, that replaces the scale' (Deleuze 1993: 69). Contrary to the scale that subsumes everything under the same categories (metres, dollars), the pendulum is sensitive to the tiniest deviation in height and weight. And even the scale itself and its corresponding principles experience a crisis: 'we shall multiply principles – we can always slip a new one out from under our cuffs – and in this way we will change their use' (ibid.: 67). To experiment with the social, which is the foolhardy principle of this book, is to configure the social scientist along with the philosopher as a lover, or, as a friend. Terrifying as it is, one must 'reach that twilight hour when one distrusts even the friend' (Deleuze and Guattari 1994: 2). In this twilight of combat the relevance of Deleuze's slogans is tested: 'Thought should be thrown like a stone by a war-machine' (Deleuze and Parnet 1987: 31).

Everything is political. No, we are not too proud to resort to slogans. If social analysis aims at being non-transcendent and hostile to any image of thought, it should effect a diagonal movement between an actualised history and the event of the problem produced by the analysis, an event that is 'immaterial, incorporeal, unlivable: pure *reserve*' (Deleuze and Guattari 1994: 156). It is the concept itself that is able to bring the problem through its critical thresholds towards the problematic, where it will revolt. That is why the intuitive, critical method of creating concepts is so vital to Deleuze and Guattari (ibid.: Chapter 1). The problematic is realised in a milieu as a revolutionary becoming, a conjunction of philosophy, or of the concept, with the present milieu, designating the birth of a *political philosophy* (ibid.: 100). Social analysis seen from this point of view is the analysis of the event as a multiplicity, or the analysis of the sayable and the visible and their interrelation as fundamentally *ontological modalities* of signs.

The twentieth century will not likely be called the Deleuzian century. The deadly limbo of the twenty-first century is a more plausible candidate, faced with the withering of civil society, fascism in the streets and in our daily practices, mutant flows of migrations on account of exploitation, and a rampant, world-integrated capitalism deterritorialising the *socius*, the need for an at once critical and affirmative social science should be apparent. This need has hardly been satisfied, and, even more disturbing, the analysis of the social has in recent years lost a great deal of its enunciative force. This is why we at the same time have witnessed a search for new approaches that are able to convey a higher degree of concreteness and precision in the social scientific approach to the emergence, production and organisation of the social. A number of the chapters deal with organisation theory, and the tendency of a sadly diminishing return is especially visible when the concern is research within management and organisation. Here, German phenomenology and especially French post-war philosophy have been dominant in the attempt to revitalise the discourse. It seems nevertheless as if these new approaches remain caught in the resentment typical of the academic showdown: negation rather than affirmation, destruction rather than creation. Hence, the quest of *thinking anew* is lost at the outset: Oedipus got us again.

Perhaps this is because contemporary social analysis is still concerned with what Foucault characterised as 'disciplinary societies' (Deleuze 1992b). They focus on binary segmentations of the social field (as for instance in dualisms of dominant and dominated) even though the flow of capital and the fluidity of its organisational principles is guided by quite different kinds of segmentations and different kinds of power relations: those of biopolitical production and of the re-production of life itself (Hardt and Negri 2000: 24). It is a power that does not just produce segmentations, organising only the movements of the body, but also functions as a virtual and immanent self-circulation of thoughts and actions within the body under the auspices of humanistic 'freedom'. In this sense, external disciplinary authority has become an internal principle of regulation and control in the social *bios* as such, not so much in its actualised institutions and organisations, but directly in relation to the transformation of their flows of matter and function, where their expressions and contents emerge. It is as Maurizio Lazzarato points out in his discussion of the difference between disciplinary societies and control societies, 'the non-relation as the informal "outside", a virtual, an event' which is confined by the biopolitical sphere Deleuze calls the societies of control.

When the biopolitical power-function works directly on the plane of matter-function it is not enough to construct social analysis solely on epistemological premises, which is to say, as a specific perspective or gaze. Such epistemological premises only focus on the sayable and the visible, and not the ontological modalities of signs that are produced in the actualisation of the social. We are, so to speak, in need of another analytical project, which one could call the constitution of social analytics that seriously engages itself in the fact, there are statements (*énoncés*) which have their own materiality, and it is by this existence of signs, as order-words, that we indeed are able to speak of a societal body. Social analytics is therefore a diagnostics of signs and their materiality. This line of thought is indebted to the somewhat overlooked third part of Foucault's *The Archaeology of Knowledge* (1972), where Foucault already sketches the problem that was to become central for Deleuze and Guattari, namely, the problematisation of the verb 'to be'.

> The threshold of the statement is the threshold of the existence of signs. Yet even here, things are not so simple, and the meaning of a term like 'existence of signs' requires elucidation. What does one mean when one says that there are signs, and that it is enough for there *to be* signs for there *to be* a statement? What special status should be given to that verb *to be*? (Foucault 1972: 84–5)

It is from the plane of the sign-materiality (which is really the plane of immanence), and not the plane of organisation that a new composition of social analyses must arise, a tactics that engages directly in and on the order-word.

Traditionally the social sciences have concerned themselves with the order of things, to deploy a Foucauldian pun. Deleuze and Guattari, however, turn our attention away from the plane of organisation, where a constant inscription and apparent stabilisation is taking place. Entities are thereby erected by different sedimentary processes: subjects (consider the efforts of Descartes), social contracts (Hobbes) and stabilised 'social facts' (Durkheim).

So this book should serve two purposes. First, it seeks precision in the comprehension of the multiplicity of the social, that is, the *process of the becoming of the social* itself. Second, it explores the consequences of such an approach in regard to specific studies, that is, it seeks to develop the contours of a *new social analytical practice*. This implies, in Deleuze and Guattari, an overflight with infinite speed or what Jameson calls 'stereo-scopic thinking' (1990: 28ff.) indicating possible counter-actualisations in which a nomad science, as developed in *A Thousand Plateaus*, plays a crucial role. Social analysis must be thought of as pure affirmation that displays the strength of the radicalism implied in a Deleuzian approach to critique while at the same time practising it. In other words, the *raison d'être* of this collection of texts is to explore how the work of Deleuze and Guattari can be put to work, rather than to display what it means. It is not a book in the growing group of introductions and interpretations. They have their own *raison d'être* considering the vast scope and unparalleled complexity of Deleuze's and Guattari's independent works, as well as their collaborations. At the same time, however, they also have their pitfalls: a reduction of complexity instead of a humble respect for the irreducible, a translation of concepts instead of a creation of concepts, a plane of scholastic organisation instead of a line of flight.

The trick is to start in the middle, where things pick up speed. The middle is necessarily constituted by the already familiar distinctions of social science, and to pick up speed is to re-create its concepts from within. The aim is not so much *novelty* as precision and consistency; that is, the aim is greater *creativity* when compared with the practice of social science to which we have grown accustomed. Growing accustomed is ultimately a reductionist and stratifying stance while the analysis provided by Deleuze and Guattari, especially in *A Thousand Plateaus*, performs its critique via affirmation (that is, a re-creation of the collective enunciation). When they take up the work of sociologist Gabriel Tarde, who had been almost completely forgotten thanks to the efforts of Emile Durkheim, the point is to show that beneath the dominant tradition within social science, preoccupied with order, stability and purity, another stream exists, a real flow of creative conceptualisations of the social, which is accessible through the concepts of belief and desire (Deleuze and Guattari 1987: 219ff.). This is also what happens in Deleuze's monographs, which document and affirm the existence of a viable alternative to the hegemonic history of philosophy, a virtual multiplicity of ideas, accessible by an imaginative, intuitive and counter-commonsense reading of the history of thought. Just as philosophy must be counter-actualised to release its real forces, the social sciences are in need of an equivalent re-creation.

The first section of the book is concerned with Order and Organisation. It does not only engage in order in the sense of *mot d'ordre*, that is, the order-words or precepts, the stratifying force embedded in every statement, but also order in its common and almost too familiar sense, as it unfolds its existence on an everyday battlefield, or, rather, as it constitutes a battlefield of social analysis. Either the concept of order is valued for its structural lucidity and its organisational capacity, often appearing as the central concept for general social analyses, or it is perpetually deconstructed using every tool available to the analyst. For that reason alone, Paul Patton's conceptual cartography in regard to the concept of order is vital for everyone conducting social analysis. Order is what protects us from chaos (which in its ultimate sense is death), but more importantly, order as it is found in the Stoic tradition has an immanent *tonos*, a tension that at once moves towards a fixation of thoughts, actions and passions and simultaneously dissolves this fixation, then becoming a structural principle of a different nature. By this token, Patton takes us through the concept of order to the diagrammatic principle of the social, that of the abstract machine, which constitutes and organises the pathologies of our time and which becomes the ontological foundation for the work to be done through its differentiating nature. This ontological foundation belongs as much in the first section as in the book as a whole.

Sure, we always make love with worlds. But as certain: we always fuck it up. Order constantly breaks down; indeed, all abstract machines only work by way of breakdowns (Deleuze and Guattari 1984). These breakdowns are signalled by fear and trembling in the work of Søren Kierkegaard (1983), which Jacques Derrida reads in a thoroughly Deleuzian manner.

I tremble at what exceeds my seeing and my knowing [*mon voir et mon savoir*] although it concerns the innermost parts of me, right down to my soul, down to the bone, as we say. Inasmuch as it tends to undo both seeing and knowing, trembling is indeed an experience of secrecy or of mystery, but another secret, another enigma, or another mystery comes on top of the unliveable experience, adding yet another seal or concealment to the *tremor*. (Derrida 1995: 54)

This reading could also be the epigraph of Torkild Thanem and Stephen Linstead's chapter on the trembling organisation, a chapter that situates the organisation in a continuous transition between the virtual and the actual. The virtual is what Derrida calls 'another mystery', that comes on top of our (already) unliveable experience. Yet the virtual is as real as the actual, as Marcel Proust notoriously put it; the virtual is 'real without being actual, ideal without being abstract' (Deleuze 1994: 208).

Beginning with one of the cornerstones in Deleuze's work, namely, Henri Bergson, Thanem and Linstead highlight the fact that while organisation is not opposed to change, neither is it synonymous with order. Rather, there exist two types of organisation within the theory of multiplicity: one is immanent to life itself, a vitalistic, virtual organisation that is always embedded in *durée*, and another is a spatial multiplicity of exteriority, actualised in scientific clock time. The second, spatial type of organisation is partly responsible for the erection of the strata. But there is no need for frenzied artistry or orgiastic excesses in order for us to evoke the multiple because desire is a much more skilful engineer than the masters of our present predicament. This lets non-organisation express that which 'exceeds my seeing and my knowing', as Derrida put it, which is the autopoiesis of the virtual: trembling, dangerous and joyful.

Moving from the question of what concepts mean to what they do, we are not only engaged in application, but are moved onward and toward the challenge of transferability, which at once inaugurates its own expression and its own field of intervention in a dramatic staging of sense (as explored in Deleuze 1990). Martin Kornberger, Carl Rhodes and René ten Bos develop this line of investigation, deploying the rhizome as it rises *inside* the dominant image of the modern, hierarchical and organic corporation. Thus they produce the image of the 'Organisation-without-Organs' as actualised by Charles Bukowski's literary alter ego, Chinaski. In the vibrant body of Chinaski, subtracted and expanded by the intermingled actions and passions of the mail carrier, we get the sensation that even in the most rigid segmentarity of the expressive flow of organisation, in the hierarchical sedimentation, there is a forceful flow of proliferating lines, always escaping the apparatuses of capture by virtue of its performative nature. If Patton gives a precise and conceptual configuration of order, Kornberger, Rhodes and ten Bos offer the body of Chinaski as a life unfolding through the ordered arena of the organisation, always engaged in processes of deterritorialisation and reterritorialisation, reaching out towards the Organisation-without-Organs.

Order and Organisation are not separate affairs, but engage in numerous becomings. The same goes for Subjectivity and Transformation, which is the theme of the second part of the book. Everything happens in the middle and only the neighbour matters, the middle is where things pick up speed. There is here no lack of Deleuzian slogans to express an idea that goes to the heart of a historical libidinal materialism; indeed, it was already formulated in Deleuze's book on Hume: 'relations are always external to their terms' (1991: 66). This means that individuals and society, the subject and 'the social', are not only empirically inseparable, but are in fact 'strictly simultaneous and consubstantial' (Massumi 2002: 68ff.). Hence, the experiences of subjectivity in social institutions and organisations must concern the states *in between* subject-positions, that is, must concern change. Peter Lohmann and Chris Steyaert's chapter, 'In the Mean Time', endeavours to do exactly this: to produce what they call an exploratory politics of change. The setting is a large organisation in the electricity industry called ELEC, which is faced with the rampant deterritorialising forces of the market and struggling with deregulation and massive layoffs. And, as it were, a perpetually changing organisation. While traditional theorising on change is occupied with control and command, Lohmann and Steyaert deploy a concept of desire that is pure production and excess. The startling story of an accountant from ELEC, whom the change processes push to his ultimate limits, explores and expresses the conditions of the social as it becomes actualised in bodies: 'The body is never in the present, it contains the before and the after, tiredness and waiting' (Deleuze 1989: 189), and, obviously, despair. An accountant might appear substitutable and perhaps even insignificant to the large bureaucracies of the world, yet the small and trivial, as Nietzsche understood, is often the unexpected locus of force, that is, the locus of the people to come.

This people yet to come keeps asking the nagging question, how do we regain our lost place in life? Instead of tracking this question down through well-worn utopian paths, Thomas Bay takes an empirical approach in his chapter. His case is right under our noses since the one who has, by all social indicators, lost a place in life is the beggar. Could we kiss a beggar, or perhaps make love with him or her? In Bay's chapter, begging is constructed as the non-thought within economic thought, or as the absolute and constitutive outside of economy, an outside without which economy would not be an economy, that is a law, *nomos*, of the house, *oikos*.

This confronts us with a Deleuzian reading of Adam Smith. This is most timely, as neo-liberalism only seems to (superficially) know the Smith of *The Wealth of Nations*, and not the Smith of *The Theory of Moral Sentiments*. Bay knows both and on this firm footing he shows that the contractarian theories of society remain in the negative. Deleuze's reading of Hume reveals society not as a set of limitations but as an ongoing 'institutional invention', which must continuously experiment with transformations of our 'limited sympathy' into 'extended generosity'. This schism is traced to the core of legal society, the *nomos*, which signifies both law as limitation and as expanding distribution: *nōmos* and *nomōs* – 'norms of power . . . norms of life' (Deleuze 1992a: 268). Such an experiment gives a whole new meaning to the notion of 'living economically', not least in present-day western societies that celebrate the spirit of capitalism but seem unable to enjoy it because they are permeated with Max Weber's Protestant, that is, Calvinist, ethos. It is here that the beggar might not 'be abolished', as Nietzsche somewhat disconcertingly suggested, but rather be seen as a virtuality with the force to amend radically our power to be affected. This suggestive reading also confirms the intimate relationship between Deleuze and Derrida (explored in Patton and Protevi 2003); it also calls forth what may be their joint utopia, where one gives without expecting returns of investment, a hospitable economy as the initiator of what the present begs so desperately for, namely, the people to come.

There can be no talk of subjectivity and transformation without a discussion of the notion of technology.[2] What, then, is the conception of technology in this volume, and what are its political implications when a recourse to Enlightenment and humanism is no longer possible? This question is taken up by Chris Land in his chapter on cyborgs and organisation. As seemingly radical post-human theories are shown to be subject to 'cosmic evolutionism' and hence reductionism and ideology (Deleuze and Guattari 1987: 49), Land develops the notion of a thorough '*trans*-human becoming', avoiding both post-humanism as well as anti-humanism. As a consequence, the prime signifier (the face) is transformed into a probehead, and the powerful anthropomorphic stratum is deterritorialised so as to re-materialise signs within a substrate of matter. Deleuze and Guattari are also here working as geophilosophers drawing maps of technology laid out on the plane of consistency (cf. the efforts in Sørensen, forthcoming).

'Language is a virus,' said William Borroughs. But the technical social machines of content that works in tandem with the semiotic collective machines of expression are not only viral they are also, on Land's construal, imperialist. Thus, any absolute deterritorialisation becomes a matter of *leaving*. It is time to lose face, suggests Land, and it is time, again quoting Burroughs, to get off this stinking, cop-ridden planet.

A volume on Deleuze and the social will have to include essays taking as points of departure Deleuze's manifold works on art, which he couples directly with the outside. The section Art and the Outside ventures directly into film and the cinema, areas where Deleuze's desire for a reinvention of the world, for a virtualisation of what we see, remained immanent. He invested much of his hope in film and TV, hopes which were largely shattered. Ian Buchanan ventures, nevertheless, into this politically permeated, if not utopian, field. While a number of the chapters in the volume deal with Deleuze's question of how it might be possible again to believe in this world, Buchanan's chapter proceeds from a stark assertion. Post-war Europe, whose ruins and wastelands have now spread like toxic moss across the known universe (to use a Jamesonian image), is a stage that has been cleared. Its people are missing and it looks to us now like a bad film.

The worst thing about this emptiness, this *placelessness*, is its complete lack of an outside, a claustrophobic construction masterly engineered in Hitchcock's films. In the 'non-places' of motels, hotels and malls, no actors move across the field, only mutant seers. What they see are shopping centres eating up places to inhabit and labour-time in which to live. Liminal spaces, which, in Buchanan's analysis, are precisely spaces of belief, have all been vaporised. The continuous existential 'undoing' of these spaces can adequately be expressed by a careful and critical reading of the concepts of deterritorialisation and reterritorialisation. But territory, Buchanan argues, is not primary a placial concept. Rather, it refers to an organisation of desire that may well have a placial dimension, but primarily has to do with our beliefs and allegiances and the ritual and bodily marks that express our social existence. As capitalism frees uncoded flows, 'we' seem to be left with no means to recode and re-ritualise our lives. How can one believe in a world in which the richest 500 are collectively worth more than the poorest 2 billion? Buchanan's own answer is immanent: keep mapping the fields.

The attempt to map the social field has, in recent decades, moved towards expressionism, if you like. This movement seems obvious, once we take into account the fact that aesthetic expressivity has always been about life as it is actualised in affects that move beyond the self-conscious subject. This enables aesthetic expressivity to conjoin but also to confront the biopolitical power of contemporary social production, not only confining the body in circuits of regulation, but also controlling the incorporeal constitution of sense (cf. Deleuze 1990). This is why one cannot say that art has wholesale become a willing servant to world-integrated capitalism, even though the idealistic and romantic idea of the artist as a critical voice is long gone, or, what would be still more horrifying, has reappeared in the technologies of modern management. Rather, we want to emphasise the more subtle point that when aesthetic expression is actualised as an affective ambience it carries a unique resistance in the midst of the biopolitical field. It is this understanding of resistance and counter-actualisation in the centre of order and things that becomes crucial in the constitution of a new social analytical practice, not in the sense that investigation and diagnostics should become artistic expression, but more in the sense that the modalities of art should become a form of biopolitical combat understood as an active ethics of being, far removed from any moral propositions and judgements.

This combat implies a passage to the critical. Deleuze has become increasingly fashionable as one of the few remaining critical voices, too often riding the same bandwagon as Foucault in this regard. Everywhere there is the reduction of the real work of the apparatus to the chatter of discursive formations, a D-formation if you will, a tidy corner in the ongoing academic discourse. Indeed, in his interview with Claire Parnet, Deleuze said that becoming a university professor did not make him especially happy: 'it was simply a normal career'. Like Kafka's famous mouse, however, Deleuze had a talent for 'making a ceremonial performance out of doing the usual thing' (Kafka 1996). There is always a need to sharpen the cutting edges of the machines, to reinvent the critical voice, even if it is as small as Josephine's piping among the greater 'clamour of being'. It was Deleuze's conceptual activism which originally created the fashion for this 'ordinary' song, though his contemporaries perhaps found the military metaphor of the Foucauldian *dispositif* more exciting. As we see it, however, the fashion for military metaphors was always in somewhat poor taste. 'There is a war,' as Leonard Cohen pointed out; it is quite real; and the D-function is a war machine, *no metaphor*.

Understood as a conceptual investigation it certainly appears to be a difficult task to reinvent the D-function, but the difficulties double when one realises that any passive and/or purely scholastic execution of the programme results in transforming Deleuze and Guattari's authorship into a cathedral filled with black holes and white walls (Deleuze and Guattari 1987: 167ff.), haunted by empty signifiers. All this would turn Deleuze into history, rather than into an experimental persona. Such pitfalls are avoided in Éric Alliez's chapter. With a combination of conceptual precision and investigative vitalism, Alliez develops the relation between *Anti-Oedipus* and *The Logic of Sense* in a discussion with Alan

Badiou and Slavoj Žižek on the question of being and, hence, on the question of the political. Alliez re-vitalises the critical and experimental force of *Anti-Oedipus*, showing that it is in *Anti-Oedipus* that the onto-logical monism of Deleuze's biophilosophy becomes a 'biopolitical fact', connecting the univocal plane of the living to desire, to a no less than uni-versal process of production.

The 'current condition', as Marx would have it, of this production is capitalism. The Deleuzian answer is resistance, that is, creativity and affir-mation within the multiplicity of social dramas. The section on Capitalism and Resistance aims at radically broadening the scopes of our current dramas. However, as Maurizio Lazzarato shows in his chapter, disciplin-arity works by exactly conditioning and confining *the outside*. Yet, even as capitalism has found new technologies of capture and of imposing the consumer's free will and deep humanism, the event itself breaks free and forms new monads. The difference between disciplinary societies and control societies is the role the informal 'outside' plays as a virtuality. The production of subjectivity is no longer bound to the disciplinary power that only knows the body and the individual (as in Taylorism and the earlier western welfare regimes), but subjectivity is now submersed and moulded by the biopolitical power that is aimed at 'whatever' multiplicity that passes through the societal body, that is, a global mass specific to life as such. This changes the aim of any social analysis away from binary seg-mentarity towards the concept of 'modulation' in respect to the open and smooth space of control societies; or in short, the modulation of life and the living itself. With Tarde's notion of the public sphere as a gigantic, instantaneous brain, the 'thought brain' from *What is Philosophy?* has received the analytical counterpart necessary for 'whatever' resistance.

Few notions in the work of Deleuze and Guattari have received more attention than that of the nomad. Nomadism has been applied widely and sometimes wildly. While tempered and consciously avoiding this tempta-tion, Holland's chapter brings the concept of the nomad into contact with citizenship. Taking up the distinction between royal science and nomad science, Holland explicates its social consequences, as the two modes of knowledge have different relations to *work*: royal science deterritorialises labour, and makes the intellectual dependent upon the state's power, while nomad science preserves knowledge within the practice of its production (the body without organs is, as might be recalled, not a concept but a set of practices, cf. Deleuze and Guattari 1987: 149–50). Likewise, according to Holland, with jazz and classical music: the manner in which these two musical forms contribute to the organisation of the social field as such is suggestive to the nature of social organisation in general.

A prime social theorist, who is undergoing a revival in social theory, Mary Parker Follett is singled out as what could be called a nomad management theorist, operating with the group rather than the individual, enabling the emergence of horizontal rather than vertical relations of authority. Here arises a concept of 'power-with', which allows us to understanding nomadic, participatory democracy in action. There also arises a welcome occasion to pit Follett (and Deleuze) directly against Carl Schmitt's construction of sovereignty in terms of the enemy – friend distinction. A no less than musical, nomadic form of citizenship, based on group-alliances, is, both on a local and a global level, a faithfully Deleuzian answer to this *impasse*.

Jussi Vähämäki and Akseli Virtanen pose the problem of resistance in terms of multiplicity, overruling the long tradition of establishing binary dualisms of inclusion/exclusion in the social sciences, whether as a strategy that implies the notion of disciplinary societies (Foucault), or the foundation of functional differentiated systems (Niklas Luhmann), or aimed directly at a specific 'object' of social analyses such as the oppressed and/or marginalised social groups imposed by the politics of equality and equal rights. In whatever form this binary segmentation is put to work, it presupposes a conceptualisation of change and history as underpinned by a linear time frame. Such image of history and change is contested by Vähämäki and Virtanen's chapter, where change is developed as creativity without reason and cause, directly related to the effective and affective force of the multitude. In this sense, the concept of multiplicity it brought to bear on capitalism and the problem of change, that is, revolution. Not so much in the sense that it erects a justified or moral rightful political voice, but more in the sense that it points to our understanding of the specific changeable (revolutionary) force we with Marx may call 'living labour': a power that exceeds its historical predicament, but nevertheless conditions our present time, that is, the temporality of a 'we', a people to come.

Revolutions have their contexts, often overlooked in the heat of the moment. Likewise, in analyses of the social from the perspective of Deleuze and Guattari, their 'theory' or perhaps, 'theories' are often either not connected to other social theories at all or are merely linked to the ones that Deleuze and Guattari themselves draw on, for example, Marx, Nietzsche, Blanchot and Tarde. Niels Albertsen and Bülent Diken set out to ameliorate this situation in their chapter named 'Society with/out Organs' in the final section of this volume, Social Constitution and Ontology.

As flux and fluids seem to be what high capitalism thrive on, it is also the base of Deleuze and Guattari's theory of the social (as well, of course, as the mental). Between chaos and consistency, this flux, comprising of different flows, cut off and conjoined by different machines, stabilises into assemblages of matter and form, content and expression. These categories enable Albertsen and Diken to follow the geophilosophical slogan and draw what we consider to be the first of its kind: *a map of Deleuze and Guattari's ontology*. It consists of two axes, one as a continuum between order and chaos, and one as a continuum between purity and heterogeneity. This enterprise gives ample opportunity for comparing a Deleuzian ontology with the one developed by Niklas Luhmann (and to a lesser extent those developed by Pierre Bourdieu and Bruno Latour). It also, if only indirectly, points to the shortcomings of a purely functionalist (e.g., a purely Luhmannian) approach to the problems in the social sciences as they are faced with global streams of capital, rapid changes and mass migration: how should a sober nomadology be deployed when everybody is becoming nomad?

Much contemporary social analysis is exclusively occupied with epistemological premises and presuppositions, thus either neglecting any elaboration of the ontological qualities of Being or unconsciously importing an empty ontology and therefore reducing the univocality of Being to the everyday quarrels of social science in general. In both cases we end up with pure abstractions that mask the fact that any distinction presupposes a totalitarian image of identity from where the differential nature of Being becomes deducted. In the final chapter, written by Manuel DeLanda, we are directly faced with this problem in terms of how we are to analyse the differential properties of scale at work inside the societal body, that is, how are we to avoid the reductionism embedded in the distinctions of scale when we trace and analyse the moveable lines of society? DeLanda goes a long way towards showing that the answer is to deploy the notion of the assemblage for each of the singular, individual entities that comprises each 'level' of the scale, in effect warding off any essentialist presuppositions. DeLanda thus inaugurates a transmission of social ontology into concrete social analysis. He does this by incorporating two strong insights: one is the already noted Humean slogan of the 'exteriority of relations', which leads to a new vibrant empiricism; the other is the assemblage-theory, in which the assemblage constitutes the decisive materiality of the social bios, yet is run through by abstract machines of various kinds.

This transmission must, finally, be placed in the foreground in the creation of a new social analytics, emphasising the ontological constitution of the virtual-real, which becomes the prime diagrammatic component in what could be considered 'empirical'. This liberates the analysis from the fixated anthropological gaze that Foucault warned against, and redirects our attention towards the empirical particles of the virtual, which remain, as indicated earlier, ' "[r]eal without being actual, ideal without being abstract"; and symbolic without being fictional', just as if 'the object had one part of itself in the virtual into which it plunged as though into an objective dimension' (Deleuze 1994: 208–9).

This brings the series of chapters (some will call it a book) to an end. Deleuze and Guattari are quite explicit on this question of series and ends. 'If you're not in some series, even a completely imaginary one, you're lost' (1987: 518). It is, in other words, time for *you* to enter into *your* series (even if it is a completely imaginary one) and find a problem worth problematising. Since problems travel with the abstract machines of a mediating language, which relentlessly threatens to restrict us to 'the lowest level of our virtuality', you must be careful (Massumi 1992: 40). There is more to life than compliance and rejection.

Our advice is to start with a small thing. First realise that we are in a social formation; then see how it is stratified for us and in us and at the place where we are. Next, descend from the strata to the deeper assemblage (cf. Sørensen 2005, if in doubt as to how to proceed). From here, you will have to make the assemblage *pass over to the side of the plane of immanence*. That's the hard part. Tip it gently; don't use a sledgehammer but a very fine file. Count the connections in the assemblage (there will be several), find the rhythm of its trembling (for it *will* tremble), slip into its mean time (for there is always time). Finally, create immanent revolutions (small ones) and lines towards the outside (fast ones) in order to deterritorialise and connect again with an outside.

It is here, when you see the plane at its horizon, that the body without organs reveals itself for what it is: connection of desires, conjunction of flows, continuum of intensities (Deleuze and Guattari 1987: 161). It is here that you enter your becoming *along with the problem that you are problematising*. It is a pure process or a movement with infinite speed, a molecular transmutation that runs from the subject towards a line of flight. Any productive encounter between Deleuze and the social must travel this way. You may, of course, have to repeat the operation.

References

Buchanan, I. (2000), *Deleuzism: A Metacommentary*, Edinburgh: Edinburgh University Press.

Deleuze, G. (1989), *Cinema 2: The Time Image*, trans. H. Tomlinson, Minneapolis: University of Minnesota Press.

Deleuze, G. (1990), *The Logic of Sense*, trans. M. Lester with C. Stivale, New York: Columbia University Press.

Deleuze, G. (1991), *Empiricism and Subjectivity: An Essay on Hume's Theory of Human Nature*, trans. C. V. Boundas, New York: Columbia University Press.

Deleuze, Gilles (1992a), *Expressionism in Philosophy: Spinoza*, trans. M. Joughin, New York: Zone Books.

Deleuze, G. (1992b), ' "Pourparlers" – Postscript on the Societies of Control', trans. M. Joughin, *October*, 59.

Deleuze, G. (1993), *The Fold: Leibniz and the Baroque*, trans. T. Conley, Minneapolis: University of Minnesota Press.

Deleuze, G. (1994), *Difference and Repetition*, trans. P. Patton, New York: Columbia University Press.

Deleuze, G. and Guattari, F. (1984), *Anti-Oedipus*, trans. R. Hurley, M. Seem and H. R. Lane, New York: Viking Press.

Deleuze, G. and Guattari, F. (1987), *A Thousand Plateaus*, trans. B. Massumi, Minneapolis: University of Minnesota Press.

Deleuze, G. and Guattari, F. (1994), *What is Philosophy?*, trans. G. Burchell and H. Tomlinson, New Columbia: University Press.

Deleuze, G. and Parnet, C. (1987), *Dialogues*, trans. H. Tomlinson and B. Habberjam, New York: Columbia University Press.

Derrida, J. (1995), *The Gift of Death*, trans. D. Wills, Chicago: University of Chicago Press.

Foucault, M. (1972), *The Archaeology of Knowledge*, trans. A. M. Sheridan Smith, New York: Pantheon.

Hardt, M. and Negri, A. (2000), *Empire*, Cambridge, MA: Harvard University Press.

Jameson, F. (1990), *Late Marxism: Adorno, or, the Persistence of the Dialectic*, London: Verso.

Kafka, F. (1996), 'Josephine the Singer or the Mouse Folk', in *The Metamorphosis and Other Stories*, New York: Dover.

Kierkegaard, S. (1983), *Fear and Trembling: Repetition*, trans. H. V. Hong and E. H. Hong, Princeton, NJ: Princeton University Press.

Massumi, B. (1992), *A User's Guide to Capitalism and Schizophrenia*, Cambridge: MIT Press.

Massumi, B. (2002), *Parables for the Virtual: Movement, Affect, Sensation*, Durham and London: Duke University Press.

Patton, P. (2000), *Deleuze and the Political*, London: Routledge.

Patton, P. and Protevi, J. (2003), *Between Deleuze and Derrida*, London: Continuum.

Sørensen, B. M. (2005), 'Immaculate Defecation: Gilles Deleuze and Félix Guattari in Organization Theory', in C. Jones and R. Munro (eds), *Contemporary Organization Theory*, Oxford: Blackwell.

Sørensen, B. M. (2006), 'Defacing the Corporate Body. Or, Why HRM Needs a Kick in the Teeth', *Tamara: Journal of Critical Postmodern Organization Science*.

Notes

1. In fact, stratification is a possible malady of any assemblage. A family could suffer from being family-bodies, that is, bodies in a hierarchical and Oedipal relation – too close, too broken – instead of being bodies in diverse conjunctions: brother, sister, whore, Outside, as it is expressed in Kafka's writings.
2. In the series on Deleuze of which the present book is a part a much timely addition on Deleuze and technology is forthcoming.

Part I

Order and Organisation

Chapter 1

Order, Exteriority and Flat Multiplicities in the Social

Paul Patton

Order and Chaos

In *What is Philosophy?* Deleuze and Guattari suggest that all thinking is a way of bringing order out of chaos, whether it takes place in the form of art, philosophy or science. Each of these distinct ways of thinking imposes its own kind of order in accordance with the different materials and methods it brings to the task: percepts and affects in the case of art, concepts in the case of philosophy, functions in the case of science. Order is what protects us from chaos. It enables us to recognise ourselves, each other and the world in which we live. In the absence of the order brought to our perceptions by the pure concepts of human understanding, Kant argued, we would be confronted with nothing more than a disorderly manifold or multiplicity of such perceptions. Order among our percepts and concepts enables us not merely to survive but to conceive and pursue projects which give meaning and purpose to our lives.

However, order can also imprison us in fixed and immobile patterns of thought and action, inhibiting creativity or change. Deleuze and Guattari cite a text of D. H. Lawrence on the source of poetry:

> people are constantly putting up an umbrella that shelters them and on the underside of which they draw a firmament and write their conventions and opinions. But poets, artists, make a slit in the umbrella, they tear open the firmament itself, to let in a bit of free and windy chaos and to frame in a sudden light a vision that appears through the rent – Wordsworth's spring or Cézanne's apple, the silhouettes of Macbeth or Ahab. (Deleuze and Guattari 1994: 203–4)

In these terms, understood as the underside of the umbrella that shields us from chaos, opinions and conventions are the enemy of creativity in all its forms. Opinions and conventions of course occur in a variety of forms, depending upon whether we are talking about theoretical disciplines such as philosophy or science, aesthetic and technical practices such as the various kinds of art, or the forms of practical reason found in ethics and politics. Deleuze and Guattari define everyday opinions as functions linking perceptual properties of things to particular perceptions or affections, and both of these to subjects of a certain kind: 'faithfulness of dogs, detest: dog-haters'; 'foul smell of cheese, love it: bon vivants' and so on. These may be supposed to follow a similar pattern in politics, philosophy, science and art, where opinion and orthodoxy are no less common. In each case, opinions involve associations of ideas that form elements of functions linking certain postulates, doctrines or artistic techniques to affects and subjects of certain kinds. In this manner, they define conservative as opposed to revolutionary thinkers, renegades or apostates as opposed to traditionalists in a given discipline: 'figurative painting, detest: modernists'; 'linguistic determination of categories, abhor: anti-relativists' and so on.

For Deleuze and Guattari, the tendency of thought towards opinion is anathema. They adhere to a Nietzschean image of thought as creation and regard the struggle against chaos as secondary to the more profound struggle against opinion: 'the misfortune of people comes from opinion' (Deleuze and Guattari 1994: 206) That is why they defend a 'utopian' conception of philosophy that bears only a critical relation to the present and that calls for 'a new earth and people that do not yet exist' (Deleuze and Guattari 1994: 108). Their appeal to a 'people to come' does not imply a determinate future form of society. It can only be understood in the sense of Nietzsche's overman or Derrida's absolute future, namely as an appeal to the structural form of a perpetually open future. This is a future that can never be attained but only approached by way of recurrent detours through the chaos that is warded off by opinion. Progress in art, science or philosophy always involves upheavals in thought that allow glimpses of the chaos beyond. Artistic genius, abnormal science and genuine philosophy all seek to 'tear open the firmament and plunge into the chaos' (Deleuze and Guattari 1994: 202).

In each case, the momentary upheaval is resolved by the elaboration of a new style of art, a new philosophical, political or scientific paradigm that involves casting a certain kind of plane over chaos. In the case of philosophy, Deleuze and Guattari call this a plane of immanence or pre-conceptual image of thought that defines what it means to think and what form will be assumed by the concepts produced on this plane. Since these concepts provide the tools with which the philosopher thinks and describes the nature of the world, the construction of concepts on a plane of immanence is indistinguishable from the construction of a world in thought:

> In the end, does not every great philosopher lay out a new plane of immanence, introduce a new substance of being and draw up a new image of thought . . . (Deleuze and Guattari 1994: 51)

The different planes of immanence constructed in the history of philosophy are never produced in isolation from one another or from other ways of thinking such as science, art, religion or the law. They are never constructed in isolation from the social milieu in which philosophical thinking takes place. Deleuze and Guattari argue that certain contingent features of social life in ancient Greece provided the conditions under which philosophical thought could emerge: a particular form of sociability, a certain pleasure in forming and breaking associations and a taste for the exchange of opinions through conversation (Deleuze and Guattari 1994: 87–8). More generally, they argue that all philosophy is geophilosophy in the sense that it is marked by certain features of the time and place in which it is carried out. French, German and English philosophies all bear the stamp of the history and spirit of the people concerned, their respective judgements as to what is right, good or true which form the basis of settled philosophical opinions. In this sense, all philosophy is bound to the social milieu in which it takes place.

The history of philosophy offers us many examples of different planes and different worlds. In *Difference and Repetition*, Deleuze characterises the tradition of thought which has dominated philosophy since Plato in terms of its commitment to a form of thought modelled on the activity of recognition, to a concept of truth as representation and to the implicit presupposition that thought has a natural affinity with the truth such that only error requires explanation by reference to the effect of extrinsic forces. This tradition purports to find the ground of the order and connection of ideas in the order and connection of things and states of affairs, or vice versa in the case of Kant and the idealist tradition he inaugurated. This image of thought is at once both a philosophical defence of orthodoxy and a representation that has acquired the status of orthodoxy. It has become a philosophical opinion so evident that it does not require justification. Every rational and sensible person agrees that the goal of thought is to represent reality: only a madman or a postmodernist would suggest otherwise.

In response, Deleuze points out that it is ultimately a matter of ethico-political choice how the world appears in thought. The Platonic world of forms and their copies, defined by its hostility towards the fluid world of simulacra, gives expression to a particular moral vision of the world that favours stability and hierarchy within the person as well as within society (Deleuze 1994: 127). However, Nietzsche reminds us that there are no moral facts only interpretations of phenomena and the history of philosophy offers many alternatives to the stable order of things connected and governed by causal laws. While this has been the dominant conception within the tradition of representational thought derived from Plato, Deleuze points out that there are intimations of another conception of the world even within Plato's *Dialogues*, namely the artistic conception of the world as an unstable and shifting play of appearances, rather than essences, that is expressed in the shifting world of simulacra. It is 'a more profound and more artistic reality' than the static world of forms or kinds able to be captured once and for all in thought (Deleuze 1994: 3). He proposes an image of thought more in tune with such an artistic conception of the world. This is an image of thought modelled not on recognition but on creative thought. Its paradigm is not the activity of employing common words to designate things in accordance with established practice ('snow is white') but the activity of an apprentice struggling to come to terms with an unfamiliar milieu or material. It is governed not by the will to truth but by the desire to solve a problem. It is an image of thought as embedded within and provoked by forces external to the thinker. It is a non-representational image in that it does not see the aim as the re-creation in thought of the order of a pre-existing natural world. Rather, while it recognises the inescapability of such thinking for everyday social life, it sees the highest aim of thought as breaking through the firmament of existing opinion in order to give expression to a new conception of the natural as well as the social world.

In other words, Deleuze and Guattari's social and political philosophy presupposes a novel plane of immanence and a new image of thought. It leads to an original conception of social order and social being. To appreciate how their new image of thought affects their conception of social order, consider the difference between states and war machines that lies at the heart of their macro political social theory. The trans-historical conception of the state proposed in *Anti-Oedipus* is fragmented in *A Thousand Plateaus* into concepts of historically specific forms of state (archaic empires, early modern monarchies, capitalist states etc.) and a concept of the state as an abstract machine of capture which may be realised in thought as well as in economic, legal or political structures.[1] In its pure form, capture involves the constitution of a general space of comparison and the establishment of a centre of appropriation. The constitution of all adult heads of households on a given territory as subjects of a sovereign power and a corresponding obligation to pay taxes is one example of such capture; the extraction of ground-rent from tenants on the basis of a comparison between the productivity of different portions of land is another. Abstract machines of capture are associated above all with processes of territorialisation and reterritorialisation. The abstract machines of metamorphosis and transformation that Deleuze and Guattari call 'war machines' are the source of such movements of deterritorialisation.

In its pure form, the state is an apparatus of capture which always involves the constitution of a field of interiority. This is a well-defined entity that incorporates the constant features of all empirical forms of state. Despite the differences between ancient empires, early modern monarchies or contemporary democratic states, they all share a *'unity of composition'* (Deleuze and Guattari 1987: 427). By contrast, there is no such unity of composition among war machine assemblages. Deleuze and Guattari provide no definitive list of characteristics of the war machine. Instead, they outline a number of defining characteristics by means of a series of axioms and propositions, which they proceed to demonstrate using empirical material drawn from the study of mythology, literature, anthropology, historical epistemology and the history of philosophical images of thought. Since there is no reason to suppose that this series is closed, the war machine is not a well-defined entity. The first axiom of Plateau 12 asserts the exteriority of the war machine in relation to the state, by which they mean that it is in all respects 'of another species, another nature, another origin' than the state apparatus (Deleuze and Guattari 1987: 352). In other words, war machine assemblages are a fundamentally different kind of thing to forms of state. They are the expression of a peculiar kind of abstract machine which 'exists only in its own metamorphoses' (ibid.: 360). As such, the war machine is more like a process of continuous variation or the differential repetition of an event than a well-defined object.

The essentially diverse character of the war machine makes it a paradoxical 'object' from the standpoint of the traditional understanding of concepts and concept formation. The war machine is not the kind of thing of which there can be a concept in the traditional sense of a series of features or marks that will determine necessary and sufficient conditions for something to be an assemblage of this kind. It is incapable of being captured in a stable concept, where this implies the specification of necessary and sufficient conditions for something to fall under a given concept. The problem, then, is to arrive at a way of thinking the war machine that is adequate to its nature:

> the exteriority of the war machine in relation to the state apparatus is everywhere apparent but remains difficult to conceptualize. It is not enough to

affirm that the war machine is external to the apparatus. It is necessary to reach the point of conceiving the war machine as itself a pure form of exteriority, whereas the state apparatus constitutes the form of interiority we habitually take as a model, or according to which we are in the habit of thinking. (Deleuze and Guattari 1987: 354)

This problem arises because the traditional understanding of concepts as the constitution of a form of interiority in thought is modelled on the state form understood as an apparatus of capture. Deleuze and Guattari point to the manner in which the traditional representational image of thought expresses the essence of the state form in general (ibid.: 374ff.).[2] The problem of how to give conceptual expression to a pure form of exteriority therefore calls for another, non-state style of thought which Deleuze and Guattari call 'nomad' thought. This is a mode of thinking which delineates its object not by conceptual capture but by retracing a line of continuous conceptual variation through the various kinds of content addressed in this plateau: the two poles of sovereignty identified in Dumézil's studies of Indo-European mythology, the games of chess and go, the different styles of epic drama found in Shakespeare and Kleist, and so on. In this manner, the war machine concept is indeterminate or inexact in a way that parallels the differential and dispersed nature of the object. It is a mobile concept that reproduces in its form the exteriority of the war machine.

The difference between the concepts of state and war machine thus provides a striking illustration of Deleuze and Guattari's preferred form of conceptualisation. Two conclusions may be drawn from this example. The first is that the contrast between state and nomad thought, or arborescent and rhizomatic thought, implies an altogether different kind of world in each case. The second is that the sense in which *A Thousand Plateaus* provides an original conception of social being and social order is inseparable from the mode of thought developed in the course of the book. That is why, paradoxically, although the social, social relations and social formations are everywhere in *A Thousand Plateaus*, there is no concept of the social as such.

Machinic Philosophy and/of the Social

Paradoxes aside, it is to *A Thousand Plateaus* that we must turn for Deleuze and Guattari's concept of the social and for the kind of order presupposed by this concept. *What is Philosophy?* provides little help in this regard.[3] As noted above, the concept of the social is present throughout *A Thousand Plateaus*. All of the domains of human experience discussed in the book are understood in relation to the social milieu in which they occur. Thus, for example, desire is social in the sense that particular desires are constructed on a plane of consistency, or BWO (body without organs), that has irreducibly social dimensions. These may be features of the physical or social environment of individuals, such as Little Hans's efforts to create rhizomatic connections to the world outside his family home (Deleuze and Guattari 1987: 14), or the military and religious organisation of the Wolf-Man's obsessions (ibid.: 34). Or they may be the socio-economic underpinnings of collective desires such as courtly love, various kinds of becoming-animal or micropolitical fascism. Similarly, language is social in the sense that all speech is the product of collective assemblages of enunciation and bound up with the transmission of the 'order-words' current in a given society at a given time (ibid.: 79). Technology is social in the sense that it is not the material object that determines whether an axe serves as a tool or a weapon but the collective assemblage or machine in which it functions: 'not the technical machine, itself a collection of elements, but the social or collective machine, the machinic assemblage that determines what is a technical element at a given moment, what is its usage, extensions, comprehension, etc' (ibid.: 398). Even knowledge has an irreducibly social element to the extent that the differences between 'nomad' and 'royal' science are bound up with the different collective assemblages in which they are developed and deployed (ibid.: 361–80).

In each case, the social dimension of desire, language use, technology or knowledge is explained by reference to a particular kind of assemblage. The concept of 'assemblage' thus provides a kind of formal structure to the conception of the social laid out in the course of the successive plateaus. *A Thousand Plateaus* repeats or reiterates a concept of assemblage in relation to each of the different fields of experience discussed: machinic assemblages of desire, collective assemblages of enunciation, musical and pictorial assemblages, and so on. However, the concept of assemblage is itself subject to variation: sometimes Deleuze and Guattari point to the internally divided nature of assemblages themselves. These are defined along two axes, one referring to the range of discursive and non-discursive components, the other referring to the nature of the movements to which the assemblage gives rise. On the first axis, assemblages are both assemblages of bodies and matter and assemblages of enunciation or utterance. On the second axis, they comprise both the constitution of territories and fields of interiority and the lines of flight or deterritorialisation along which the assemblage breaks down or becomes transformed into something else. Every assemblage has both movements of reterritorialisation, which tend to fix and stabilise its elements, and '*cutting edges of deterritorialisation*, which carry it away' (Deleuze and Guattari 1987: 88).

It is the latter movements that are constitutive of any assemblage. The articulation of the corporeal and discursive elements of a given assemblage 'is effected by the movements of deterritorialisation that quantify their forms. That is why a social field is defined less by its conflicts and contradictions than by the lines of flight running through it' (ibid.: 90). Understood in terms of the interaction of assemblages, social formations are defined 'by *machinic processes*' rather than by modes of production (ibid.: 435). In these terms, the economic determinism of the structural Marxist concept of society is replaced by a concept of social life as defined by a series of interlocking, overlapping, discrete systems of regulation of desire, language, thought and behaviour. However, since there will always be an open-ended set of such systems there is no unitary concept of society as such. Capital provides an overarching system of coordination, but this is understood in terms of an apparatus of capture which affects but does not control all of the assemblages which operate in a given social formation (see below).

Sometimes, Deleuze and Guattari draw a contrast between two kinds of assemblage: on the one hand, extensive, molar assemblages that are unifiable, totalisable and organisable; on the other hand, molecular assemblages that are neither unifiable nor totalisable but chaotic. These two kinds of assemblage may be characterised in a variety of ways: for example, in terms of the contrast between arborescent and rhizomatic systems. Arborescent systems are 'hierarchical systems with centres of significance and subjectification' (Deleuze and Guattari 1987: 16). They are 'unifiable' objects in the sense that their boundaries can be clearly defined and their parts connected according to an invariant principle of unity. They embody the principles of organisation found in modern bureaucracies, factories, armies and schools, in other words, in all of the central social mechanisms of power. By contrast, rhizomes are indeterminate objects that embody the more fluid principles of organisation found in social or cultural movements. They have more in common with packs or bands rather than with the structured crowds or mass phenomena described by Canetti (Canetti 1962). They lack principles of unity or connection such as central axes or invariant elements. They are determined rather by 'magnitudes and dimensions that cannot increase in number without the multiplicity changing in nature' (Deleuze and Guattari 1987: 8).

These two kinds of assemblage are like poles or tendencies in terms of which empirical organisations may be evaluated. In this manner, Deleuze and Guattari's concepts provide a language in which to analyse the character and evolution of actual social organisations. Consider a further characteristic of rhizomatic assemblages, namely the degree to which they are flat in the sense that they are never subject to overcoding or to a 'supplementary' dimension but rather 'occupy all of their dimensions' (Deleuze and Guattari 1987: 9). An assemblage that was flat in this sense would be one that was subject to no constraints other than those derived from its primary objective. It would be a purely functional assemblage such as a business organisation unencumbered by considerations of morality or social responsibility, a military organisation unencumbered by political constraints, or an individual defined by a sole activity like the principal character of Fitzgerald's novella, *The Crack-Up*, who resolves to become a writer pure and simple, and in the process becomes 'no more than an abstract line' (Deleuze and Guattari 1987: 199). It is clear that no empirical organisation or individual person could ever be completely 'flat' in this sense of the term. It may be that in recent years there has been a shift away from strongly hierarchical and centred forms of organisation in the direction of flatter and more decentred forms, and that in one sense this does involve freeing the organisations concerned from extraneous constraints. However, it would be a mistake to conclude that this was necessarily an improvement or an increase in freedom, either of the agents involved in their operation or of their clients.

A further characteristic of rhizomatic multiplicities, which is related to their degree of flatness, is their mode of relation to the outside: rhizomatic assemblages are defined 'by the abstract line, the line of flight or deterritorialisation according to which they change in nature and connect with other multiplicities' (Deleuze and Guattari 1987: 9). We can suppose that, minimally, this implies that rhizomatic organisations will not just be responsive to other organisations and environmental conditions outside themselves, but that they will adapt in ways determined by their own internal propensities for change, or the lines of flight of which they are capable. However, such variation is consistent with a considerable degree of continuity of content and structure, whereas in the extreme or limit case, an organisation might be supposed to exist independently of any internal continuity. In this case, the organisation has become pure function, existing only in relation to the outside. This is how Deleuze and Guattari define the organisation that is the key to their ethical and political outlook and which they define in terms of its independence of all forms of capture: the nomadic 'war machine'. It is not enough, as we saw above, to conceive of this war machine as external to all forms of apparatuses of capture: it is necessary to conceive of the war machine as itself 'a pure form of exteriority' (ibid.: 354). But how are we to understand this pure form of exteriority: as a realisable form of organisation, as a limit co-extensive with the death of any functional empirical organisation, or as an abstract machine that finds expression in processes of metamorphosis and transformation?

Another variation on the distinction between two kinds of assemblage appears in the form of the distinction between molar and molecular lines or between macropolitical and micropolitical levels of social analysis. This is not simply a difference in scale but a difference in kind. It refers to the different ways in which social and political life is played out: first, with reference to conflicts between molar social entities such as social classes, sexes and nations and, second, at the molecular level in terms of social affinities, sexual orientations and varieties of communal belonging. The microsociology of Gabriel Tarde dealt with this molecular level of social life and offered an alternative to class analysis. In these terms, with regard to the 1789 revolution 'what one needs to know is which peasants, in which areas of the south of France, stopped greeting the local landowners' (Deleuze and Guattari 1987: 216).[4]

How are we to understand the relation between these two kinds of assemblage or two levels of social life? On the one hand, they appear to involve irreducibly different kinds of entity such that there is no possibility of conversion of one into the other. They correspond to different kinds of constituents of our everyday world involving different modes of individuation: a season or a time of day is not identified in the same manner as a chemical element or a legal subject. Different societies, or different social spheres within the same society, may have a preponderance of one mode of individuation over the other: pre-modern as opposed to modern societies, disciplinary institutions or bureaucracies as opposed to social, artistic or religious movements, and so on. On the other hand, Deleuze and Guattari make it clear that they are not proposing a dualism between two kinds of assemblages or machines. Rather, they insist on the interpenetration and co-implication of the two kinds of assemblage: tree structures have their rhizomatic offshoots and rhizomes have their own points of arborescence. There are only different dimensions of one and the same assemblage. From this perspective, there are not so much different kinds of thing as different ways of understanding the same things. In this sense, they refer to different underlying forms of order that provide the basis for two distinct but not mutually exclusive readings of the world.

Abstract Machines and Virtual Multiplicities

In order to resolve this apparent conflict between two ways of perceiving the relationship between the different kinds of assemblage, we need to consider another dimension of the assemblages themselves. While assemblages are more or less concrete arrangements of things, their mode of functioning cannot be understood independently of the particular kind of abstract machine that they embody. Abstract machines are always singular and immanent to a given assemblage. They are virtual machines that do not exist independently of the assemblages in which they are actualised or expressed, but they are also vital to the operation of those assemblages (Deleuze and Guattari 1987: 100). They are endowed with a directive power that Deleuze and Guattari distinguish from other models of causality in suggesting that an abstract machine 'is neither an infrastructure that is determining in the last instance nor a transcendental Idea that is determining in the supreme instance. Rather, it plays a piloting role' (ibid.: 142).[5] Abstract machines are thus virtual machines in the sense that the software program which turns a given assemblage of computer hardware into a certain kind of technical machine (a writing machine, calculating machine, a machine for representing three-dimensional objects and so on) is a virtual machine that governs the functionality of the assembled components.

This conception of the directive role played by the abstract or virtual machines that inhabit actual assemblages recalls the conception of a transcendental field that Deleuze outlines in Chapter 4 of *Difference and Repetition*. The constituent elements of this field are virtual multiplicities or structures in the sense that they are composed of purely formal elements defined by the reciprocal relations between their component elements. In the case of language, for example, the ultimate signifying units or phonemes are defined by their reciprocal relations to other phonemes. In the case of the economic structure of human societies, the relations of production and corresponding property relations likewise form a system of 'differential relations between differential elements' (Deleuze 1994: 186). Defined in this manner, a structure will be 'an internal multiplicity – in other words, a system of multiple, non-localisable connections between differential elements which is incarnated in real relations and actual terms' (ibid.: 183). The suggestion that the elements of these virtual structures or multiplicities are 'incarnated' in actual terms and relations points to their ontological status in *Difference and Repetition*. These structures are the 'more profound' real elements that, Deleuze had argued in Chapter 1, must be determined as abstract and potential multiplicities in order to enable an account of a world of free differences (ibid.: 50). On the one hand, these positive and differential elements provide the key to his conception of difference 'in itself'. On the other, they are the bases of the differential ontology outlined in this book.

In terms of this ontology, everything that exists incarnates a structure of some kind, and there will be as many kinds of structure as there are distinct kinds of matter and thought. Living organisms, languages and societies are all expressions of particular kinds of structure. Language in general may be regarded as a solution to the problem of how to communicate an infinite variety of semantic contents using a relatively small number of signifying elements. The Idea of language as such will therefore be a virtual structure that includes all of the relations between signifying elements that may be actualised in particular languages. Determinate sets of relations between phonemes will be incarnated in particular natural languages that amount to particular, determinate solutions to the problem of language as such. Similarly, as Marx showed, human societies may be regarded as solutions to the fundamental problem of the survival and reproduction of the species in the form in which this arises for human beings, namely the constitution of a mode of production of necessary means of subsistence. The Idea of society as such will therefore be a virtual set of indeterminate relations between means of production, direct and indirect producers, and consumers, while particular Ideas of society will involve an actual set of determinate social relations. These relations in turn will determine the 'synthetic and problematising field' (Deleuze 1994: 186) to which that society's economic, juridical and political arrangements constitute solutions. The crucial events that mark the history of a society will represent the emergence of actual solutions to its economic or other problems, or the replacement of one set of solutions by another.

The characterisation of the virtual multiplicities which populate the transcendental field or plane of immanence outlined in *Difference and Repetition* relies upon a particular sense of the term 'multiplicity' derived in the first instance from Riemann's mathematical typology of multiplicities or 'manifolds'.[6] In contrast to Kant's use of this term to refer to the unintelligible chaos of sensory intuitions in abstraction from the ordering principles of the understanding, Riemann uses the term to refer to the organising principles of any collection of elements however disparate. As such, a multiplicity is not 'a combination of the many and the one, but rather an organization belonging to the many as such, which has no need whatsoever of unity in order to form a system' (Deleuze 1994: 182). Multiplicities can henceforth be categorised according to the different kinds of relation between their components. Riemann contrasted metric multiplicities, such as lines of different magnitudes where there was a common standard of comparison, and non-metric multiplicities where there is no common measure and where comparisons between elements can only be effected by indirect or qualitative means. Meinong and Russell provided further examples of this distinction in contrasting magnitudes with distances and intensities which are not metric but comparable only to the degree that one element is included within another but in such a way 'that what is divided changes in nature at each moment of the division, without any of these moments entering into the composition of any other' (Deleuze and Guattari 1987: 483). Deleuze points to examples from other domains such as the movements of horses, which can be divided into several qualitatively distinct gaits – walk, trot, lope, canter and so on – where there is an order between them but where the individual gaits do not form part of the succeeding gait: a canter is not made up of walking plus trotting.

Bergson transformed this classification of different kinds of multiplicity to his own ends in arguing that the ontological distinction between duration and extensity corresponds to a distinction between qualitative and quantitative multiplicity.[7] Deleuze argues that, for Bergson, the extensive or objective reality of things takes the form of 'numerical multiplicity', where this is understood as the kind of multiplicity that divides by differences in degree and where the process of division does not involve changes in kind. Arithmetical number is an example of this kind of multiplicity: numbers are infinitely divisible but the outcome is always further numbers of the same kind. Space is another example. By contrast, another type of multiplicity 'appears in pure duration: It is an internal multiplicity of succession, of fusion, of organisation, of heterogeneity, of qualitative discrimination, or of *difference in kind*; it is a *virtual and continuous* multiplicity that cannot be reduced to numbers' (Deleuze 1988a: 38). Bergson draws examples of such multiplicities from the domain of consciousness, where a complex feeling may contain a number of elements imperfectly perceived but where, once these elements are distinctly perceived by consciousness, the feeling inevitably changes its nature.

It is apparent that Deleuze and Guattari employ a version of the Bergsonian distinction between two kinds of multiplicity as part of the logical framework for the theory of assemblages in *A Thousand Plateaus*. Arborescent assemblages correspond to quantitative multiplicities whereas rhizomes are qualitative multiplicities in which there is no possibility of comparison according to a single standard:

> the point is that a rhizome or multiplicity never allows itself to be overcoded, never has available a supplementary dimension over and above its number of lines . . . Multiplicities are defined by the outside: by the abstract line, the line of flight or deterritorialization according to which they change in nature [i.e. metamorphose into something else] and connect with other multiplicities. (Deleuze and Guattari 1987: 9)

In their discussion of pack, herd and swarm multiplicities typically found in cases of becoming-animal, they point out that these continually cross over into one another as in the case of werewolves that become vampires when they die. As such, these mythological pack animals illustrate the transformative character of all qualitative multiplicities:

> Since its variations and dimensions are immanent to it, *it amounts to the same thing to say that each multiplicity is already composed of heterogeneous terms in symbiosis, and that a multiplicity is continually transforming itself into a string of other multiplicities, according to its thresholds and doors.* (Deleuze and Guattari 1987: 249)

Just as the differences between arborescent and rhizomatic multiplicities correspond to the differences between numerical and qualitative multiplicities, so the differences in kind between micropolitical and macro political analysis are explicitly related to the distinction between the kinds of multiplicity drawn by Bergson:

> We are doing approximately the same thing when we distinguish between arborescent multiplicities and rhizomatic multiplicities. Between macro- and micro-multiplicities. On the one hand, multiplicities that are extensive, divisible and molar; unifiable, totalizable, organizable; conscious or pre-conscious – and on the other hand, libidinal, unconscious, molecular intensive multiplicities composed of particles that do not divide without changing in nature, and distances that do not vary without entering another multiplicity and that constantly construct and dismantle themselves in the course of their communications . . . (Deleuze and Guattari 1987: 33)

Finally, just as Bergson viewed qualitative multiplicities as associated with the ontologically primary realm of duration, and just as problematic Ideas or Structures formed the fundamental elements of Deleuze's differential ontology in *Difference and Repetition*, so Deleuze and Guattari treat rhizomatic, molecular and micropolitical assemblages as prior to arborescent, molar and macropolitical assemblages, and the abstract machine of mutation as prior to the abstract machine of overcoding. If they sometimes speak as if there were but a single Abstract Machine of which all concrete assemblages were more or less complete actualisations, this is because for them the function of mutation, metamorphosis and the creation of the new is ontologically primary. This priority is implicit throughout the reiterated theory of assemblages in *A Thousand Plateaus*, even though it is only occasionally made explicit. We saw above that rhizomatic multiplicities are defined not by an internal principle of unity but by the line of flight or deterritorialisation according to which they metamorphose. Elsewhere, Deleuze and Guattari differentiate their conception of assemblages from that of Foucault in similar terms. Given this conceptual connection between absolute deterritorialisation and qualitative assemblages, they assert the ontological primacy of both when they refer to the priority of the movement of absolute deterritorialisation, describing this as 'the deeper movement . . . identical to the earth itself' (Deleuze and Guattari 1987: 143).

Order and Action

On this basis, we might suppose that there is a consistent ontology of qualitative and quantitative multiplicities throughout Deleuze's work. *Difference and Repetition* outlined a metaphysical conception of the world in which the actual, quantitative nature of things may be traced back to the qualitative multiplicities that populate its plane of immanence. In parallel fashion, the theory of assemblages in *A Thousand Plateaus* offers a differential ontology conforming to the same structural principles: it is the abstract machines of mutation and deterritorialisation at the heart of every assemblage that form their most profound 'inner nature'. Understanding Deleuze and Guattari's concept of order in this way enables us to answer the questions raised above about the relations between the different kinds of assemblage, line or process. It matters little whether we say that there are two distinct kinds of assemblage or two different dimensions of one and the same assemblage. What is important for Deleuze and Guattari's conception of social being is, first, the primacy of the abstract machines of mutation and deterritorialisation; and second, the fact that both dimensions, or both kinds of assemblage, must be supposed to be present in any given state of affairs.

This is how we should understand the distinction between macro- and micropolitics.[8] Tarde's microsociological approach shows that events and processes at the macro political level do not occur independently of affective changes in a given population. The schizoanalytic study of desire shows that micropolitical phenomena do not occur independently of the implication of individuals and groups in public life, institutions and organisations. It follows that social organisations and public institutions must be understood to combine elements of both kinds of assemblage and both kinds of process. Deleuze and Guattari suggest as much in their comments on Kafka and the different kinds of segmentarity that we find in social space:

> It is not sufficient to define bureaucracy by a rigid segmentarity with compartmentalization of contiguous offices, office manager in each segment,

and the corresponding centralization at the end of the hall or on top of the tower. For at the same time there is a whole bureaucratic segmentation, a suppleness of and communication between offices, a bureaucratic perversion, a permanent inventiveness or creativity practiced even against administrative regulations. (Deleuze and Guattari 1987: 214)

Everything may be conceived from both points of view. Animals, people, events and social processes may be understood now in one way, now in the other. Persons may be conceived, as they are for legal and political purposes, as re-identifiable subjects whose identity remains constant throughout their lives. Biometric technology merely provides the means to attach that identity more firmly to individual bodies. Alternatively, persons may be conceived as moral and social entities defined in terms of their ends, beliefs and desires, such that when these undergo sudden or far-reaching change we can say that they are no longer the same person. Scott Fitzgerald's novella and Kieslowski's film, *Three Colours Blue* present us with protagonists who become or attempt to become different persons in this sense. Understanding these characters, or indeed ourselves, as qualitative multiplicities allows us to appreciate the attractions as well as the dangers of such transformation. In the same way, events may be understood in terms of lived experience and linear time, or they may be understood in themselves or in their 'becoming' and their 'specific consistency' which escape history altogether (Deleuze and Guattari 1994: 110). To understand events in this way is not simply to inhabit them and to appreciate their internal complexity, it is also to appreciate the ways in which fragments of the past, or the future, are active in the present. To understand both dimensions of the event is another way to be aware of both the possibilities for change and the forces that make it difficult to free ourselves from the past.

In the end, the value of this philosophy of multiplicities lies less in the field of empirical social analysis than in that of practical reason. We should not forget that, despite the wealth of empirical detail employed in the presentation of their concepts in *A Thousand Plateaus*, Deleuze and Guattari always describe their work as philosophy. *What is Philosophy?* is explicit that such philosophical concepts should not be confused with empirical or scientific ways of thinking. Scientific concepts are defined in terms of more or less stable and quantifiable components and relations to other concepts while philosophical concepts are defined in terms of their propensity for transformation and the 'consistency' of their non-quantifiable components. In these terms, they contrast the scientific characterisation of a bird, which refers to species and genus and distinguishing features, with the philosophical concept, which comprises 'the composition of its postures, colours and songs' (Deleuze and Guattari 1994: 20). What then is the interest in seeing the world in one of these ways rather than the other? The answer can only be pragmatic and refer us back to our interests as social agents engaged in the world. The bird as assemblage or ritornello is not simply part of an aesthetic vision of the world: it is a differential assemblage defined by its internal and external relations and subject to change along any of these lines. The primary interest served by sedentary or scientific thought in its settled phases is to remind us that there are degrees of immobility and immutability in things. Understanding how these operate and how they relate to one another is a condition of effective action. However, the overriding interest of Deleuze and Guattari's nomad thought is to understand how the immobility and immutability in things might be unhinged so that new kinds of individual and social being can emerge. Everything changes, however slowly or however few and far between are its lines of flight or deterritorialisation. The order implied by the primacy of qualitative multiplicities reminds us that the world is in motion and that nothing is immobile or immutable.

References

Ansell Pearson, K. (1999), *Germinal Life: The Difference and Repetition of Deleuze*, London and New York: Routledge.

Canetti, E. (1962), *Crowds and Power*, trans. C. Stewart, London: Victor Gollancz Ltd.

Deleuze, G. (1988a), *Bergsonism*, trans. H. Tomlinson and B. Habberjam, New York: Zone Books.

Deleuze, G. (1988b), *Foucault*, trans. S. Hand, Minneapolis: University of Minnesota Press.

Deleuze, G. (1993), *The Fold: Leibniz and the Baroque*, trans. T. Conley, Minneapolis and London: University of Minnesota Press.

Deleuze, G. (1994), *Difference and Repetition*, trans. P. Patton, London: The Athlone Press.

Deleuze, G. (1995), *Negotiations, 1972–1990*, trans. M. Joughin, New York: Columbia University Press.

Deleuze, G. (1996), 'L'actuel et le virtuel', appendix in G. Deleuze and C. Parnet, *Dialogues*, 2nd edn, Paris: Flammarion.

Deleuze, G. and Guattari, F. (1987), *A Thousand Plateaus*, trans. B. Massumi, Minneapolis: University of Minnesota Press.

Deleuze, G. and Guattari, F. (1994), *What is Philosophy?*, trans. H. Tomlinson and G. Burchell, New York: Columbia University Press.

Patton, P. (2005), 'Deleuze and Democratic Politics', in L. Tønder and L. Thomassen (eds), *Radical Democracy: Politics between abundance and lack*, Manchester: Manchester University Press, 50–67.

Turetzky, P. (1998), *Time*, London: Routledge.

Notes

1. Deleuze and Guattari's concept of 'abstract machines' is explained further below.
2. Applying their concept of the state form as involving two poles or types of capture to the image of thought, they point out that 'it is not simply a metaphor when we are told of an *imperium* of truth and a republic of spirits. It is the necessary condition for the constitution of thought as principle, or as a form of interiority, as a stratum' (Deleuze and Guattari 1987: 375).
3. The different objects of philosophy, art or science are not discussed, or only mentioned in passing, in this relentlessly meta-philosophical book. Nevertheless, in the context of discussing the differences between the conceptual personae found in philosophy and the psychosocial types found in sociology, Deleuze and Guattari remark that social fields comprise not only structures and functions, but also three kinds of 'movements that affect the Socius': the constitution of territories along with the processes of deterritorialisation and reterritorialisation that affect them (Deleuze and Guattari 1994: 67–8).
4. Deleuze and Guattari acknowledge Gabriel Tarde (1843–1904) as the author of a 'microsociology' in which the social is considered from the perspective of infinitesimal gestures which form waves of influence both beneath and beyond the level of the individual, and 'differences' and 'repetitions' that elude the dialectic of identity and opposition. See Deleuze 1994: 25–6, 76, 307, 313–14, 326; Deleuze 1988b: 36, 142; Deleuze 1993: 109–10, 154; and Deleuze and Guattari 1987: 216, 218–19, 548, 575.
5. 'There is no doubt that an assemblage never contains a causal infrastructure. It does have, however, and to the highest degree, an abstract line of creative or specific causality, its *line of flight or deterritorialisation*; this line can be effectuated only in connection with general causalities of another nature' (Deleuze and Guattari 1987: 283).
6. One of Deleuze's last published texts begins with the claim that 'Philosophy is the theory of multiplicities' (Deleuze 1996: 179). Similarly, in *Negotiations* he comments: 'I see philosophy as a logic of multiplicities' (Deleuze 1995: 147).
7. Bergson's distinction between two types of multiplicity and its relation to his theory of duration is discussed in Turetzky 1998: 194–210. On Deleuze's use of Bergson's concept of multiplicity and his relation to neo-Darwinism, see Ansell Pearson 1999: 155–9.
8. I argue for this way of understanding the relation between macro- and micro politics in Deleuze and Guattari in Patton 2005.

Chapter 2

The Trembling Organisation: Order, Change and the Philosophy of the Virtual

Torkild Thanem and Stephen Linstead

Deleuze has argued that with a few exceptions such as Bergson, philosophers, despite their concern with concepts, have neglected the concept of philosophy itself. If so, then this is even more true for organisation theorists, who have been obsessed with what organisations do, but have taken the concept of organisation largely for granted. Again with few exceptions (e.g. Cooper 1986; Cooper and Burrell 1988) they have rarely asked what organisation is, or questioned the ontological status of organisation. Yet although much of Deleuze's work, especially that with Guattari, is about organisation, especially the economic organisation of capital and the conditions of production and signification, much of this is implied or inferred, or at a remote level of abstraction. A search of the indices of critical commentaries on Deleuze yields only minimal reference to the concept 'organisation', if it appears at all. So the aim of this chapter is to progress the project of interrogating the ontological status of organisation, by rendering explicit the idea of organisation that can be read implicitly within – or read into – the work of Deleuze (cf. Knights 2004).

Certain commentators undertaking the task of ontological interrogation (e.g. Burrell 1997, 1998; Chia 1999) have argued that organisation is the *opposite* of change, with change as pure flow and process. They have argued against linearity as deathly, a stoppage of the innate vitality of process, and for non-linear conceptualisations of change, such as Deleuze and Guattari's (1983, 1984, 1987) rhizome and Bergson's *durée*. However, it is possible to read Bergson – as we believe that Deleuze (1988) in fact does – as arguing that organising processes are an act of reply to specific experience which *remains in conversation with its object and changes along with it* (Linstead 2002). Thus change and organisation cannot be opposed – change itself is a result of organisation and organisation is a product of change which is itself in change. Bergson did not stop at being the philosopher *of* change, but conceived of philosophy as being itself *change* – rather than becoming imprisoned in its own intellectual and rationalistic overcodings and alienated from experience and the body. In this chapter we argue that Deleuze takes Bergson further in his consideration of the nature of philosophy, its relation to the body and to experience, and develops a Bergsonian path between phenomenology and structuralism which is sensitive to both but fully embraces neither – as Bergson puts it, a *partial realism* neither subjective nor objective, realist nor idealist (Bergson 1999: 86; Colebrook 2002: 1–3). This enables us to make the paradoxical assertion that organisation is not opposed to change, but organisation *is* change.

In the first part of the chapter we clarify the relationship between organisation and *order*, terms which are usually taken to be synonymous. We begin by developing our discussion of the concept of organisation in Deleuze and Bergson, and particularly in terms of its relation to the concepts of order and desire in Deleuze and Deleuze and Guattari. We discover that in terms of micro and macro processes, these two concepts are of considerable importance to Deleuzian thought, although the meso territory of organisation theory and neo-insitutional economics is less well covered. We find that organisation may have aspects which are both deadening and antithetical to change, and yet are an essential part of the constant and often infinitesimal movements that themselves create change from the flows of desire. We expand on this double sense of organisation in the first part of the chapter. Bearing this understanding of organisation in mind, the rest of the chapter puts organisation theory in contact with two themes central to Deleuzian philosophy – the view of *philosophy as concept creation* and *the concept of the virtual* – which in turn are utilised to ask what organisation is and how it can be studied.

In the second part of the chapter, we argue that insofar as philosophy should preoccupy itself with the creation and invention of concepts, a *philosophy of organisation* needs to be constructed from *the concept of organisation*. More precisely, a philosophy of organisation must create and invent *new* concepts of organisation – and must therefore itself be continually reinvented. Extending this Deleuzian–Bergsonian approach, this may involve pursuing the *connections* between the concept of organisation, the empirical field of organisation, and the concept and empirical field of non-organisation.

In the third part of the chapter we take up Deleuze's concept of the virtual, another Bergsonian legacy, as a tool for investigating non-organisation and the relationship between organisation and non-organisation. As such, the virtual draws attention to the forces that subvert and disrupt, escape, exceed and change organisation, thus making possible a new concept of organisation, which is both autopoietic and autosubversive – not fixed, but in motion, never resting, but constantly *trembling*.

Organisation, Order and Desire

Henri Bergson implicitly uses the term *organisation* in two ways and we can see the same distinction running more explicitly through Deleuze's work. For Bergson, organisation is *life itself* (Linstead and Mullarkey 2003). Wherever we find an *organism* we find it organising itself and its environment – taking this, leaving that, reproducing, transforming and excreting, evolving, connecting and even socialising. Beginning from a position that organisation is a *sign* of life, Bergson ends up using the terms almost interchangeably. This sense of *vital organisation* stems from an intimate engagement and creative evolution with the environment, and is embedded in experienced duration, lived time, or *durée*. The life form that organises is organised, is *within* organisation. The other type of formal organisation – ordering, measuring, abstracting, acting at a distance – is typically associated with scientific clock time, the abstracted experience which is by definition outside *durée*, or attempts to be. It is the critique of this form of organisation in Bergson and Deleuze that has led some commentators (e.g. Chia 1999) to oppose organisation to change, but this is only part of the story. Whilst the dead hand of organisation might be an appropriate metaphor for formalistic and abstracted understandings of organisation (Burrell 1997), our readings of Bergson and Deleuze offer a way of revitalising the concept.

Deleuze connects this dualistic view of organisation to another Bergsonian concept, multiplicity. He argues that in Bergson there are two types of multiplicity:

> one is represented by space . . . It is a multiplicity of exteriority, of simultaneity, of juxtaposition, of *order*, of quantitative differentiation, of *difference in degree*; it is a numerical multiplicity, *discontinuous and actual*. The other type of multiplicity appears in pure duration: it is an internal multiplicity of succession, of fusion, of *organisation*, of heterogeneity, of qualitative discrimination, or of *difference in kind*; it is a *virtual and continuous* multiplicity that cannot be reduced to numbers. (Deleuze 1988: 38)

The first kind of multiplicity is the kind which Bergson finds in Einstein and mathematical relativity (Bergson 1999). It spatialises thought by setting phenomena out as though on a laboratory table, treating aspects of consciousness like objects of physics, moments of time as separate positions (Linstead 2002). Multiplicity in this regard accepts that things change over time, but treats time as it would treat space. For example, it is quite reasonable to use the same metric for heat and cold, regarding cold as an absence of heat. An object cannot be hot at the same time as it is cold – its capacity to withstand a multiplicity of temperatures can therefore only be demonstrated sequentially. This holds for the human sensation of temperature too – although parts of our body might be hot whilst others are cold, a singular part is not both hot and cold at the same time. Heat and cold are intensive properties – they don't add to each other but average out across the system (DeLanda 2002: 59–61). But is human happiness equally capable of being viewed as an absence of sadness? We all have experiences which are tinged with, or even lie between both, moments when we do not know whether to laugh or cry. They are present together within us, not as external objects acting upon us with separate influences, and happy/sad cannot be collapsed like heat/cold into the simultaneity of the single metric of temperature, a terrain through which we move like mercury moving up and down the thermometer scale. They are therefore extensive – they can be and are split as different qualities. The virtual shifting and becoming of mood is relational and qualitative, irreducibly experienced and intuited rather than measured and calculated.

Michael Hardt is emphatic in calling the first example a *multiplicity of order* and the second a *multiplicity of organisation*, both of which he distinguishes from Hegelian dialectic, which is 'unable to think multiplicity at all because it recognises neither differences of nature nor differences of degree' (Hardt 1993: 13). Deleuze uses this recognition to create a non-dialectical politics of multiplicity, advocating a pluralism of organisation (based on enfoldedness, relational connections and becoming) against a pluralism of order (based on positions, interests and governmentality). So the concept of organisation does have critical ontological significance in Deleuze – it is not set against change, but it is distinguished from the ordering excesses of formal organisation. And it is so set insofar as it embodies desire, whilst ordering arrangements seek to repress and eradicate desire; indeed as Guattari notes, desire could be 'more realistic, a better organizer and a more skilful engineer, than the raving rationalism of the present system' (Guattari 1984: 86; see also DeLanda 2002: 160; Goodchild 1996: 158).

The Geological Organisation

The ideas of order and organisation can also be seen in the geological approach which Deleuze and Guattari take to stratification. The extended

Bergsonian idea at play here is that biological and social and economic life can be seen to form in the same way as geological strata form, with the same type of sorting and amalgamating processes and the same type of crossings between strata. But as DeLanda (1999, 2000) argues, this is not a purely metaphorical approach – what can be discerned is a deep isomorphism which links geology and society, making possible what he calls a mineralisation of history, which reveals the same set of processes operating behind them, the same 'engineering diagram', 'blueprint' or as Deleuze and Guattari put it 'abstract machine' at work behind the structure-generating processes.

In *A Thousand Plateaus* Deleuze and Guattari (1987) theorise the emergence of two types of structures (there are other possibilities) – what they call *strata* (trees, hierarchies or arboreal structures), which emerge from homogeneous elements, and *self-consistent aggregates* (rhizomes, which DeLanda (1999: 120) calls *meshworks*), which emerge from the articulation of heterogeneous elements. Georges Bataille argued that the problem of restricted economy was that it wrestled the heterogeneous into the homogeneous and could not accommodate the creative articulations of endogenous desire. Deleuze and Guattari take this further, arguing that the dichotomy can be applied across biology, physical chemistry and human institutions. DeLanda illustrates this by identifying processes common in the physical world (his example is the formation of geological strata) to the development of hierarchical structures – sorting/sedimenting and cementing/consolidating, the latter facilitated by a third joining substance such as silica or hematite. This *double articulation* is referred to by Deleuze and Guattari as *content* or *territorialisation* and *expression* or *coding*. This is not the old distinction between substance and form (in Aristotelian hylomorphism substance is simply formed content), as DeLanda points out:

> Sedimentation is not just a matter of accumulating pebbles (substance) but also entails sorting them into layers (form), while consolidation not only effects new architectonic couplings between pebbles (form) but also yields a new entity, sedimentary rock (substance). (DeLanda 1999: 123)

The formation of social strata, that is, social classes, exhibits the same 'abstract machine' at work. We speak of such development whenever a society presents a variety of differentiated roles to which not everyone has equal access, and the ruling elite preserves for itself access to those roles controlling key natural, material and human social and cultural resources. Social role differentiation may be the result of the intensification of energy flows in a society – for example, a charismatic leader emerging in pre-modern society – but the sorting of those roles into ranks on a scale of prestige requires the emergence of specific group dynamics (ibid.: 124). The emergence to hegemony of one group may cede them the power further to restrict access to the roles that they occupy, and their criteria for sorting the rest of society into less highly ranked sub-groups begin to crystallise. As Eisenstadt argues:

> it is from such crystallization of differential evaluation criteria and status differences – such as segregating the lifestyles of the different strata, the process of mobility between them, the steepness of the stratificational hierarchies, some types of stratum consciousness, as well as the degree and intensity of strata conflict – develop in different societies. (Eisenstadt quoted in DeLanda 1999: 124)

Roles therefore sediment through sorting and ranking processes in most societies, but they are not an autonomous dimension of social organisation in all societies – the intensity of in-group dynamics of elites may vary considerably, surpluses may not be allowed to accumulate (as in the potlach) and kinship or alliance relationships may prevail over social roles. Here is where the second operation of *codification* is necessary to consolidate the loose accumulation of roles into a social class. This operation legally or religiously interprets the new criteria and establishes the elites as the bearers of the new culture, the 'legitimators of change and delineators of the limits of innovation' (DeLanda 1999: 124).

When turning to the development of meshworks of heterogeneous elements, Deleuze and Guattari identify three types of actions. First, a set of heterogeneous elements must be brought together through an *articulation of superpositions*, interconnections among diverse but overlapping elements. Second, *intercalary elements* effect this interlock as local connectors (e.g., as catalysts between two or more others). Finally these interlocked heterogeneous elements must be capable of endogenously generating stable behavioural patterns, at regular temporal or spatial *intervals*. The growth of these meshworks is by *drift*, a result of the cumulation of adjacent interactions. This is less well developed than the double-articulation model of strata but the importance of non-homogenising articulation is no less.

DeLanda (1999: 128) considers pre-capitalist markets to be an example of a socio-cultural meshwork. With pure barter, complementary demands must be matched, closely, by chance. When money is introduced, diverse demands can be matched at a distance as money acts as the intercalary element which translates demand and price into relations of value. It also allows demands to become substitutable among diverse elements, or goods, which have the same value. Of course, this only holds when there is no wholesaler hoarding or dumping stock, or no guild controlling price setting. Markets do in these conditions generate endogenous stable states, especially when commercial centres form trading circuits and cyclic price waves occur. But neither meshworks nor hierarchies occur in pure forms, as even goal-determined bureaucracies exhibit some drift and even small markets have some hierarchical elements. Social capital is the product of networks giving rise to hierarchies, and where bureaucracies co-exist (e.g. various government and academic groups) they tend to form a mesh-work of hierarchies through local and contingent links for inter-agency collaboration (DeLanda 1999: 128–9). Markets also stratify, with the more abstract money markets on top, luxury goods in the middle, and basic commodities (e.g. grain) on the bottom. Societies therefore consist of changing mixtures of meshworks and strata that occur in more or less stratified states, rather than exclusive states. Indeed, contexts which favour highly stratified forms can be thought of as *striated* space, where contexts favouring low stratification are *smooth* space.

The flow of self-organising reality, animated by desire, or relatively unformed and unstructured matter-energy flows from which these forms emerge is the *Body without Organs (BwO)*. The idea of organisation which Deleuze and Guattari are often seen to oppose derives from their view of *organ*isation and the *organism* which fixes the role and function of *organs*, locking them into one particular role and disallowing multiple functions and multiple combinations of organs into different *desiring machines* (think of the allowed combination of hands, mouth, digestive system and anus as a defecation or waste machine; then consider the combination of mouth, hands and anus in different ways as erotic organs as a pleasure-machine, which is still illegal in several parts of the world). The organism is a result of the organisation of the *Body without Organs* (see Brewis and Linstead 2000; Linstead 2000).

> The organism is not at all the body, the BwO; rather it is a stratum on the BwO, in other words, a phenomenon of accumulation, coagulation and sedimentation that, in order to extract useful labour from the BwO, imposes on it forms, functions, bonds, dominant and hierarchized organisations, organised transcendences . . . The BwO is that glacial reality where the alluvions, sedimentations, coagulations, foldings and recoiling that compose an organism – also a signification and a subject – occur. (Deleuze and Guattari 1984: 159)

Let's consider this last point more closely, as Deleuze and Guattari explicitly construct a theory of escape from the dominant powers of society by reinvesting desire within the social formations that both produce and repress it. Their view of desire is as an immanent force, which is repressed by the illusion of desire wanting something outside of itself – a need to be satisfied or 'displaced representation' – rather than being sufficient in its own exuberance (Goodchild 1996: 146). Although stratification is necessary for the world to appear in the first place, it works by displacing desire onto an object outside itself, by channelling it and investing it in representations, or simulacra. Simulacra are signs produced by machinic formulations which are not those that have produced the desire, and so they can only *conjugate* with desire and not connect. To connect, both terms would need to be changed by the coming together, but in conjugation the simulacrum onto which desire is attached – the image of a face, a product, a model body, capital itself – is not changed. Desire and simulacra form constants by being coupled, repeated and reproduced as a formula until, in effect, what is conventionally desirable appears to be a natural desire. So we desire to be taller, have bigger muscles, want the bigger office, the faster car – and when we attain these things experience that familiar feeling of emptiness. But nevertheless, these constants then form the sediment of social strata, a common bonding of social aspiration. The conjugations of desire hold society together, but this is not productive – only when a desire is connected to another desire could this be so. Power then operates through stratification and conjugation whilst connection destratifies as it occasions mutual deterritorialisation between desires – literally releasing them into each other.

Social strata are created by two processes, subjectification and significance, underlain by a third – organisation. Subjectification positions the subject through grammar, constructing relations not through the content or meaning of language but through the way in which it orders and positions its speakers and sets out their choices for them – they may enter into these forced, conjugated choices or be silent. Along with these grammars are also produced chains of signification (or *signifiance*), with normative interpretations of subjectivity and understanding. So the use of a particular expression evokes a set of rules to be followed and a customary or dominant meaning or chain of meanings. Deleuze and Guattari talk of *order*-words which both give commands/judgements and establish positions within a system – what they call a *major* language which is concerned with ordering activities like extracting constants, homogenising, centralising, standardising and establishing positives and negatives. Of course, following Canetti, they recognise that a command to conform (like the roar of a lion) is also a warning of failure to comply and an invocation to flee. Thus there opens up an opportunity for a *minor* language – which changes the meaning of statements by creating new connections, subverting and multiplying meaning and establishing *lines of flight* (Jackson and Carter 2004).

Behind subjectification and signification, organisation proceeds through two forms of segmentation – the molar and the molecular. Molar segmentation operates through large groupings, the sort that are often statistically manipulated, such as binary sex distinction. Circular segments occur where dispersed groups defer to a centre or state – McDonaldisation would be a circular molarity, as could economic globalisation. Linear segments link units through equivalence and translatability – wage-regimes link monetary markets to production systems which link to consumption segments (Deleuze and Guattari 1987: 217). Molar segmentation operates according to an organising machine that is exterior to the process which generated the segments in the first place, and is distal in its operations. It creates regularities and institutions as building blocks of society. Molecular segmentation operates through interaction and contiguity, working through self-organising systems which lie alongside each other, catalyse and interact, and act relatively – switching roles from product to catalyst, content to expression, in shifting *assemblages*. Where molar segments are reterritorialisations concerned with unity and identity, based on universalised distinctions and categorical boundaries, and are subjugated to an external authority, molecular segments are subject only in relation to productive processes lying alongside them, where the product of such interaction influences the process, as in *autopoiesis* (Goodchild 1996: 159–60).

Power, then, operates in society through subjectification and signification, which themselves depend on *organisation*, which operates through the orderings and reorderings of molar and molecular segmentarity. These operations are reciprocal, supple and subtle – those subject to power do not passively submit to it, nor do they desire repression due to some deep ontological insecurity, nor are they the dupes of ideology:

> Desire is never separable from complex assemblages that necessarily tie into molecular levels, from microformations already shaping postures, attitudes, perceptions, expectations, semiotic systems, etc. Desire is never an undifferentiated instinctual energy, but itself results from a highly developed, engineered setup rich in interactions: a whole supple segmentarity that processes molecular energies . . . (Deleuze and Guattari 1987: 215)

Further, although the molar and the molecular are in relation, this is not a simple reciprocity.

> [T]he stronger molar organisation is, the more it induces a molecularisation of its own elements, relations and elementary apparatuses . . . The

> administration of a great organised molar security has as its correlate a whole micromanagement of petty fears, a permanent molecular insecurity, to the point that the motto of domestic policymakers might be: a macropolitics of society by and for a micropolitics of insecurity. However . . . molecular movements do not complement but rather thwart and break through the great world-wide organisation. (Deleuze and Guattari 1987: 215–16)

Thus capitalism engenders privatisation, performance-related pay and personal key success factors under the scrutiny or in the name and in the interests of the owners of the means of production; totalitarianism is a different kind of personal and micropolitical insecurity under the constant real or imagined scrutiny of the state in the name of the People and in the interests of the Party powerful. But society is not, as in Marxism, defined by its contradictions – it is defined by its lines of flight, which are quantum and molecular and leak between linear or circular molar segments, because:

> There is always something that flows or flees, that escapes the binary organisations, the resonance apparatus, and the overcoding machine . . . Power centers are defined much more by what escapes them or by their impotence than by their zone of power. (Deleuze and Guattari 1987: 216–17)

This for us is crucial – that which is not powerful nevertheless is able to reinscribe itself on power, in a minor way, and as a consequence all our concepts not only relate to but are shaped by their responses to and relations with that which they are not. This will be important for the ideas we develop in the next section, but before we do, let us briefly take stock. At this point, we can see that, for Deleuze, organisation is about order, order is about power, and power is about impotence – from which multiplicities following molecular flows of desire can create change. Although there is little direct theorising about organisations as such in Deleuze, we have found that we have much material available for our conceptual assemblage if the task of embarking on a Deleuzian philosophy of organisation/s is to begin. What we now need to consider more fully is the nature of that task.

The Work of Philosophy: Concept Creation

In *What is Philosophy?* Deleuze and Guattari argue that philosophy is 'the art of forming, inventing, and fabricating concepts' (1994: 2). Following this idea, they go on to outline a complex set of related premises that govern the process of concept creation. First, the concept needs *conceptual personae* – a supporting cast of thinkers, similar to the cast of actors or *dramatis personae* in a play. Appositely, Deleuze and Guattari trace the notion of conceptual personae to the ancient Greek understanding of the philosopher as friend (that is, the friend of wisdom and concepts). In contrast to the sage in other civilisations, the Greek philosopher does not possess wisdom, but seeks wisdom by constantly creating and inventing, re-creating and reinventing concepts. Given the intensity with which wisdom is sought, the philosopher is not merely a friend, but the lover and claimant of concepts who operates in constant rivalry with other lovers and claimants.

This characterisation of the philosopher as suitor underlines the dynamic and uncertain nature of what it means to do philosophy. Since the philosopher is constantly inventing concepts and challenging previously invented concepts, no one philosopher may exercise total conceptual control – final definitions are unattainable. The concept's autopoietic nature reinforces this indeterminacy. Concepts are self-positing. However, concept creation and self-positing are not mutual exclusives, and Deleuze and Guattari assert that 'The concept posits itself to the same extent that it is created' (ibid.: 11). Consequently, the philosopher can only potentially *have* the concept, its power and its competence.

From this starting point Deleuze and Guattari declare that 'There are no simple concepts. Every concept has components and is defined by them' (ibid.: 15). In other words, the concept is a *multiplicity*, that is, a whole, but a fragmentary whole. As a whole, the concept is able to totalise its components, but as a fragmentary whole, this ability is limited. And since it is only through its fragmented nature that the concept can 'escape the mental chaos constantly threatening it, stalking it, trying to reabsorb it' (ibid.: 16), its ability to do this is also limited. The wholeness and fragmentation ascribed to the concept is therefore not a leap towards order and closure, but a recognition of the concept's *openness*.

The concept's openness is reinforced by its relational nature. The concept is not absolute and on its own, but becomes what it is in relation to others and anomalies – specifically other concepts and particular problems, which are pre-conceptual (Surin 2002). Consequently, the discovery of a new problem would change the nature, role and meaning of a concept. While reinforcing the indeterminate nature of the concept, this means that Deleuze and Guattari avoid turning the concept into an abstract entity confined to the domain of ideas. Since concepts are connected to pre-conceptual problems, they speak of the world. And insofar as concepts are dynamic, they speak of possible worlds. This is the power of the concept: not just to express what exists here and now, but what might possibly exist in the future. It is through this assertion that Deleuze and Guattari's philosophy of concept creation extends into an ontological project. Openness, relation, connection, dynamism, possibility. It is by creating concepts that Deleuze (sometimes with Guattari) rethinks life and embodiment, for example (Massumi 1992; Rajchman 2000): it is by inventing different conceptualisations of organisation that organisation theorists might be able to rethink organisation. Rather than attempting a detailed account of what a new concept of organisation might look like – we have identified some Deleuzian elements which can inform such a project in the first part of this chapter – we now turn to certain epistemological and ontological conditions that may be taken into account when creating new concepts of organisation.

Creating new concepts of organisation is not just a matter of a pure theorising as if they were isolated from the rest of the world. Organisation needs to be conceptualised in relation to pre-conceptual and post-conceptual problems and experiences of organisation. Just as power is defined by what escapes it, its *impotence* (or non-power), a philosophy of organisation needs to be developed in relation to a *non*-philosophy of organisation that respects it, welcomes it, and complements it. At the same time, if appreciating organisation as a matter of change, a philosophy of organisation must be developed in relation to a philosophy of *non-organisation*. Briefly, this means developing a philosophical appreciation of the forces that disrupt, undermine, exceed and change organisation. In empirical terms, this may include forces of disease, madness, alternative sexualities and natural catastrophes. In cosmological terms, it includes all the forces of exhaustion and disintegration, affectivity and creativity, which make things as we 'normally' know them melt into air and become something entirely different (see Thanem 2004). It may be argued that non-organisation, through his rethinking of Bergson's concept of the virtual, marks the very starting point of Deleuzian philosophy of becoming. The virtual is both organisational and non-organisational, and as a matter of non-organisation, the undivided Whole of the virtual puts organisation into a larger context that destabilises specific organisational phenomena and organisation in general. Both these elements in Deleuzian philosophy destabilise organisation on two levels: epistemologically, by undermining the power of any one conceptualisation of organisation, and ontologically, by undermining the power of organisation itself. It is because of this epistemological-ontological fold that thinking organisation in relation to the virtual might enable the creation and invention of a new concept of organisation.

The Virtual

Deleuze first deals with the concept of the virtual in his essay 'Bergson's Conception of Difference' (1999 [1956]), returns to it in *Bergsonism* (1988 [1966]), and expands on it in relation to the concept of the event in *Difference and Repetition* (1994 [1968]). This last move is important, and before examining the virtual in more detail we shall therefore turn to the event, which later enables us to extract specific considerations from Deleuzian philosophy of becoming in an effort to understand issues of organisation.

Deleuze's concept of the event is more open yet more specific than that implied by commonsense dictionary definitions. An event is not simply something that happens, such as an organised social occasion, a public lecture or an item in a sports programme. What makes an event is none of the above, but the capacity to open up the future and make things happen. In other words, the event is defined as event by virtue of its capacity to *change*, to make a difference. As the event is different from what already exists, and as it sticks out from the mundane and the regular, it marks a rupture or discontinuity in history. But by opening up the future, the event takes its differential nature beyond the moment of its own realisation, promising further differentiation. The event is therefore a matter of continuity as well as discontinuity, a point that Deleuze largely inherits from Bergson. The role of continuity in Deleuze's thinking of the event now leads us to the virtual and its relation to the *actual*, which is a radical alternative to conventional philosophies of being that tend to think in terms of the real and the possible, where the real is what exists here and now, and the possible is what can exist. In this frame of thought the possible is always determined by the real in such a way that what can exist always depends on what already exists. Possible events to be realised in the future therefore depend upon the events that are realised in the present – they may be consequentially or even causally connected. Imagine a pendulum which, given time, moves from one end of a continuum to another. By knowing the pendulum's current and previous positions we can predict its next position. By knowing what event is real here and now, we can predict what possible events will be realised in the future. Conventional thinking therefore progresses from the real (a real state of affairs) towards the realisation of the possible. But as we shall see below, Bergsonian and Deleuzian thinking moves in the opposite direction, from the virtual to the actual and the actualisation of the virtual.

Whereas the possible is opposed to the real and 'the process undergone by the possible is . . . a "realisation" ', the virtual is not even engaged in a relationship with the real (Deleuze 1994: 211). Contrary to most dictionaries, which tend to define the virtual as *almost* existing or *almost* real, Deleuze's conceptualisation of the virtual implies no sense of inferiority. The virtual is in no respect less than the real, but more, and 'possesses a full reality by itself' (ibid.: 211). Crudely speaking, this reality possessed by the virtual is the universe, the one and the all, which means that the virtual *is* everything and that it is *in* everything. The extended and undivided world of the virtual is then related to the actual, and the process undergone by the virtual is not one of realisation, but actualisation. The virtual should therefore not be confused with popular or mainstream references to virtual organisations and virtual reality that confine the virtual to recent developments in information technology, thus considering it as less than the real since it is held to remove social and organisational experience from face-to-face interaction (for a view that attempts to bring recent technological advances face to face with recent philosophical advances, see DeLanda 2002).

In *Bergsonism*, Deleuze argues that it is the *élan vital* (Bergson 1911) which enables the actualisation of the virtual. Boundas insists that the '*Élan vital* is not an occult power, but rather the name of the force(s) at work each time that a virtuality is being actualised' (1996: 91). In Deleuze's own words, 'The *élan vital* . . . designates the actualisation of this virtual' (1988: 113). As noted above, as the virtual undergoes the process of actualisation or differenciation, it is manifested as different things that differ from one another. But since these things are actualities (rather than things as such), they are not established with stable boundaries and fixed identities and they do not enjoy the same status as they would within a philosophy concerned with the real state of affairs. This is because the virtual, with its undivided yet differentiated nature, continues to exist in the actual. In order to understand how the virtual continues to exist in the actual, it is necessary to re-invoke the concept of the event.

Deleuze does not speak of the actualisation of the virtual in terms of the thing, but in terms of the event. Every actualisation of the virtual is an event, and the concept of the event (as opposed to the thing) goes to highlight that the actual does not fix and determine what has undergone actualisation. Hence, the actualisation of the virtual is not a matter of closure, but openness because the event taking place with the actualisation of the virtual never terminates its connection to the extended and indeterminate world of the undivided virtual Whole. Thus far, Deleuze agrees with Bergson. But as well as recognising movements from the virtual to the actual, Deleuze insists that we must equally recognise movement in the opposite direction, from the actual to the virtual:

> The real [that is, the actual in this context] is not only that which is cut out according to natural articulations or differences in kind; it is also that which intersects again along paths converging toward the same ideal or virtual point. (Deleuze 1988: 29)

This is Deleuze's point of departure from Bergson (Hardt 1993: 19–21; Ansell Pearson 1999: 74–5; Grosz 2000: 228) and Bergson's restriction of intensity to virtual, intensive differences in kind. According to Ansell Pearson (1999: 75), this move beyond Bergson is important because the absence of intensity from the actual would lead to a 'thermodynamic race to the grave' that would annul the different tendencies inherent in the virtual. Deleuze holds that *within* every actualised event there is a virtual pure event, which maintains the connection between the actual and the extended world of the virtual (Williams 2000). Consequently, the actual is subjected to continuous change and modification and can only enjoy a temporary and momentary existence as a singular event. But instead of approaching entropy, it can recombine with different virtual tendencies and become something else. Although the pages displaying this text could catch fire, blow away with the wind, disappear into the bottom of some filing cabinet, or rot and dematerialise, they could also be used to support a broken leg on a rickety desk, or be turned into new paper upon which a different sort of text could be printed. Alternatively, in the realm of formal organisations, the machinery of a printing company gone bust may be taken over by political radicals using it to publish anti-capitalist posters and leaflets. Or the devolution of organisational decision-making may go so far that it slips out of the hands of senior management who find company policy subverted by white-collar workers paying more attention to customers they can empathise with than the interests of company executives and shareholders. Similarly, in the realm of social organisation and body politics, the privatisation of public health may go so far that citizens start completely to ignore advice from the public-health authorities on how to organise one's body, lifestyle, eating habits and sex-life in the pursuit of good health, and instead connect to bodily desires that fatten, starve, infect or excessively invigorate the body.

Given that the actual springs out of the virtual, it is never *pre-formed* along these lines. The kind of actualisation undergone by the virtual in order to become actual is far from obvious. Unlike the real, which is 'the image and likeness of the possible that it realises, the actual . . . does *not* resemble the virtuality that it embodies' (Deleuze 1988: 97). Hence, 'actualization . . . are a genuine creation. The Whole must *create* the divergent lines according to which it is actualized and the dissimilar means that it utilizes on each line' (Deleuze 1988: 106). As a consequence, actualisation is a matter of creation, which means that the virtual '*must create* its own terms of actualization' (Hardt 1993: 18). This is also the challenge for organisation and organisations. If we are to follow Deleuze's argument, organisations must create their own terms of actualisation. Organisations must become creative. In much of the creativity literature in the management field this becomes an empty cliché, valorising the capacities of the individual entrepreneur, inventor or strategist. Not so for Deleuze.

Following Bergson, Deleuze (1988) argues that the creative act takes the form of creative evolution, which effectively decentres the individual and the organisation. Deleuze's most important contribution here is to investigate creative evolution in relation to the virtual and to show how the creative evolution of the Bergsonian organism is due to the connection between the actual organism and the virtual Whole. Without collapsing the concept of organisation into the concept of the organism, this enables us to see how the creative evolution of an organisation is not due to the organisation alone, but to the connection between the actual organisation and the virtual Whole. Since organisations are always in creative evolution, successful or otherwise, it becomes difficult to maintain the mainstream view that organisations exist as stable bounded entities and the attitude that the only processes that matter are the processes of organisation that make organisational entities possible. In addition to its organisational tendencies, the virtual Whole embodies tendencies of non-organisation that disrupt the actualisation of processes and boundaries of organisation. These non-organisational forces do not constitute the virtual as such, but are actualisations of the virtual. The significance of the virtual when thinking about organisation is that the future of organisation is completely open. Ignoring the virtual and the non-organisational actualisations that may emerge from it risks restricting the change to which organisation is subjected. It risks exaggerating the endurance and stability of the organisational processes that make organisations come into being.

Non-organisation should therefore not be confused with the concept of disorganisation. As opposed to disorganisation, which is simply that which is organised differently (by unusual means and in the pursuit of unusual ends), non-organisation is not reducible to organisation. Instead, it refers to that which is not organised, but nevertheless caught up with organisation in a complex and intricate relationship. Non-organisation is the dynamic forces that exist independently of organisation in that it subverts and resists, contradicts and interrupts, escapes, precedes and exceeds organisation. It is part of the rhizomatic movement of desire which is both imperceptible and yet makes its presence felt. And as such, as a Body without Organs (or Organisation without Organs) it is capable of changing organisations and even making organisations disappear, at least in the form that we tend to know them (see Thanem 2004).

Conclusion

In conclusion, we must acknowledge that there is a danger with this position. Embracing this concept of the virtual could open up so much that everything evaporates and the concrete organisational forces that keep things in their place are underestimated. This does not mean that understanding organisation and non-organisation as actualisations underpinned by the virtual is wrong or inadequate. Nor does it imply a blanket rejection of or opposition to realism. It simply means that such a supple understanding needs to be used with some caution and not constructed as a displacing representation of organisation. By acknowledging that organisation is not all that exists in the world and that organisational arrangements cannot last forever, resting as they do on molecular accomplishments, it can serve an important role in unwresting the reified ontological status that mainstream organisational research typically attributes to organisations, and adding greater depth, clarity and possibility to those approaches which already consider organisation with greater subtlety. Rather than writing off organisation as such, it can help us view organisations and organisational activities in a broader context of constant change that is not reducible to action, function, structure, information, economics or language – but is itself a matter of change (Tsoukas 2005). Bergson (1911) spoke of creative evolution as constituting a different, non-spatialised order, a creative vital order involving the challenge faced by life to find ways to resist inorganic, unorganised, spatial matter. To Bergson, the self-organised body of the organism, then, provides ways in which life becomes liveable, inventing and evolving in open-ended creative evolution. As it does so, according to Deleuze, the stabilising plane of consistency and the plane of organisation will constantly move against each other – destabilising and stabilising, perpetually trembling. Deleuze invites us to develop organisation theory that does not define its objectives in terms of explanation, prediction, interpretation or representation, which are the dominant concerns of existing organisation theory, but itself trembles. Whilst mainstream organisation theory might see this as a trembling with fear, we see it as the excited trembling of anticipation.

References

Ansell Pearson, K. (1999), *Germinal Life: The Difference and Repetition of Deleuze*, London: Routledge.

Bergson, H. (1911), *Creative Evolution*, trans. A. Mitchell, New York: Holt.

Bergson, H. (1999), 'A letter from Bergson to John Dewey', in J. Mullarkey (ed.), *The New Bergson*, Manchester: Manchester University Press.

Boundas, C. V. (1996), 'Deleuze-Bergson: An Ontology of the Virtual', in P. Patton (ed.), *Deleuze: A Critical Reader*, London: Blackwell.

Brewis, J. and Linstead, S. (2000), *Sex, Work and Sex Work*, London: Routledge.

Burrell, G. (1997), *Pandemonium: Towards a Retro-Organization Theory*, London: Sage.

Burrell, G. (1998), 'Linearity, Control and Death', in D. Grant, T. Keenoy and C. Oswick (eds), *Discourse and Organization*, London: Sage.

Chia, R. (1999), 'A Rhizomic Model of Organizational Change: Perspective from a Metaphysics of Change', *British Journal of Management*, 10: 3.

Colebrook, C. (2002), *Gilles Deleuze*, London: Routledge.

Cooper, R. (1986), 'Organization/Disorganization', *Social Science Information*, 25: 2, reprinted in J. Hassard and D. Pym (eds) (1990), *The Theory and Philosophy of Organizations*, London: Routledge.

Cooper, R. and Burrell, G. (1988), 'Modernism, Postmodernism and Organizational Analysis: An Introduction', *Organization Studies*, 9: 1.

DeLanda, M. (1999), 'Immanence and Transcendence in the Genesis of Form', in I. Buchanan (ed.), *A Deleuzian Century*, Durham, NC: Duke University Press.

DeLanda, M. (2000), *A Thousand Years of Non-Linear History*, Cambridge: Swerve Editions, MIT Press.

DeLanda, M. (2002), *Intensive Science and Virtual Philosophy*, London: Continuum Press.

Deleuze, G. (1988), *Bergsonism*, trans. H. Tomlinson and B. Hammerjam, New York: Zone Books.

Deleuze, G. (1994), *Difference and Repetition*, trans. P. Patton, London: Athlone.

Deleuze, G. (1999), 'Bergson's Conception of Difference', trans. M. McMahon, in J. Mullarkey (ed.), *The New Bergson*, Manchester: Manchester University Press.

Deleuze, G. and Guattari, F. (1983), *On the Line*, trans. J. Johnston, New York: Semiotext(e).

Deleuze, G. and Guattari, F. (1984), *Anti-Oedipus: Capitalism and Schizophrenia*, trans. R. Hurley, M. Seem and H. R. Lane, London: Athlone.

Deleuze, G. and Guattari, F. (1987), *A Thousand Plateaus: Capitalism and Schizophrenia*, trans. B. Massumi, Minneapolis: University of Minnesota Press.

Deleuze, G. and Guattari, F. (1994), *What is Philosophy?*, trans. G. Burchell and H. Tomlinson, London: Verso.

Goodchild, P. (1996), *Deleuze and Guattari: An Introduction to the Politics of Desire*, London: Sage.

Grosz, E. (2000), 'Deleuze's Bergson: Duration, the Virtual and a Politics of the Future', in I. Buchanan and C. Colebrook (eds), *Deleuze and Feminist Theory*, Edinburgh: Edinburgh University Press.

Guattari, F. (1984), *Molecular Revolution: Psychiatry and Politics*, trans. R. Sheed, Harmondsworth: Penguin Books.

Hardt, M. (1993), *Gilles Deleuze: An Apprenticeship in Philosophy*, Minneapolis, MN: University of Minnesota Press.

Jackson, N. and Carter, P. (2004), 'Gilles Deleuze and Felix Guattari', in S. Linstead (ed.), *Organization Theory and Postmodern Thought*, London: Sage.

Knights, D. (2004), 'Writing Organization Analysis into Foucault', in S. Linstead (ed.), *Organizations and Postmodern Thought*, London: Sage.

Linstead, S. (2000), 'Dangerous Fluids: The Organization without Organs', in J. Hassard, R. Holliday and H. Willmott (eds), *The Body and Organisation*, London: Sage.

Linstead, S. (2002), 'Organization as Reply: Henri Bergson and Casual Organization Theory', *Organization*, 9: 1.

Linstead, S. and Mullarkey, J. (2003), 'Time, Creativity and Culture: Introducing Bergson', *Culture and Organization*, 9: 1.

Massumi, B. (1992), *A User's Guide To Capitalism and Schizophrenia: Deviations from Deleuze and Guattari*, Cambridge: MIT Press.

Rajchman, J. (2000), *The Deleuze Connections*, Cambridge: MIT Press.

Surin, Kenneth (2002), ' "*Delire* is World-historical": Political Knowledge in *Capitalism and Schizophrenia*', *Polygraph*, 14.

Thanem, T. (2004), 'The Body without Organs: Nonorganizational Desire in Organizational Life', *Culture and Organization*, 10: 3.

Tsoukas, H. (2005), 'Afterword: Why Language Matters in the Analysis of Organizational Change', *Journal of Organizational Change Management*, 18: 1.

Williams, J. (2000), 'Deleuze's Ontology and Creativity: Becoming in Architecture', *Pli: The Warwick Journal of Philosophy*, 9.

Chapter 3

The Others of Hierarchy: Rhizomatics of Organising

Martin Kornberger, Carl Rhodes and René ten Bos[1]

In his preface to *Anti-Oedipus*, Michel Foucault suggests that Deleuze and Guattari answer questions less concerned with *why* things might be so, and more concerned with *how* to proceed. The procession that he identifies is the employment of desire in political action against (at least) the 'fascism in all of us, in our heads and in our everyday behaviour, the fascism that causes us to love power, to desire the very thing that dominates and exploits us' (Foucault 1983: xiii).

Fascism comes in many incarnations. As Deleuze and Guattari (1987) enumerate, this includes '[r]ural fascism and city or neighbourhood fascism, youth fascism and war veteran's fascism, fascism of the Left and fascism of the Right, fascism of the couple, family, school and office' (Deleuze and Guattari 1987: 214). It is the fascism of the office and the organisation that we wish to address in this chapter. We understand this fascism to operate on what Deleuze and Guattari refer to as a 'molecular' level. It is, in other words, a fascism that is already active prior to its organisation or normalisation on the 'molar' level of the state. It is, therefore, a kind of microfascism which Deleuze and Guattari understand as 'cancerous body rather than a totalitarian organism' (Deleuze and Guattari 1987: 215). This does not, of course, entail that particular organisations cannot be 'molar' or normalising forces. It is rather to acknowledge also that in organisational settings fascism has its own rhizomatics. Moreover, the notion of corporate organisation as 'the natural' order of work is itself a multiplicity of empirical organisations that communicate with each other so as to resonate *organisation*. This resonation is particularly vibrant when it comes to the idea of hierarchy as a form of order desired in organisations. While it acknowledged over and over again that hierarchy (or stratification) is not necessarily detrimental – one has to 'respond to the dominant reality' and 'mimic the strata' for reckless destratification is simply suicidal (Deleuze and Guattari 1987: 160

see also 40, 161). Nonetheless this hierarchy is a desire to repress desire in the name of centrality and control. Hierarchy is therefore aporetic: while it is not necessarily bad for you, it also opens the door to some kind of fascism (which in spite of certain seductiveness can be very bad for you).

To enable us to think about the social order of organisations we deploy some ideas and concepts from Deleuze in relation to Charles Bukowski's novel *Post Office* (1980 [1971]) and use this book as a means of exploring the world of organisations and hierarchies. In connecting Deleuze and Bukowski we want to entangle this novel with a story about hierarchy more generally – a story which has, in the modern era, seen hierarchy as the most dominant and naturalised (albeit contested) order of organisation. We create connections between *Post Office* and a variety of discourses that have emerged on the topic of hierarchy in organisations. In effect, we wish to subvert conventional perspectives on organisations by producing a text that expands the concept of organisation in such a way that its content is no longer limited to hierarchy as the only or dominant possible order.

The most dominant contemporary image of organisations has been that of a hierarchical 'organic organisation' (Burns and Stalker 1961; de Geus 1999). This organisation is considered as a whole composed of parts (organs) which are hierarchically organised and which operate together according to a central plan. This organisation is akin to a unitary body made up of organs (Hoskin 1995) that should function perfectly in relation to each other in order to carry through that which is dictated by the head. Organisations are conceptualised as interiority in *the* image of order. Conversely, what 'is outside is less ordered, less understood, the outside is a threat for the inside' (Weiskopf 2002: 85). Thus 'the assumption of boundaries has been the basis for constituting the organization as entity' (Malavé 1998: 111) and their orderly nature. Historically, the concepts of organisation, order and hierarchy have become axiomatic. The readings of Weber's (1978) bureaucracy as iron cage and Taylor's (1947) scientific management as hierarchical and rational structuring devices have levelled the playing field for the taken-for-granted perspective on 'hierarchy = organisation = order'. Put simply, the organisation is understood as rationally designed, separated from its environment, a problem-solving tool, driven and determined by pre-given goals imposed by an environment of markets, stakeholders, functional needs, and so on. The design of organisations obeys a model that 'aspires to certainty and control, and makes ambiguity and spontaneous cooperation suspect if not undesirable . . . It is built on a disdainful conception of human nature as suffering from "limited rationality" . . . it dreams of a world that is perfect but dead' (Czarniawska 2003: 361).

For Deleuze and Guattari the pervasiveness of this image of order is not something to admire. As they famously stated: 'We're tired of trees. We should stop believing in trees, roots, and radicles. They've made us suffer too much. All of arborescent culture is founded on them, from biology to linguistics' (Deleuze and Guattari 1987: 15). But what then for organisations, those infernal trees inscribed in hierarchy charts end-lessly drawn and redrawn in the hope that structures will provide answers to questions never quite articulated? Can and should we hope for some way out of this organisational arborescence? While attesting to the arborescence of bureaucracy, Deleuze and Guattari tell us that bureaucracies 'can begin to burgeon nonetheless, throwing out rhizome stems, as in a Kafka novel' (ibid.: 15) – or in our case a Bukowski novel.

Chinaski Interrupts

We now turn to Charles Bukowski's novel *Post Office* as our literary guide to hierarchy. We have chosen Bukowski for this purpose not only because his book has work and hierarchy as its central themes, but also because he clearly belongs to that 'strange Anglo-American' literary trad-ition whose practitioners – Melville, Lawrence, Lowry, Miller, Kerouac and others – 'know how to leave, to scramble the codes, to cause flows to circulate, to traverse the desert of the body without organs' (Deleuze and Guattari 1983: 132–3). They engage in 'stoned thinking based on intensively lived experience: Pop Philosophy' (Seem 1983: xxi).

During his life, Bukowski produced more than forty-five books. These included collections of poetry, short stories and novels. Through his work and life Bukowski earned his reputation as a hard-drinking, hard-fighting and hard-writing man whose depiction of the underside of American post-war life is second to none. As well as working and earning some money as a writer, Bukowski was also employed for eleven years in the US postal service as a mail deliverer and clerk – his experience of organisations is, if anything, empirical. He quit this job to become the often impoverished down-and-out writer for which he is better known. As a full-time writer, Bukowski's first novel was *Post Office* and it is through its roughly autobiographical character of Hank Chinaski that Bukowski tells of his life and work experience during this time.

Post Office is about one person's problematic relationship (to say the least) with the hierarchy of a particular organisation as it is conceptu-ally imposed on him. In Deleuze and Guattari terms, the book deals with hierarchy by creating disruptions, crossing flows, following desire and deterritorialising. In a general sense, this deterritorialisation is about 'the movement by which "one" leaves the territory. It is the operation of the line of flight' (Deleuze and Guattari 1987: 508). More specifically, however, Bukowski's is not a form of negative deterritorialisation that is 'immediately overlaid by reterritorializations' (ibid.: 508). Instead it emerges as a more nomadic deterritorialisation, which, while never escaping the possibility and lure of reterritorialisation, expresses a profound unrest with a world 'as the object of a mortuary and suicidal organization surrounding it at all sides' (ibid.: 511).

The first page of Bukowski's novel *Post Office* is a transcription of the official code of ethics of the United States Post Office, Los Angeles, California, dated 1 January 1970. This code talks of how postal employees (presumably including Chinaski) have 'established a fine tradition of faithful service to the nation' (Bukowski 1980: 1). It refers to the 'unwavering integrity', 'complete devotion', and 'the highest moral principles' required of postal employees and how they must act with 'honor and integrity worthy of the public trust' (ibid.: 1). In reading the story of Henry Chinaski, the postal employee, we soon find that this code is not something he cares for. Indeed, the position of this code – a pure bureaucratic document, an apparatus of territorialisation – at the beginning of the novel foreshadows how the novel itself will problematise such attempts of despotic encoding.

The story of *Post Office* starts when Chinaski takes a job as a mail carrier when the postal service needs extra workers to deliver Christmas cards. It ends, when, following a range of disciplinary actions against him, he resigns and decides to write a (this) novel – a decision that becomes the eruptive line of flight breaking him free from the hierarchy. In the intervening period we are told of Chinaski's world of hard drinking, failed marriages and racetrack gambling – and, of course, his problematic relationship with the hierarchy in which he works and which constrains his nomad desires. At the beginning of the story Chinaski works as a substitute mail deliverer who fills in for the regular carriers who, for reasons of sickness and so on, are not able to work. Each morning he reports to the post office at 5 a.m. (usually after having been up late drinking) and waits to see if there is work for him. The supervisor, Johnstone, takes a dislike to Chinaski and stops giving him work, but as Chinaski says to one of his buddies, 'I don't care. I'm not kissing his ass. I'll quit or starve, anything' (Bukowski 1980: 11). He refuses to be subjugated by the concepts of work and organisation as they are put to him – he refuses to give in to the supervisor or even to acknowledge his position. Failing to get through to

Chinaski, eventually Johnstone starts giving him the most difficult routes in order to 'break' him. As Chinaski narrates:

> The sweat dripping, the hangover, the impossibility of the schedule, and Johnstone back there in his red shirt, knowing it, enjoying it, pretending he was doing it to keep costs down. But everybody knew why he was doing it. Oh, what a fine man he was! (Bukowski 1980: 13)

Regardless, Chinaski proceeds without bowing down to 'the Stone', without rendering himself 'below', without succumbing to the hierarchical apparatus. He is screamed at by householders and chased by dogs bearing fangs, but he figures 'it was gung ho for a new man, especially for one who drank all night, went to bed at 2 a.m., rose at 4:30 a.m. after screwing and singing all night long, and, almost, getting away with it' (Bukowski 1980: 14). He is continually 'written up' (a literal attempt at inscription) for any misdemeanour from being late back from his route or placing his cap in the wrong place in the office. Johnstone continues to give him the hardest routes.

Chinaski does not play the dominant game that he is presented with at work – in particular, he does not respect the concept of 'organisation as hierarchy'. Even the most modest attempt at deference to Johnstone's superior hierarchical position might have ensured an easier life for Chinaski – but he is without compromise. What then might a worker who is *not* like Chinaski be like? Who might be the territorialised worker? Bukowski illustrates this when he introduces the character Matthew Battles – Johnstone's favorite 'sub' (i.e. substitute mail carrier).

> The Stone's favorite carrier was Matthew Battles. Battles never came in with a wrinkled shirt on. In fact everything he wore looked new, was new. The shoes, the shirts, the pants, the cap. His shoes really shined and none of his clothes appeared to have ever been laundered even once. Once a shirt or a pair of pants became the least bit soiled he threw them away.
> The Stone often said to us as Matthew walked by:
> 'Now there goes a carrier!'
> And The Stone meant it. His eyes damn near shimmered with love. (Bukowski 1980: 25)

Here Chinaski presents us with an image of what two of us have referred to as the pure and exemplary worker (ten Bos and Rhodes 2003) – the kind of worker he cannot and does not want to be. He knows too that such purity is impossible as Matthew later gets arrested for stealing money.

As the story proceeds, Chinaski continues to deliver the mail, but never gives in to the call for dedication or respect to the hierarchy. He says:

> I remember one of the older carriers pointing to his heart and telling me.
> 'Chinaski, someday it will get you, it will get you right here!'
> 'Heart attack?'
> 'Dedication to service. You'll see. You'll be proud of it.'
> 'Balls!'
> But the man had been sincere. (Bukowski 1980: 28)

Despite his disrespect for hierarchy, Chinaski does understand – fully in line with Deleuze and Guattari's understandings in this regard – what it can do. This is illustrated in his depiction of another carrier whose name was George Greene, a man who was known to all as G.G. G.G. was in his late sixties and had worked as a carrier for more than forty years. His face was

> wrinkled into strange runs and mounds of unattractive flesh. No light shone from his face. He was just an old crony who had done his job: G.G. The eyes looked like dull bits of clay dropped into eye sockets. (Ibid.: 35)

Chinaski has no respect for G.G. Despite the man's pride and dedication to the job – indeed, one of the beneficial things that bureaucracy can bring to a person – Chinaski's verdict is merciless: '[H]is life hadn't been a brave one' (ibid.: 36). Eventually, when he is unable to meet a deadline for inserting junk-mail circulars in his planned route, G.G. 'flips out' at work and is never seen again – as if to work outside of the order of organisation was an unbearable possibility. As Chinaski puts it:

> The 'good guy'. The dedicated man. Knifed across the throat over a handful of circs from a local market – with its special: a free box of brand name laundry soap, with a coupon, and any purchase over $3. (Bukowski 1980: 39)

After three years as a substitute mail carrier Chinaski gets promoted to being a 'regular' full-time worker. He sourly comments on this:

> Somehow, I was not too happy. I was not a man to deliberately seek pain, the job was still difficult enough, but somehow it lacked the old glamour of my sub days – the not-knowing-what-the-hell was going to happen next. (Bukowski 1980: 39)

For a moment the territorialisation of Chinaski seems imminent, but the possibility of this is too much for his nomad soul – he immediately resigns. He starts working as a small-time professional gambler and then as a clerk in an art store, but annoyed with his new boss, he applies for a job back in the postal service as a clerk (rather than a carrier) after someone tells him that it was an easy job. He was wrong. The job involved working long twelve-hour night shifts sorting mail – he stays in this job for twelve years. Like before, he continues to get written up for infringements of the post-office rules. During a counselling session the following conversation takes place:

> 'Mr Chinaski, you are saying, "Fuck the post office!" '
> 'I am?'
> 'And, Mr Chinaski, you know what that means?'
> 'No, what does it mean?'
> 'That means, Mr Chinaski, the post office is going to fuck *you*!'

He continues to get counselled and to receive disciplinary warnings from the post office – which, for the most part, he ignores. Finally he resigns – he leaves quietly. The book closes with Chinaski deciding to write a novel – despite all the attempts he didn't get fucked.

Hierarchy

Leaving Bukowski for a while, we now move across to look at a different way of understanding hierarchy. The cultural antecedents of hierarchy primarily associate it with relative closeness to god. Etymologically, hierarchy derives from the Greek word *hierarkhia* meaning the rule of a high priest (*ta hiera* – sacred rites, and *archeia* – to lead or rule). The use of hierarchy as the ranked organisation of persons or things emerged in the early seventeenth century, based on the earlier use of hierarchy to denote a ranked division of angels. According to this, angels are grouped into three classes: the angels of pure contemplation, the angels of the cosmos and the angels of the world. Within each of these classes were three choirs starting with Seraphim, then Cherubim and eventually working its way down to the relatively lowly Archangels and Angels. Each class of angels has its own designated role and function. The angels of pure contemplation govern all creation, the angels of the cosmos govern the cosmos and the angels of the world govern the world (Connell 1995). Within this hierarchy, the role of the angels is to act as mediators between god and mortals. The angels' duty is to bring human prayers to heaven and to return god's answers to earth (Guiley 1996). The ranking of angels is from highest to lowest – above the angels is pure divinity and the throne of god and below the angels is the world of mortals. This origin of hierarchy is generally attributed to the fifth-century theologian who adopted the name Dyonisius the Areopagite. It was used 'to define and describe an organization structure based on the top-down delegation of power and determination of functions' (Iannello 1992: 15). Hierarchy, in this sense defines beings (both heavenly and mortal) in terms of their position between god and the inevitable sin of humanity.

In tracing the development of hierarchy throughout the ages, and with a more organisational focus, Bernhard and Glantz (1992) state that rigid hierarchies of work organisation ascended as a form of social organisation in line with the invention of systemic agriculture. With the industrial revolution, the notion of hierarchy moved on from the state and the church to the workplace. In this process, although organisations did not invent hierarchy, they perfected it as a means of control and rationalisation and as a way of differentiating and stratifying rights, privileges and authority (Perrow 1992). Most famously, Weber (1947) argued that the hierarchy of authority in the workplace is a means to achieve control over people's behaviour for the purpose of efficiency. In this context, some believe that hierarchy is a natural form for organisations – a thing that emerges free from human intervention and is indeed *natural* – it comes from nature, from god. Even critics of traditional hierarchical models such as Halal (1996) argue that 'some hierarchy will always be needed because the universe is naturally organised in a hierarchical fashion' (Halal 1996: 28). In their advocacy of the utopia of the 'boundaryless organisation' Askenas et al. (1995) have proposed that '[h]ierarchies are necessary, inevitable and desired fixtures for organizational life' (Askenas et al. 1995: 33). Nature takes the blame again – *all god, no responsibility.*

Even more forcefully, Jacques (1996) has argued that managerial hierarchies are a direct reflection of fundamental differences in the nature of human capability – with people rising to more senior positions because they have naturally superior capabilities. On this basis, he proposes a 'universally applicable organisational structure' that will maximise efficiency and competitiveness as well as ensure the 'release of human imagination, trust and satisfaction at work' (Jacques 1996: 2). Precisely like the celestial hierarchy that presaged it, such a hierarchy is based on the natural superiority of those 'higher up' and their role in providing deliverance for those 'lower down' – as if the more senior one is as a manager, the closer one is to god, and, of course, there must be angels in the boardroom. Even the discovery of the 'informal organisation' by Elton Mayo and his Hawthorne collaborators did not extinguish the fiery desire for hierarchy – they suggested that this hierarchy rather than the informal organisation is essential to organisational goal achievement (Iannello 1992).

In the next section, we will discuss how Bukowski and Deleuze reject this simplistic and heavenly up–down imagery in favour of a more horizontal concept of organisation – a perspective of plateaus. Drawing on this, our connection with Bukowski is one that provides the opportunity to explore one's 'potential becoming to the extent that one deviates from the [hierarchical or stratified] model' (Deleuze and Guattari 1987: 105). In Chinaski we find a nomadic man in a hierarchised world – one who does not classify himself according to the dominant organisational concept in which he finds himself, but yet one in which he does find himself nonetheless. Although he is ill-fitted to his job and is constantly at odds with those defined by the hierarchy as his superiors, he does not resist authority as much as he tries to refuse to recognise it, or refuse to play its game. He deals with hierarchy not by moving up or down, but by moving out. Rather than being a freedom fighter seeking liberation from hierarchy, Chinaski enacts what we analytically can term a *rhizomatics of organisation*.

Towards a Rhizomatic Organisation

Deleuze and Guattari question radically the very concept of the 'signifying totality' (1987: 4) that dominates and organises contemporary thinking. As we have suggested, the very idea of thinking of organisation in terms of order, stability and stratification is an instance of such a signifying totality and we wish to suggest that Chinaski refuses to accept this totality (rather than accepting it and trying to escape from it in the vain hope of finding liberation). To interrupt this totality, to subvert and pervert the aborescent schemes that dominate our lives and that condemn us to a rigid and segmented existence, the concept of organisational rhizomatics might be invoked.

An organisation, conventionally understood as being essentially arborescent, seeks to define itself on the basis of a central mode of signifying practice – one where 'all roads lead back to Rome' and where Rome is inevitably the 'top' of the organisation – the home of the self-proclaimed angels scrambling to get closer to god. Organisation has the desire to coordinate activities within pre-set boundaries such as the code of ethics cited at the beginning of *Post Office*. Organisation conceived in this way appears in the form of what Deleuze and Guattari call 'the state apparatus' for it strives for a universality that defines 'goals and paths, conduits, channels, organs, and entire organon' (Deleuze and Guattari 1987: 374).

In contrast, in conceiving organisation as potentially rhizomatic, it is important to note that the distinction between the rhizomatic and the arborescent is one that is constructed for the purposes of being able to conceive of their relation rather than them being independently opposed models. To this point, Deleuze and Guattari show that 'there are knots or arborescence in rhizomes, and rhizomatic off-shoots in roots' (ibid.: 20). It is this very point that suggests the practicality of a rhizomatic conception of organisations – that is, even in the most conventional and rigid hierarchy one can expect to find rhizomes which demonstrate a creative potential for exploring new territories.

Chinaski is such a rhizomatic offshoot in the post office. What we take from his example is that hierarchy is not sufficiently problematised through a focus on humanistic liberation. It is rather that Chinaski's behaviour seems to subvert the formalities and centripetalisation of being organised. Note, however, that his behaviour is not independent of the hierarchy, but that it is rather connected to it in a non-hierarchical manner: it is a mutation of hierarchy's purity that favours connection and movement outside organic unity. The rhizome that Chinaski opens up might be expected thus to contain 'lines of segmentarity according to which it is stratified, territorialized, organized, signified, attributed, etc., as well as lines of deterritorialization down which it constantly flees' (ibid.: 9). More specifically, Chinaski shows us that organisation as hierarchy and centrality can never live up to its own claims to divine stratification because the potential for destratification and movement outside of the territories defined by the centre is always immanent. Even the post office is an organisation made up of heterogeneous elements and disparate connections that multiply and variegate.

Being in such an organisation does not necessarily entail flowing with the centralised rules and listening to the commands of those 'higher up' the hierarchy. Instead, there is always the possibility to follow the rhizome stemming from bureaucracy. This might be achieved by following what Deleuze and Guattari call 'lines of flight' – movements of desire that enable 'one to blow apart strata, cut roots, and make new connections' (Deleuze and Guattari 1987: 15) and that challenge the hegemony of the hierarchical signifier. Such lines of flight can depart from or infiltrate the traditions of western bureaucracy and its agrarian origins. What we wish to suggest is a nomadology of organisations as a means of exploring their immanent rhizomatic potential – at its extreme, as we explore below, an Organisation-without-Organs. Deleuze and Guattari's concept of nomadology is entwined with that of rhizomatics, deterritorialisation, and the following of lines of flight. Such a nomadology is one that opposes the plans for destinations to fixed points and instead follows lines of flight that prevent organisation from establishing itself on firm structural ground.

The transformation of organisation from arborescence to rhizomatic is performative as much as it is structural. Organisations, as they are encountered by the lonely travellers within them, do not appear as fixed things (in spite of their unmistakable power) but rather as assemblages of ideas, experiences and representations. Yet, thinking rhizomes while working in a sweatshop would no doubt not be sufficient to ease the boredom and the pain of one's tasks. On the other hand, not following lines of flight, not trying to deterritorialise from the daunting shadow of a hierarchy could only ever be to resign oneself to the imposed limitations of the organisational state apparatus.

What we want to suggest with the concept of rhizomatic organisation is not that a change of the rules can achieve more (or less) egalitarianism within a hierarchical setting. Instead, with this concept we wish to invoke the idea that organisation might very well not be doing anything, might not be directed towards a goal, might in this sense not be operative or productive at all. Organisations are loci where madness, disgust, desire, anxiety, lust and other kinds of deterritorialisation do occur. These are the dimensions that Chinaski opens up. What this points to is a concept of hierarchy that tries to see arborescence as a problematic mutation of the rhizome rather than the rhizome as the evil other of the arborescent organisation. Hierarchies may not cease to exist but that does not mean that there is only one way of connecting with them or that there are not multiple ways of interrupting them. In fact, people constantly escape hierarchies – the manager who negotiates a golden hand shake before he leaves the hierarchy; the worker who smokes dope while unloading a truck; or the student who downloads his essay from www.easyessay.com – they all connect hierarchy to other lines, interweave and mingle the strict order of things with other elements and create a line of flight.

The Organisation-without-Organs

Organisations are always to some extent unmanaged, disorganised and without a unitary organisation of organs. If they weren't, there would be nothing to organise in the first place (Cooper 1990; Munro 2001). They mix and intermingle with other elements, be it people, artefacts or other organisations. What we wish to explore now is how this immanent becoming of organisation might lead, as its ultimate consequence, to organisational death. There is a common sense that would disagree – organisations should be built to last forever, at least in the managerial eye. Although they are designed and conceptualised along the lines of the metaphor of the living (and thus dying) world, they transcend individual mortality and create an aura of eternity. This is what Levine (2001) calls the fantasy of inevitability in organisations. Part of this fantasy is the widespread narcissistic opinion that organisations are unique even if there are many similar organisations offering similar products. Such organisations cannot face the fact that they will eventually collapse, and that other (dis)organisations will replace them. If this is correct, then the biggest threat and challenge to management thinking must be organisational death – a fact that is hard to accept:

> The capacity to acknowledge the inevitability of death is, then, the other side of the capacity to give up prior assumptions, to refuse to know the shape of life before life has taken shape. (Levine 2001: 1262)

The fantasy of immortality, fed by vision and mission statements, and institutional pressure to imitate others' behaviour (DiMaggio and Powell 1983) make strategy the vade-mecum of managers. Yet, the experience of organisational change can be similar to the 'death and dying . . . of terminally ill patients' (Zell 2003: 73).

Perhaps, organisations do not die. Being blissfully unaware of their immanent end, they are not what Heidegger referred to as being-towards-death. Yet, saying that organisations cannot die doesn't preclude that they cannot cease to live. In fact, organisations cease to exist continuously. If we examine the Fortune 500 companies, we can see this. Since 1970, between 30 and 50 per cent of the Fortune 500 companies disappeared every ten years or so. If you take the list of the top twelve companies in 1900, only one single organisation – General Electric – is still enjoying business as usual (see Tidd et al. 2001: 17). The same seems to be true for smaller, less-equipped companies – they too are constantly threatened by the danger of perishing (for one of the few studies on this topic, see Haveman 1993).

Obviously, death represents the ultimate collapse of the hierarchy; it is the most radical form of its transformation since it is a transformation to non-existence. On this basis, we might ask how the dream of immortality relates to the inevitability of 'death'. In other words, what is the relation between order and disorder, between organisation and disorganisation, between purity and impurity? What we can see in *Post Office* is an event that constantly escapes the hierarchical, ordered organism, something that lives inside it, feeds on it like a parasite, but constantly fights and rebels against it. It connects with other flows and brings in new, alien elements that disturb its smooth functions. Deleuze and Guattari's concept of the 'Body without Organs' will help us to understand this reality. Our proposal here is to retain yet transform the notion of 'organisation as organism' by working towards a discussion of the concept of the 'Body without Organs' (BwO) and the translation of it into the concept of 'Organisation-without-Organs' (OwO). Invoking OwO is, we suggest, a radical consequence of organisational rhizomatics. Although the concept was introduced to the study of organisations by Cooper and Burrell in 1988, it has not been picked up widely (nor wildly; see Linstead 2000). To be clear as a concept, OwO does not mean that an organisation's organs are erased:

> The organs are not its enemies. The enemy is the organism. The BwO is opposed not to the organs but to that organization of the organs called the organism. (Deleuze and Guattari 1987: 158)

The OwO transforms the organisational hierarchy and its organic organisation and alters its identity dramatically. A Chinaskisation of organisation! Further, employing the concept of the OwO, we have to bear in mind one caveat: taken by themselves, the organic organisation and the OwO are both dead ends. One leads into death through order, the other one leads into death through chaos. As indicated above, destratifying is ambiguous and even dangerous:

> Staying stratified – organized, signified, subjected – is not the worst that can happen; the worst that can happen is if you throw the strata into demented or suicidal collapse, which brings them back down on us heavier than ever. (Deleuze and Guattari 1987: 161)

This OwO is not about celebrating chaos over order, but rather (like Bukowski) it is about exploring analytically organisations at their extremes – when they find themselves in the vicinity of death, which can be understood either as a radical transformation of their identity or as their eradication.

Looking at organisational discourse and at the *Post Office* as exemplary case study, it can be said that management and organisation theory is obsessed by a transcendental rationality that can be traced back to a Cartesian origin where mind controls matter, and the head (management) controls and directs the organisation (body, employees) and the bits and pieces are hierarchically structured in between like obedient angels. In response to this, we seek to criticise this image and defer it simultaneously by working up to the concept of the OwO in relation to those people who find themselves within an organisation. By rhizomatically following his lines of flight, Chinaski refuses the ideology of the organisational 'we' and refuses to identify himself with the office. Arguably, he is part of the organisation, but he constantly deterritorialises it and transformes it into an OwO. Implicitly, this means that no one can know what the organisation actually is or what it will do. Chinaski was simply not predictable. If management assumes that it has the power to make the corporate body speak or to silence it, to move and to stop it, it also assumes that without such thought, the body would be inert, only passively reacting to environmental changes. Such is an organised body, (in)formed by a transcendent power. But what is the experience of an organisation that is not determined by a mastermind or a master plan?

No one knows what a body can do without it being determined by the mind. If people claim that this or that action of the body springs from the mind, which has command over the body, 'they do not know what they say, and they do nothing but confess with pretentious words that they know nothing about the cause of the action, and see nothing in it to wonder at' (Spinoza 1883: 108). Many things happen in organisations which management would never have dreamed possible without its direction. In fact, one could say that *organisation is what happens while management is busy making other plans*. Chinaski is but one example of the myriads of immanent events that unfold in and on organisations, transforming it into an OwO.

Our thesis is that the body of an organisation and its organs can and do achieve things which management, captive in its prejudices, has never dreamt of. Such an understanding puts the emphasis on the body rather than on the mind. According to such an immanent understanding, learning and change is rather a physical becoming than just a mental adoption. Hierarchies cannot learn or change in a Deleuzian sense, since they react allergically to every unfamiliar element. Chinaski is a good example: the hierarchy tries to cope with him employing a mixture of either rejecting (expelling) him or converting (disciplining) him according to its rules and procedures. But what it cannot do is connect with the strange element that he is and that he introduces. The hierarchy would take on an entirely different shape. Ultimately, however, the hierarchy cannot learn. Its only way to experience radical change is when it ceases to exist.

Implications

Chinaski seems relatively unique in his willingness and capability to live an extreme form of rhizomatic life. It is indeed problematic to see his rupture with the post office as some form of exemplar of how one might deal with the demands that organisation might place on people at work – demands to be subjectified, defined, stratified within the closely defined territory of the organisation. If arborescence demands that we be imitators of pre-existing models, Chinaski stands firmly against such imitations. He refuses to copy the rules and the structures in the comportment of his own life and follows his desires with a minimum of structure. However, Chinaski is not fighting against forces or resisting heroically but he uses the forces like a surfer. This is what Deleuze refers to as a 'combat-between', namely 'the process through which a force enriches itself by seizing hold of other forces and joining itself to them in a new ensemble: a becoming' (1997: 132). By way of such a connection to the organisation Chinaski produces a body without organs that consists of intensities in a constant state of becoming. This is not an easy option. To live his life might actually be unbearable. The absence of structure, the willingness to follow desires, and the revolt against hierarchy require so much fluidity that the very subject who experiences it might almost cease to be.

Why then look to Chinaski? Our answer is that in his extremity, Chinaski provides possibilities for action that for many of us might be unthinkable. Indeed, where we have many organisational models that suggest extreme forms of hierarchical being – the organisation man, the exemplary worker, the human resource (for example) – we have few that propose the opposite extreme (see ten Bos and Rhodes 2003). Our proposal is that Chinaski is one such example – one that in a flight from hierarchical life enables us to see life more clearly and helps us to forge more rhizomatic paths through it. Thus just as 'you never reach the Body without Organs' (Deleuze and Guattari 1987: 150), so too the extreme behaviour of Chinaski is a liminal experience, something that cannot be reached by many. Nevertheless, his behaviour demonstrates the disorganisation of rhizomatics and, consequently, articulates a new other for organisational hierarchy – an idea of how to proceed. On an organisational level, the concepts of hierarchy and OwO challenge established images of organisational change. On a more general level, organising is always about organising the differences between alternative orders, whether they are hierarchies, rhizomes or OwO. With Deleuze we can understand the very idea of differences between orders:

> The idea of disorder appears when, instead of seeing that there are two or more irreducible orders (for example, that of life and that of mechanism, each present when the other is absent), we retain only a general idea of order that we confine ourselves to opposing to disorder and to thinking in correlation with the idea of disorder. (Deleuze 1988: 19–20)

Thus, an analytic of the social informed by Deleuze and Guattari emphasises the nuances between things rather than categorising things. Beside these lines of flight, such an analytic of the social would accelerate our thinking and push it out of stagnation and habit. As common Cartesian sense tells us, thinking is cutting, dividing, separating, in order to gain control. With Deleuze and Guattari we can understand the overarching desire and driving force behind such thinking:

> We require just a little order to protect us from chaos . . . All that the association of ideas has ever meant is providing us with these protective

rules – resemblance, contiguity, causality – which enable us to put some order into ideas, preventing our 'fantasy' (delirium, madness) from crossing the universe in an instant. (Deleuze and Guattari 1994: 201)

It is not chaos but our ways and attempts to control it that inhibits the creation of intelligent thinking and lively theory. To map unknown terrain, to create new places, to defer perception, we need fantasy, imagination and a joyful technology of foolishness. Therefore we can conclude with Deleuze and Guattari that it 'is as if the *struggle against chaos* does not take place without an affinity with the enemy, because another struggle develops and takes on more importance – the struggle *against opinion*, which claims to protect us from chaos itself' (Deleuze and Guattari: 1994: 203). While remaining ambiguous towards chaos, an analytics of the social informed by Deleuze and Guattari would unambiguously explore new ways of thinking and conceptualising it. A rhizomatics of organising might be but one way of doing so.

References

Ashkenas, R., Ulrich, D., Jick, T. and Kerr, S. (1995), *The Boundaryless Organization: Breaking the Chains of Organizational Structure*, San Francisco: Jossey-Bass.

Bernhard, J. G. and Glantz, K. (1992), *Staying Human in the Organization: Our Biological Heritage and the Workplace*, Westport: Praeger.

Bukowski, C. (1980 [1971]), *Post Office*, London: Alison and Busby.

Burns, T. and Stalker, G. M. (1961), *The Management of Innovation*, London: Tavistock.

Connell, J. T. (1995), *Angel Power*, New York: Ballantine Books.

Cooper, R. (1990), 'Organization/Disorganization', in J. Hassard and D. Pym (eds), *The Theory and Philosophy of Organizations: Critical Issues and New Perspectives*, London: Routledge.

Cooper, R. and Burrel, G. (1988), 'Modernism, Postmodernism and Organizational Analysis: An Introduction', *Organization Studies*, 9: 1.

Czarniawska, B. (2003), 'Forbidden Knowledge: Organization Theory in Times of Transition', *Management Learning*, 34: 3.

de Geus, A. (1999), *The Living Company: Growth, Learning and Longevity in Business*, London: Nicholas Brealey.

Deleuze, G. (1988), *Bergsonism*, trans. H. Tomlinson and B. Hammerjam, New York: Zone Books.

Deleuze, G. (1997), *Essays: Critical and Clinical*, trans. D. W. Smith, and M. A. Greco, Minneapolis: University of Minnesota Press.

Deleuze, G. and Guattari, F. (1983), *Anti-Oedipus: Capitalism and schizophrenia*, trans. R. Hurley, M. Seem and H. R. Lane, Minneapolis: University of Minnesota Press.

Deleuze, G. and Guattari, F. (1987), *A Thousand Plateaus: Capitalism and Schizophrenia*, trans. B. Massumi, Minneapolis: University of Minnesota Press.

Deleuze, G. and Guattari, F. (1994), *What is Philosophy?*, trans. H. Tomlinson and G. Burchell, New York: Columbia University Press.

DiMaggio, P. and Powell, W. (1983), 'The Iron Cage Revisited: Institutional Isomorphism and Collective Rationality in Organizational Fields', *American Journal of Sociology*, 48: 2.

Foucault, M. (1983), 'Preface', in G. Deleuze and F. Guattari, *Anti-Oedipus: Capitalism and Schizophrenia*, Minneapolis: University of Minnesota Press.

Guiley, R. E. (1996), *Encyclopedia of Angels*, New York: Facts on File.

Halal, W. E. (1996), *The New Management: Democracy and Enterprise are Transforming Organization*, San Francisco: Berrett Koehler.

Haveman, H. (1993), 'Ghosts of Managers Past: Managerial Succession and Organizational Mortality', *Academy of Management Journal*, 36: 4.

Hoskin, K. (1995), 'The Viewing Self and the World We View: Beyond the Perspectival Illusion', *Organization*, 2: 1.

Iannello, K. P. (1992), *Decisions without Hierarchy: Feminist Interventions in Organization Theory and Practice*, New York: Routledge.

Jacques, E. (1996), *Requisite Organization: A Total System for Effective Management Leadership for the 21st Century*, Arlington, VA: Cason Hall.

Levine. D. (2001), 'The Fantasy of Inevitability in Organizations', *Human Relations*, 54: 10.

Linstead, S. (2000), 'Dangerous Fluids and the Organization-without-Organs', in J. Hassard, R. Holliday and H. Willmott (eds), *Body and Organization*, London: Sage.

Malavé, J. (1998), 'From Bounded Systems to Interlocking Practices: Logics of Organizing', in R. Chia (ed.), *In the Realm of Organization: Essays for Robert Cooper*, London: Routledge.

Munro, R. (2001), 'Unmanaging/Disorganisation', *ephemera critical dialogues in organization*, 1: 4.

Perrow, C. (1992), 'Small Firm Network', in N. Nohria and R. G. Eccles (eds), *Networks and Organizations: Structure, Form and Action*, Boston: Harvard Business School Press.

Seem, M. (1983), 'Introduction', in G. Deleuze and F. Guattari, *Anti-Oedipus: Capitalism and Schizophrenia*, Minneapolis: University of Minnesota Press.

Spinoza, B. (1883), *Ethics: Demonstrated in Geometrical Order and Divided into Five Parts*, London: Truebner.

Taylor, F. (1947), *The Principles of Scientific Management*, New York: Norton.

ten Bos, R. and Rhodes, C. (2003), 'The Game of Exemplarity: Subjectivity, Work and the Impossible Politics of Purity', *Scandinavian Journal of Management*, 19: 4.

Tidd, J., Bessant, J. and Pavitt, K. (2001), *Managing Innovation: Integrating Technological, Market and Organizational Change*, Chichester: John Wiley.

Weber, M. (1947), *The Theory of Social and Economic Organization*, New York: Free Press.

Weber, M. (1978), *Economy and Society*, Berkeley: University of California Press.

Weiskopf, R. (2002), 'Deconstructing "The Iron Cage": Towards an Aesthetic of Folding', *Consumption, Markets and Culture*, 5: 1.

Zell, D. (2003), 'Organizational Change as a Process of Death, Dying and Rebirth', *Journal of Applied Behavioral Sciences*, 39: 1.

Note

1. The order of the authors reflects merely the arbitrariness of the alphabet rather than a hierarchy of expertise.

Part II
Subjectivity and Transformation

Chapter 4

In the Mean Time:
Vitalism, Affects and Metamorphosis
in Organisational Change

Peter Lohmann and Chris Steyaert

> Affects are the nonhuman becomings of man.
> Gilles Deleuze and Félix Guattari, *What is Philosophy?*

Demand the Impossible

We begin within a specific social field constituted by a process of organisational change, which was initiated by the current policy of deregulat-
ing the electricity industry in Europe. As we join the story, the quiet days
of monopoly are coming to an end at ELEC, a Danish utilities provider.
We focus on how employees are produced as subjects in such a context,
how they *become* subjects. We have followed developments at ELEC
during a three-year period; we have approached them from the perspective of the emotions, frustrations and struggles, the comments and hesi-
tations of its casualties, which crowd the really affective movements of
the change process. To address and analyse this social field, we want to
produce an exploratory politics of change. Such a venture, as Brian
Massumi has noted, is not without risk.

> [A]n exploratory politics of *change* is philosophy pursued by other means –
> a radical politics equal to the 'radicality' of the expanded empirical field
> itself. Radical politics is an inherently risky undertaking because it cannot
> predict the outcome of its actions with certainty. If it could, it wouldn't be
> radical but reactive, a movement dedicated to capture and containment,
> operating entirely in the realm of the already possible, in a priori refusal of
> the new. Radical politics must tweak and wait: for the coming, collective
> determination of the community. Its role is to catalyze or induce a global
> self-reorganization: tweak locally to induce globally (to modulate a slogan).
> Speaking of slogans, repeat this one: 'be realistic, demand the impossible.'
> Under what conditions could that be a formula for a *political empiricism*?
> (2002: 243–4)

Massumi's formulation has a number of important consequences for a Deleuzian reinvention of the concept of change as it appears in the so-called organisational change literature (for a representative sample see Van De Ven and Poole 1995; Weick and Quinn 1999; Sturdy and Grey 2003). First, we are interested in a radical and active formulation of change. The vast majority of the literature on 'organisational change' is merely interested in changing organisations under conditions of control and containment, holding the course prescribed by the political chart of capitalism. A Deleuzian analysis does not allow such reductionism. Second, we will connect the philosophical with the non-philosophical, as 'philosophy needs nonphilosophy to make an actual difference in the world' (Massumi 2002: 244). If we are not to miss the point of Deleuze's philosophy we must engage with it as a tool picked up by our non-philosophical hands (Deleuze and Guattari 1994: 218). Third, we connect with the empirical world and its expansion. Following Massumi above, we will 'tweak the local' and let it transform the concept of change itself, a concept that is systematically overcoded in the organisational change literature. Fourth, analysis should never be an interpretation but a *style of experimentation*. This takes place through collective enunciation, through fabulation. So we will read the responses of the organisational members at ELEC as the emergence of a collective enunciation, a slow and patient collective becoming. Fifth, Massumi's call for radicality brings us closer to the becoming-Deleuzian of this century (Foucault 1977), for, like Rosi Braidotti, we suspect that 'what is really running out of time is the possibility of inscribing Deleuze's radical project into contemporary culture *at all*' (Braidotti 2002: 87).

Experiment

Braidotti calls Deleuze's philosophy a 'high tech brand of vitalism' (2002: 73) that undoes the Hegelian trap that associates desire with lack and negativity. She summarises his vitalist empiricism and its link to affectivity as follows: 'desire as positivity, not as lack; theoretical practice as a cartography of positions; subjectivity as a passions-driven network of impersonal and machine-like connections' (ibid.: 77). These key ideas are derived from *Anti-Oedipus* and *A Thousand Plateaus*, which present a political philosophy that includes 'a concern for the political effectivity of desire and the unconscious investments which play a part in macropolitical movements, a concern for the micropolitics of social life' (Patton 2000: 6). According to Deleuze and Guattari, the problem is that we construct our society on the basis of a desire that has been turned into *interests*: 'the very first step that the platonic logic of desire forces us to take, making us choose between *production* and *acquisition*' (Deleuze and Guattari 1983: 25). As an apparently unproblematic psychoanalytic concept, desire has become equal to the Oedipal 'ME', constituting an uncritical synthesis of Freudianism perpetually hunting for that extra something, always reducing desire to a 'production of fantasy' (ibid.: 26).

Deleuze and Guattari do not deny that regaining a lost object may lead to satisfaction, but they do not consider this element to be the essence of desire. Instead they turn the attention away from the individual and towards the group in order to show that the whole Oedipal structure of desire reflects our societal paranoia and has become an instrument for interiorising social and political oppression (Genosko 1996). Lack is 'created, planned and organized through social production' (Deleuze and Guattari 1983: 28). Moreover, desire is never 'an undifferentiated instinctual energy, but itself a result from a highly developed, engineered setup rich in interactions' (Deleuze and Guattari 1987: 215). Desire is inseparable from a machinic process of production that operates on a micropolitical level to form individual perceptions, attitudes, expectations and ways of speaking (Patton 2000). These micropolitical operations are formed by capitalism, since psychoanalysis does not invent Oedipus, the mother and the father 'with the slashed, split, castrated ego, [who] are the products of capitalism insofar as it engineers an operation that has no equivalent in the other social formations' (Deleuze and Guattari 1983: 269). Negativity, the characterisation of desire as lack, is instituted through ideological means in order to rationalise a social situation of hierarchy and domination (Butler 1999), 'a whole supple segmentarity that processes molecular energies and potentially gives desire a fascist determination' (Deleuze and Guattari 1987: 215). Desire must, according to Deleuze and Guattari, be moved away from the dominant psychological theme of a 'negative theology', a theology of absence that prioritises guilt and the transcendence of the law that make desire a normative ideal (Deleuze and Guattari 1986).

Whereas the current theology of desire is reactive and anti-life, Deleuze and Guattari provide an alternative conception of desire as a productive and generative activity. Desire is free and oriented along an immanent 'line of flight', always an approximation of movement, always approaching change. Desire is never just want, lack or need (Deleuze 1995). There is not something that triggers desire to come into play; it is always in play as our *world production*. Desire is *real* and not imaginative; desire produces real connections, investments and intensive stages within and between bodies. Desire is, they continue, 'not rooted in a subject or its objectives or objects, but subjects and objects are produced by desiring machines' (Deleuze and Guattari 1994: 184). As Guattari has said later,

> It's a question of being aware of the existence of machines of subjectivation which don't simply work within 'the faculties of the soul', interpersonal relations or intra-familial complexes. Subjectivity does not only produce itself through the psychogenetic stages of psychoanalysis or the 'mathemes' of the Unconscious, but also in the large-scale social machines of language and the mass media – which cannot be described as human. (Guattari 1995: 9)

Deleuze and Guattari's understanding of machines and production is deduced from dissatisfaction with the distinction between the relatively autonomous spheres of production (man–nature), distribution (industry–nature), and consumption (society–nature). Machines are therefore not to be understood as a metaphor; machines are said to produce, as there is no such thing as independent spheres or circuits: 'production is immediately consumption and a recording process at the same time' (Deleuze and Guattari 1983: 4). Desiring machines are always coupled to one-another, the production of production, the connective nature of 'and': 'Desire constantly couples continuous flows and partial objects that are by nature fragmentary and fragmented. Desire causes the current to flow, itself flows in turn, and breaks the flow' (ibid.: 5). The world becomes an intense experience where desire enacts a principle of creativity and invention and a possibility (to manoeuvre) in free interplay with the contexts we are a part of: 'If desire produces, its product is real. If desire is productive, it can be productive only in the real world and can produce only reality' (ibid.: 26). The focus is turned towards collectivity, the other: 'Social production is purely desiring production itself under determinate conditions . . . there is only desire and *the social*, nothing else' (ibid.: 29). In this production process, desire becomes the 'productive response to life in which the force and intensity of desire multiplies and intensifies in the course of an exchange with alterity' (Butler 1999: 213).

With the comment of Félix Guattari in an interview, where he said: 'For me desire is always "outside"; it always belongs to a minority' (Genosko 1996: 213); desire, collectivity and minority are brought into a relationship. This relationship is developed in Deleuze and Guattari's study of Franz Kafka, whom they consider a prime example of 'a minor literature' (1986; see also Rodowick 1997). Kafka loved to write about servants and employees, about offices and registries. His themes are undoubtedly administrative and organisational as he connects desire with 'a most extraordinary bureaucratic machine' (Deleuze and Guattari 1987: 4).

Indeed, the standard interpretation of his work is said to exemplify the alienation and absurdity of bureaucratic and governmental 'states'. For instance, both in *The Trial* and in *The Castle*, the focus is on distancing and panoptical, judgemental and administrative systems that alienate the story's characters from themselves and from an understanding of their selves. But Deleuze and Guattari break with such a tragic and psychologised interpretation of Kafka, which is why their transformative conceptualisation becomes a productive one in terms of reaching an affirmative analysis of change processes in organisations.

Against the image of Kafka as a misanthrope, a hero only of negativity, Deleuze and Guattari (1986) read Kafka's novels in a joyous way, trying to extract its revolutionary force and to situate his writings as 'the bearer of an affirmation without reserve' (Bensmaïa 1986: xiii). The designation of Kafka's writings as a minor literature is based upon three characteristics. First, the language of a minor literature is affected by deterritorialisation. It forms that 'which a minority constructs within a major language' (Deleuze and Guattari 1986: 16) as Kafka's 'Prague German is a deterritorialized language, appropriate for strange and minor uses' (ibid.: 17). Second, in minor literatures everything has political immediacy because their texts go beyond individual (Oedipalised) concerns and turn into political programmes. There is another story in the text, one that is quivering and trembling, struggling to cut the Oedipal strings that are attached to it, a story that is a matter of life and death. Third, 'everything takes on a collective value' in minor literatures (ibid.: 17). A minor literature does not form a literature of masters but aspires to a collective and revolutionary enunciation, to the concerns of the people, of a people to come. A writer, placed in the margins of his or her community, has the possibility of expressing 'another possible community and to forge the means for another consciousness and another sensibility' (ibid.: 17). A minor literature forms a collective machine of expression. Kafka becomes K. to indicate that the individual person is not centre-stage. Rather one can see K. as 'a functioning of a polyvalent assemblage of which the solitary individual is only a part' (ibid.: 85).

A Deleuzian reading of the literature of organisational change rejects a 'major' use of it by deterritorialising it, by approaching it with political urgency, aiming at a becoming-everybody. Such a counter-actualisation redirects the Oedipalised languages in order to find new capacities, opening up 'to fluctuation, to tendencies or unrehearsed opportunities of political association and transformation' (Hughes 1997: 58). We will have to create a foreign language within the language of organisational change, to be spoken by a people that does not yet exist (Rajchman 2000).

Add to the World

So the problem is not really one of getting *inside* the company one wants to study, but one of remaining on the edge of its community. Indeed, the easy part in our case was gaining access to the emprical material we wanted to look at. ELEC itself suggested having a doctoral student present to follow and document the expected major transformation processes. The company expected that it would learn some crucial lessons from such a study, lessons that it could implement on the next available occasion, when a new cycle of change predictably descended upon the organisation. Such an invitation makes it clear that change was implicitly understood as something that had a beginning and an end, a before and an after, an old state of order and a new state of order. The change process was thought to be like crossing a body of water to dock safely at the expected destination, which would then be the 'new' organisation. It did not go as expected, however, and more than once the people involved found themselves back in the open sea. We quickly realised that the only safe place that was open to this study would be found 'in the meantime', which offered a no-place that was also a no-time, a nowhere and a never yet to come. We had entered this study in the middle, right where change becomes change. Looking only at the movements there, we soon found ourselves on the margins; and this, of course, was where we belonged.

The study found itself in the paradoxical situation that, as in most change projects, change is not really appreciated or wanted. Rather, change is conceived as something that has to be managed and controlled: it never leaves the Oedipal grip of the effective management team. Change cannot be 'open to all at any time' (Patton 2000: 83). Change becomes identified with a permanent lack, the pursuit of an unreachable 'ideal' organisation that will replace the memory of the old one. This reductionist version of change goes hand in hand with the *bon mot* that change is the only constant of our time (Braidotti 2002; Sturdy and Grey 2003). On this view, a research team like ours is required to explain and interpret the change process through terms, methods and concepts that do not themselves change. The traditional production of research is one of description and representation. But as Deleuze pointed out, 'there is a "use" of representation, without which representation would remain lifeless and senseless' (1990: 146). Such 'other', and precisely *minor*, uses of representation require us to write multiple fabulations and to fabulate multiple writings – acknowledging that the multiple of change has to be created. Massumi encourages us to redirect the concept of change as it is currently practised in the organisational change literature:

> If you don't enjoy concepts and writing and don't feel that when you write you are adding something to the world, if only the enjoyment itself, and that by adding that ounce of positive experience to the world you are affirming it, celebrating its potential, tending its growth, in however small a way, however really abstractly – well, just hang it up. (Massumi 2002: 13)

Fabulations as fictional anticipations may be what Massumi calls 'parables for the virtual'. Writing makes science joyful, transporting life into a state of a non-personal power (Deleuze and Parnet 1987).

A People to Come

To tell the story of ELEC as a fabulation is to engage in a form of heterogeneous engineering, producing an assemblage of events drawn from speeches, texts, micropractices, laws, briefings, tears, silences. In order to show an event of change-becoming-change, we must focus on the becoming minor of the employees, who form a 'groupuscule' emerging in affects and collective enunciations that are based on a conceptual induction of change as a desiring production. Braidotti warns that 'accounting adequately for changes is a challenge that shapes up long-established habits of thought' (2002: 3). This requires thinking through flows and interconnections. The point is not to represent our data, but to picture the (complexity of) processes, the 'fluid in-between flows' of observations, experiences, information (Braidotti 2002). It is quintessential to bring emotions and affects into the analysis, as they are currently missing in studies of organisational change (see Steyaert 2005). We here follow the lead of Thrift as he writes that 'the thinking of movement and motion cannot be done without considering e-motion' (Thrift 2004: 60). More importantly, affectivity is central to Deleuze's notion of becoming: affects are becomings (Deleuze and Guattari 1987: 256). Herewith Deleuze redefines, in Braidotti's words, 'the practice of theory-making in terms of flows of affects' (Braidotti 2002: 70). Affects form war machines (Deleuze and Guattari 1987) or machines of metamorphosis (Patton 2000) giving access to a people to come based on the development of a minor consciousness. This allows us to readdress the becoming of organisational change as being oriented to new peoples (Deleuze and Guattari 1994: 108).

In order to address affects, we follow and describe the many reactive and active responses in connection with the vast amount of efforts to manage the change. At ELEC, the quiet days of being a monopoly were over and life turned around a struggle of becoming competitive. In this fissure, the workings of its history became visible through how employees were moved and felt moved around. At first, employees waited and felt insecure; then they were uncertain and they confronted their uncertainty and felt irritated; later they were despondent, exhausted and anxious. The new change discourse that centred on competition and the free market received an echo, an affective silence that contained the collective enunciation of employees. Beyond their multiple individual responses they were moved by a process of waiting, confrontation and exhaustion. Managers, consultants and employees all tried to control and manage this change process, but it always escaped them. This escape is formed through multiple lines of flight that should allow us to fabulate the becoming-minor of the change process and to write a cartography of affects.

The situation at ELEC is as follows. As a result of the European Commission's electricity market directive from 1996, ELEC ventured into a series of organisational change processes under different headings. Our study followed a group of about fifteen employees over a three-year period. The becoming-minor of employees at ELEC is produced in three movements: 'waiting', 'confrontation' and 'exhaustion', which we illustrate by way of the responses of one of the employees, an assistant accountant.

First, then, there is the waiting. Shortly after the change process was announced, employees experienced that their working lives had changed in a way that many did not think was possible. Being a hundred-year-old monopolistic utility, people had always thought that they could trust 'Mother ELEC'. When you worked at ELEC, you had found a mother that would take care of you for the rest of your life. While this phrase quickly fell into disuse, people remained patient and tried to act normally, as though nothing concrete had happened so far. They in fact waited for two full years while a number of taskforces analysed and prepared the outline for a new business model, which was based on Business Process Reengineering. After the work groups had made detailed plans for each new unit, the model was officially launched a half year later. The largest blow to the organisation was the layoff of 10 per cent of the approximately one thousand employees. This sort of thing had never happened before. This response of waiting is well expressed in the statement of an assistant accountant. He went on at length, stating that during this period of insecurity he knew only what he felt.

We have been informed in a reasonable way. And I mean informed, because we have not been involved. Nobody: not the common people or common employees. The longer the process took, the more people have become frustrated. You are just told that this will happen at this date. When they make something public, you get twenty-five words in the internal newsletter that ends with 'to be continued'; you can't use that to do anything. The information takes too long to come out. Information therefore starts to spread through more informal channels. People gossip. It is a top–down monologue: 'we are going to do it like this'. There are no opportunities for dialogue and debate; there is definitely no debate. It does not add to the open process that the company claims to be engaged in. That is so inaccurate. It might be that this is more about the feelings that I have than about how things are done. It could be that these changes are all very good, like the new personnel policy. It could be that it favours us employees in areas where we have felt a need for improvement for years. We may even end up with slightly better conditions. Then it is just very irritating and harmful that we have been through all these uncomfortable feelings. Everybody searches the policy for the things they don't like or understand and then turns it against ELEC. I don't know. I just know how I feel.

There is a desire for debate in this response. It has already been initiated by the 'common people' as a kind of collective murmuring in the corridors. Thus, in the meantime, a second response follows: confrontation. As pointed out by the assistant accountant, the new business model and a new personnel policy constituted significant changes that were supposed to lead ELEC competitively into its future. However, as the government specified further regulatory demands in a new electricity act, ELEC initiated a new project called 'Qualified Development' in order to reduce costs. For employees, this new change process provoked the question of why, since the new business model had hardly been implemented. It was a double question confronting management and confronting the personal feeling of not being able to follow what happened. People felt they were being pushed around and could not understand the need for a second round of turmoil and chaos.

In the meantime, questions accumulated.

Why are they [the management] answering our questions so mysteriously? Is there something they are not telling us? If this was my company, then I would say to my employees: 'Listen, we have to do this and that; otherwise we have to fire you all.' I mean if everything else fails then why not try the truth? Then there wouldn't be this difference between what they preach and what they practise. I don't know and don't care anymore. They call it an 'open process' but nobody knows anything.

Confrontations subsequently arose on three concrete issues. The first confrontation concerns the closing-down of certain locations of ELEC:

How stupid can this be? We use a lot of time and energy discussing how much we should pay internally in rent to ELEC, on moving money between accounts in each unit. We tried to use as few square meters as possible. People, desks, copy machines, computers, archives, you name it, were moved into as few square metres as possible. The result is that large parts of our districts stand completely vacant, whereas people almost sit on top of each other in other parts of these buildings. I mean, if this kind of physical movement is the only outcome after these years of analysis, what have we come to?

The second confrontation relates to the new style of the personnel department:

I have just had it up to here. I can only laugh at their circus language. It is just so silly with all those English titles and labels. 'The Human Resources Department', they say when they pick up the phone. 'Ohhh', I say, 'What happened to our Personnel Department? As part of personnel, where am I now expected to go?' You know, had this been a football match, we would have lost. Management must be sitting behind a one-way screen. We can see what they are doing, but they do not have any feeling for how employees respond to it.

The third confrontation comments upon the new flexible work hours:

Flexible for whom? With the huge increase in home-workplaces, we work after the kids have been put to bed. Flexibility – we work long hours, and at all hours, but it is, of course, not registered anymore so we can't tell for sure. I just know what I see. Not to forget the extra two and a half hours of work we have had added since we now pay for our own lunchtime. I just know that our work conditions have worsened over the last few years.

In the meantime, a new CEO came and, with him, a new attitude. The new CEO expressed the clear goal that ELEC had to focus on 'its core business'. As a consequence, a market-based organisation emerged, operating with the lowest possible costs. A further dismantling of units and letting go of more employees were also considered necessary. The response was one of exhaustion, anxiety and loss of orientation. An internal investigation of the organisational culture, or 'management climate', of the company had been conducted and was now generally referred to as the 'climate survey'. This company survey illustrated the general 'dissatisfaction' felt by staff. We met our assistant accountant again, who had not yet been fired.

People say it might have something to do with that climate survey. The fact is that the climate is not very good at the moment, in fact it is ice-cold, except in some of the market units where there is said to be high spirits.

After thirty-six years in one place it is also hard not to have any influence on what you work with and where you do it. Just coming to this building again makes me cry. Since we moved in here, I have always worked here, it is close to my home, but along with the most recent changes, I was offered a job at a location far away from here. I am not really sure that it was an offer, that I had a choice. I could say yes or yes, please, or I would be fired. I can sit here and think that it is a job, which I have chosen myself, but in fact I have not.

As we talked he sometimes cried, paused and then continued, trying to explain the tears:

When the reorganisation happened last February and March, I needed to talk with somebody about what was happening, to gain some control. When somebody asked me about something, anything, I immediately began to cry. Even my family didn't know what was going on with me. At my request, I got a referral to a psychologist, which has helped to get me back on track again. And if it is not the mental stress caused by an uncertain future, then it is stress from the huge workload that we have to take on. I have colleagues working between fourteen and sixteen hours a day, because they cannot say no – or might be afraid of saying no. But it gets to them. They wake up one day in bed staring at the ceiling, not knowing why they are here. It will scare them, I know it from experience. As I said to one of our directors the other day, when I coincidentally bumped into him and he asked how it was going: as long as people offer resistance in a company, then things are OK, because it indicates that people care about what they are doing, but when indifference and carelessness sets in then there is a problem. And that is what is happening in ELEC, people don't care.

A Cartography of Affects

As we followed the assistant accountant and the movements of waiting, confrontion and feeling exhausted, his version of the story refers to what Braidotti calls a

[p]ractice of accountability (for one's embodied and embedded locations) as a relational, collective activity of undoing power differentials . . . [T]hey activate the process of putting into words, that is to say bringing into symbolic representation, that which by definition escapes consciousness. (Braidotti 2002: 12)

Against the overall discourse of privatisation and liberalisation repeated at forums, meetings and individual conversations, people reacted by having initial reservations, played out by waiting, then by confronting, and finally by becoming exhausted. By being moved, they created a reserve for new thoughts and actions. What was felt, undergone, sensed and suffered from had no place in official discussions and discourses; however, their accounts did allow some form of positioning. Braidotti explains how employees can collectively emerge as a whole through the process of narrating their own stories: 'Narrativity is a crucial binding force here but I interpret it as a collective, politically-invested process of sharing in and contributing to the making of myths, operational fictions, significant figurations of the kind of subjects we are in the process of becoming' (ibid.: 21–2).

Narrations related to these affective processes can be seen as a form of fabulation. The concept of 'fabulation' is a notion that Deleuze takes from Bergson (Deleuze 1988a) and that reappears in the interviews conducted between 1972 and 1990, where Deleuze makes the following pronounce-ment: 'Utopia isn't the right concept: it's more a question of a "fabulation" in which a people and art both share. We ought to take up Bergson's notion of fabulation and give it a political meaning' (Deleuze 1995: 174). While stories are a form through which the past enters the present, fabulations prioritise the future in the present, expressing a virtual multiplicity. When we met the assistant accountant on numerous occasions we were partici-pating in his fabulations. The same goes for the many other employees we met during the numerous interviews, observations and participations in meetings and forums that comprise this study.

> What we have to do is catch someone else 'telling tales,' 'caught in the act of telling tales.' Then a minority discourse can take shape: *this* is what Bergson calls fabulation. To catch someone in the act of telling tales is to catch the movement of the constitution of a people. A people isn't some-thing which is already there. A people is what is missing, as Paul Klee said. (Ibid.: 125–126)

A cartography of affects catches people in the act of telling stories, of stuttering and crying. It is about entering the echoes, perplexities and reservations that people live with. These fabulations bring to the fore the sense in which the employees at ELEC live in a language that is not their own, or who no longer even know the meaning of their own words and know only very poorly the major language they are forced to serve (Lambert 1998). The responses of 'waiting', 'confrontation' and 'exhaus-tion' counter the new language and discourse they are forced to speak and form the possibility of developing a minor language.

The assistant accountant speaks the new lingo rather well. He is as able to ask very pertinent questions, to express adequately his feelings and the general turmoil, to ask direct questions, to confront *en passant* his director and – last but not least – to make creative suggestions that those responsible seem not to think of or to listen at. These affects are silences pointing at a minor discourse opposing the establishment of an overwhelmingly present managerial discourse. The assistant accountant is not against change. He does not offer resistance. Rather, he emerges as someone that 'may actually yearn for change and transformation' (Braidotti 2002: 75). We see the affects of waiting, confrontion and exhaustion constituting the desiring processes of metamorphosis of the employees at ELEC.

We can now sum up an exploratory politics of change as a politics of desire, multiplicity and creativity, rejecting the dominant discourses, breaking it open by way of a minor language and a minor people:

> change must be judged and evaluated according to the extent to which desire, multiplicity and creativity are emancipated, to which the outcome is social relations which exist for the betterment of us all, rather than just for the favoured few, characterized by collective values and in which everything is political. (Linstead 2004: 9–10)

Organisational change is fabulated in a cartography of affects: waiting, confrontation and exhaustion. Such an affective cartography replaces the linear process of organisational change that moves from one order to a new order (Clegg et al. 2005; see also Chapter 3 of this book). The affective processes through which change emerges form a rhizomatic movement that is circular and centrifugal. What becomes relevant is, as Paul Klee says above, that a people is what is missing and the affects that come along with change processes are affirmed, particularly, in a minor language. An organisation resembles a society. Reformulating Georges Bataille, we can say that neither the organisation nor its people lack anything. On the contrary an organisation is an abundant production of surplus. Seen from such a perspective, effecting organisational change is a vitalist and affirmative micropolitical activity. Studying change is both a critical and creative analysis of organisational change, a study which implies a political ontology 'that provides tools to describe transformative, creative or deterritorialising forces and movements' (Patton 2000: 9). Waiting, confrontation and exhaustion are practices that remain, as we have argued in this chapter, political activities. They form 'meanwhiles' where '[n]othing happens . . . but everything becomes, so that the event has the privilege of beginning again when time is past' (Deleuze and Guattari 1994: 158). What change does or can do to organisations is to remove their fixed identities. This or that organisation becomes *an* organisation, written by a people to come.

Change the Change Literature

The literature of organisational change is yet to come. It can be changed: we can wait for it, we can confront it, and it may exhaust us. Tweaking the above concepts, they enable a change of the change literature itself, producing several lines of flight or recommendations, by which the future of organisational change theory can become experimental. Indeed, the Deleuzian mood is (about) to change the field of organisational change itself, to deterritorialise it, to enforce its becoming-minoritarian. To be sure, this is an all-too-rare manoeuvre in the numerous reviews of studies of organisational change (see, for instance, Van de Ven and Poole 1995; Hage 1999; Weick and Quinn 1999; Pettigrew et al. 2001). That would be the least we should expect from connecting the field of organisational change with Deleuze and Guattari: not only that the field can think its own changing, but that it changes, can transform itself, is pushed in a mode of becoming. How can we instigate an exploratory politics of change? How can we ask the impossible, continue to experiment (with concepts) and add to the world?

Ask: How does it Work?

We imagine a literature with a pragmatic focus, replacing the question of what it means with the question, how does it work? 'The only question is how anything works, with its intensities, flows, processes, partial objects – none of which *mean* anything' (Deleuze 1995: 22). This alters the importance and weight that is currently given in the organisational change literature to sensemaking (Weick and Quinn 1999), to interpretation (Deetz et al. 2000), and to communication and discourse in general (Barrett et al. 1995; Ford 1999; Sturdy and Grey 2003). Instead of asking for meaning, we would rather pose questions like: what new thoughts does it enable us to think? What new emotions does it enable us to feel? What new sensations and perceptions does it stir in our bodies? How does it work for *me*? This turns the literature of organisational change into a study of affects, not so much the study of emotions as the excluded other of rationality, but of affects in relationship to vitalism.

Increase the Connections

With the concepts of desiring production and becoming minor, we have referred to just a few concepts to connect with. We find there is an abundance of concepts for further experimentation (Deleuze and Guattari 1994: 111): becoming, event, multiplicity, nomadism, movement, flow, revolution. On top of this comes less obvious ones such as haecceity, molecularity, deterritorialisation, counterpoint, intensities, style, rhizome, rhythm, line of flight, smooth space, speed, desert, war machine . . . The series is open-ended and forms a multiplying connectivity (Rajchman 2000), a rhizomatic conjunction: 'and . . . and . . . and . . .' The series forms a 'rainbow of alternative figurations which Deleuze throws our way' (Braidotti 2002: 73).

Don't Follow the Master

It is not enough to simply import and apply some of the concepts of Deleuze and Guattari and to make them fit into the ongoing knowledge creation an academic field seems to be about. Rather such a field is itself, as Sørensen (2005) argues, created for the purpose of giving orders regarding the organisation of bodies and the administration of signs. Indeed, Carter and Jackson (2004: 124) argue that 'it is not possible to make a conventional organization theory out of Deleuze and Guattari's analysis of organizations'. 'Applied Deleuzism', as Buchanan calls it, or 'reading with Deleuze', is suggestive and experimental, rejecting 'all forms of slavishness in favour of (liberating) creativity' (Buchanan 2000: 8). How does such an un-slavish way work? Massumi gives us a first rule of thumb:

> [I]f you want to invent or reinvent concepts . . . don't apply them. If you apply a concept or a system of connection between concepts, it is the material you apply it to that undergoes change, much more markedly than do the concepts. The change is imposed upon the material by the concepts' systematicity and constitutes a becoming homologous of the material to the system. This is all very grim. It has less to do with 'more to the world' than 'more of the same'. It has less to do with invention than mastery and control. (Massumi 2002: 17)

Inspired by how Deleuze tried to de-Oedipalise and nomadise the discipline of philosophy, Braidotti argues that it is a matter of 'becoming-Deleuzians in an un-Oedipal manner', going beyond his master's voice (2002: 68). Somehow irritated by how certain (male) Deleuzian scholars enact 'with distressing seriousness the position of dutiful son' (ibid.: 86), Braidotti points (among others) at Massumi's style (see Massumi 1992 and 2002) characterised by a creative, non-Oedipalised writing that does not mimic Deleuze's texts (Braidotti 2002).

End Power Games

A Deleuzian reading and its pleasures (Massumi 1992; Braidotti 2002) resists the attempts of theory to become a royal science. What has to be rejected in the literature of organisational change is its tendency to control and regulate processes, to join and please those in power and to develop all types of planned interventions towards perfectibility (Carter and Jackson 2004). When one adheres to the majoritarian discourse, change as a becoming is already excluded. If a Deleuzian reading of organisation theory forms a minor contribution, as suggested by Carter and Jackson (ibid.), one leaves the pretension of developing a theory that can take part in the power-games of organisational life and serve someone's interests. Rather, the minoritarian as 'a potential, creative and created, becoming' (Deleuze and Guattari 1987: 106) is oriented towards powers that belong to a different realm, namely that of creation. Change, in a minoritarian sense, can thus only take the form of a creating, a becoming. Against the state apparatus-book of organisational change theory and its overcoded models of control and planned change[1] (Deleuze and Guattari 1987), an affirmative and nomadic version has to be written in a deterritorialising mode and must be defined, as Deleuze (1988b) says of Foucault, by the outside.

Make Events Work

Organisational analysis experiments with 'untimely' concepts that can act counter to our time for the benefit of a time to come (Patton 2000; for examples see Chia 1999; Tsoukas and Chia 2002; Styhre 2002; Carter and Jackson 2004). This is why theoretical action and practical action needs to be connected in a Deleuzian pragmatism which is based on the slogan that 'le multiple, il faut le faire' (Deleuze and Guattari 1980: 13). An empiricist will attempt to discover the conditions under which something new is produced, working on the assumption that things only exist as 'multiplicities'. For the empiricist, organisations are not a matter of identity, but one of the multiplicity of many dimensions. Empiricism moves research away from the totalising practice of how things are to how they may be created; that is to say how they work. Empiricism is a form of 'making events work' (Sørensen 2004).

Mind Your Health

Connecting affects to the body and to art, Deleuze and Guattari reinvigor-ate the Spinozian question about what the body can do.

[W]e know nothing about a body until we know what it can do, in other words, what its affects are, how they can or cannot enter into composition with other affects, with the affects of another body, either to destroy that body or to be destroyed by it, either to exchange actions and passions with it or to join with it in composing a more powerful body. (Deleuze and Guattari 1987: 257)

In that sense, we tweak and twist the initial concern for health that drove the pioneers of organisational change and development (for an overview, see the classic of Bennis 1993; Morgan 1997). Health and vitalism relate to affects as 'the perception of one's own vitality, one's sense of aliveness, of changeability' (Massumi 2002: 36). This is what fabulation can bring to us as a minor genre, a literature of health.

References

Barrett, F. J., Thomas, G. F. and Hocevar, S. P. (1995), 'The Central Role of Discourse in Large-Scale Change: A Social Constructionist Perspective', *Journal of Applied Behavioral Science*, 31: 3.

Bennis, W. (1993), *Beyond Bureaucracy: Essays on the Development and Evolution of Human Organization*, San Francisco: Jossey-Bass Publishers.

Bensmaïa, R. (1986), 'The Kafka-effect', foreword in G. Deleuze and F. Guattari (1986), *Kafka: Toward a Minor Literature*, Minneapolis: University of Minnesota Press.

Braidotti, R. (2002), *Metamorphoses: Towards a Materialist Theory of Becoming*, Cambridge: Polity Press.

Buchanan, I. (2000), *Deleuzism: A Metacommentary*, Edinburgh: Edinburgh University Press.

Butler, J. (1999), *Subjects of Desire*, New York: Columbia University Press.

Carter, P. and Jackson, N. (2004), 'Deleuze and Guattari: A "Minor" Contribution to Organization Theory', in S. Linstead (ed.), *Organization Theory and Postmodern Thought*, London: Sage.

Chia, R. (1999), 'A "Rhizomatic" Model of Organizational Change and Transformation. Perspective from a Metaphysics of Change', *British Journal of Management*, 10.

Clegg, S. R., Kornberger, M. and Rhodes, C. (2005), 'Learning/Becoming/Organizing', *Organization*, 12: 2.

Deetz, S. A., Tracy, S. J. and Simpson, J. L. (2000), *Leading Organizations through Transition: Communication and Cultural Change*, Thousand Oaks: Sage Publications.

Deleuze, G. (1988a), *Bergsonism*, trans. H. Tomlinson and B. Hammerjam, New York: Zone Books.

Deleuze, G. (1988b), *Foucault*, trans. S. Hand, Minneapolis: University of Minnesota Press.

Deleuze, G. (1990), *The Logic of Sense*, trans. M. Lester and C. Stivale, New York: Columbia University Press.

Deleuze, G. (1995), *Negotiations*, trans. M. Joughin, New York: Colombia University Press.

Deleuze, G. and Guattari, F. (1980), *Mille Plateaux: capitalisme et schizophrénie*, Paris: Les Éditions de Minuit.

Deleuze, G. and Guattari, F. (1983), *Anti-Oedipus: Capitalism and Schizophrenia*, trans. R. Hurley, M. Seem and H. R. Lane, Minneapolis: University of Minnesota Press.

Deleuze, G. and Guattari, F. (1986), *Kafka: Toward a Minor Literature*, trans. D. Polan, Minneapolis: University of Minnesota Press.

Deleuze, G. and Guattari, F. (1987), *A Thousand Plateaus: Capitalism and Schizophrenia*, trans. B. Massumi, Minneapolis: University of Minnesota Press.

Deleuze, G. and Guattari, F. (1994), *What is Philosphy?*, trans. G. Burchell and H. Tomlinson, New York: Columbia University Press.

Deleuze, G. and Parnet, C. (1987), *Dialogues*, trans. H. Tomlinson and B. Habberjam, New York: Columbia University Press.

Ford, J. D. (1999), 'Organizational Change as Shifting Conversations', *Journal of Organizational Change Management*, 12: 6.

Foucault, M. (1977), 'Theatrum Philosophicum', in *Language, Counter-Memory, Practice*, ed. D. F. Bouchard, trans. D. F. Bouchard and S. Simon, Ithaca: Cornell University Press.

Genosko, G. (1996), *The Guattari Reader*, Oxford: Blackwell Publishers.

Guattari, F. (1995), *Chaosmosis: An Ethico-Aesthetic Paradigm*, trans. P. Baines and J. Pefanis, Indianapolis: Indiana University Press.

Hage, J. T. (1999), 'Organizational Innovation and Organizational Change', *Annual Review of Sociology*, 25.

Hughes, J. (1997), *Lines of Flight*, Sheffield: Sheffield Academic Press.

Lambert, G. (1998), 'On the Uses and Abuses of Literature for Life: Gilles Deleuze and the Literary Clinic', *Postmodern Culture*, 8: 3.

Linstead, S. (2004), *Organization Theory and Postmodern Thought*, London: Sage Publications.

Massumi, B. (1992), *A User's Guide to Capitalism and Schizophrenia: Deviations from Deleuze and Guattari*, Cambridge: MIT Press.

Massumi, B. (2002), *Parables for the Virtual: Movement, Affect, Sensation*, Durham: Duke University Press.

Morgan, G. (1997), *Images of Organization*, London: Sage Publications.

Patton, P. (2000), *Deleuze and the Political*, London: Routledge.

Pettigrew, A. M., Woodman, R. W. and Cameron, K. S. (2001), 'Studying Organizational Change and Development: Challenges for Future Research', *Academy of Management Journal*, 44: 4.

Rajchman, J. (2000), *The Deleuze Connections*, Cambridge: MIT Press.

Rodowick, D. N. (1997), *Gilles Deleuze's Time Machine*, Durham: Duke University Press.

Sørensen, B. M. (2004), *Making Events Work: Or, How to Multiply Your Crisis*, Copenhagen: Samfundslitteratur.

Sørensen, B. M. (2005), 'Immaculate Defecation: Gilles Deleuze and Félix Guattari in Organization Theory', in C. Jones and R. Munro (eds), *Contemporary Organization Theory*, Oxford: Blackwell.

Steyaert, C. (2005), 'Affect and Fabulation in Organizational Becoming', paper presented at the First Organization Studies Summer Workshop, Santorini, June.

Sturdy, A. and Grey, C. (2003), 'Beneath and Beyond Organizational Change Management: Exploring Alternatives', *Organization*, 10: 4.

Styhre, A. (2002), 'Thinking with AND: Management Concepts and Multiplicities', *Organization*, 9: 3.

Thrift, N. (2004), 'Intensities of Feeling: Towards a Spatial Politics of Affect', *Geografiska Annaler*, 86B: 1.

Tsoukas, H. and Chia, R. (2002), 'On Organizational Becoming: Rethinking Organizational Change', *Organization Science*, 13: 5.

Van de Ven, A. H. and Poole, M. S. (1995), 'Explaining Development and Change in Organizations', *Academy of Management Review*, 20: 3.
Weick, K. E. and Quinn, R. E. (1999). 'Organizational Change and Development', *Annual Review of Psychology*, 50.

Note

1. Note that the oxymoron 'planned change' has been one of the major headings under which organisational change was described (see Bennis 1993).

Chapter 5

I Knew there were Kisses in the Air

Thomas Bay

> I am a man who has lost his life and is searching by all means possible to make it regain its place.
>
> Antonin Artaud, *Selected Writings*

How do we regain the lost place of our life? Perhaps, as Artaud's own life suggests, by incessantly searching for it, again and again experimenting with our capacities, trying to find out what our body is capable of, capable of encountering, capable of experiencing — its 'capacity to be affected' (Deleuze 1992: 217). Perhaps this is precisely what living is all about, continuously searching for places that offer new ways of living. And perhaps we even have to lose ourselves first, our bearings, our lives, in order to find new dwellings where we can come into full possession of our power of action, and where new modes of existence may be invented.

This poses a twofold problem, which I consider to be the very crisis of experience, creativity and invention, of producing new life opportunities: instigating events, complexifying encounters, offering possibilities of losing *and* finding our selves 'in this world, as it is' (Deleuze 1989: 172). Losing-and-finding our selves in this sense, becoming imperceptible, saying 'yes' to what is strange and singular in our existence, to the intensities and singularities that traverse our body, is of course extremely risky, since there is no guarantee of ever finding our way home again. This is why many of us find it safer to perform this existential practice with an eye on worlds beyond this world, to escape into worlds of abstraction providing transcendent points of reference wherefrom this world, this life, becomes judicable. The overall problem I wish to address in this chapter is that

> we no longer believe in this world. We do not even believe in the events which happen to us, love, death, as if they only half concerned us . . . The link between man and the world is broken. Henceforth, this link must become an object of belief: it is the impossible which can only be restored

within a faith . . . *We need reasons to believe in this world* . . . What is certain is that believing is no longer believing in another world, or in a transformed world. It is only, it is simply believing in the body. (Deleuze 1989: 171–2)

Believing in the body's capacities for being affected.

What we call economy is no longer economy if by the latter we understand a practice in which cultural, societal and economic matters become inseparable, a socio-cultural economy in which we live and entertain both our actual and virtual lives, support and take care of our selves. Traversing more or less every aspect of cultural and societal life, the economic calculus has transformed human interaction into an endless series of transactions, a system of reciprocal exchanges, in which nothing can be given without being returned or repaid. If the economy was once a useful tool to society, today it is the other way round: society has become an economic toolbox peopled by consumers. If this is our only way of defining the functioning of an economy – as a capacity for subordinating the vitalities of life to its own workings – and we consider this a problem, then I suggest we ask ourselves whether we can think economy beyond the universal law of exchange. Is it possible to conceive of an economy that is both *of* and *in* the future: a real, actualised economy, to be sure, but one that is still in touch with its virtual possibilities, its plane of composition? If I were to name this purely empirical plane, I would use the ancient Greek word *oikoumēne*, a human territory or dwelling where indefinite anybodies, impersonal individuations, individuals without characteristics, traits or qualities subsist before becoming personal individualisations, economic subjects.

The problem is not that of finding some sort of first economic entity from which all other economies would derive, 'but instead, the problem is to move towards something radically Other . . . We must produce something that doesn't yet exist and about which we cannot know how and what it will be' (Foucault 1991: 121). To be more explicit, we must invent an unfamiliar economy, an economy without a home or *oikos*, without a metaphysical centre or hearth, an unhoused economy, a purely nomic, that is, radically normative economy, an intensive space occupied by an imperceptible people, without determinate identities, so vague they become strangers even to themselves. Is it possible to think this economic world in such a vagabond manner, empirically, without an ever-present transcendent source of authority? I will attempt to do just this, to think differently, that is, 'to experiment and to problematize' (Deleuze 1988b: 116), the *nomos*, the conventional place of habit in and through which economic subjects tend to emerge, without resorting to metaphysical grounds. If, as

Deleuze suggests, the constitutive root of the subject is habit, if 'we are *habits*, nothing but habits – the habit of saying "I" ' (Deleuze 1991: x), and if believing and inventing is what makes the subject a subject, then I believe we must find resourceful ways of cracking this habitual 'I' up, thus allowing something new to come to pass, a new thought to occur, a new possibility for life to emerge. We must learn to believe and to invent.

I suggest we do this by staging an encounter between a 'house-holding' man and an unhoused man, between a man who lives his life according to the universal law of exchange, who considers every relation a (potential) transaction, who holds that human actions by definition are reciprocal and who will therefore return every favour, even a gift; and a man begging for a life, a man who knows how to receive without offering something in return, who stretches out his hand towards you, inviting you to learn how to give without expecting something back, hoping thereby to extract from this encounter an event – 'the most delicate thing in the world' (Deleuze and Parnet 1987: 66) – giving us a purely empirical opportunity: 'not to be unworthy of what happens to us' (Deleuze 1990: 149). In other words, I would like to arouse in you another sensibility, a different way of feeling, offering leeway, and the opportunity to call your economised self into question, to become (someone else).

My intention is to affirm the practice of begging as the non-thought within economic thought itself, the outside that always remains to be thought, that which the economy is unable to think. In this respect, a beggar could be conceived as a conceptual persona entering into economic thought to pose questions about the very idea and function of the economic, calling thereby not only economy as an image of thought into question, but staking the economy's most elementary conventions. The beggar, as a conceptual persona, is a style of thinking that imposes itself upon economic thought, marking out an existential domain, a zone of life, which threatens to tear out the very heart, if it has one, of the economic body, to completely uproot economic thinking as such, thus making it possible to conceive of economy very differently. In my view, a beggar, refusing exchange, refusing to offer something in return, provides an opportunity to rediscover a place for life in the economy itself, to search it out again, to research the question of its nature, to investigate the possibilities of restoring faith in the economy. This is my way of combating the economic forces that, perhaps, consume too much of our lives, threaten to, once and for all, take the economy away from us; it is my way of experimenting with the conditions of possibility under which new ways of living economically may arise – begging/giving as the potential becoming-other of economic exchange.

The importance of the practice of exchange for explaining human progress cannot be understated. Aristotle perceives exchange (*allage*) as constitutive not only of every form of economy, but of any kind of human association as such (Aristotle 1991: 1133b). Friedrich Nietzsche suggests that buying and selling 'are older even than the beginnings of any kind of social forms of organization and alliances' (Nietzsche 1967: 70). According to Adam Smith, what defines the very essence of man is his 'propensity to truck, barter, and exchange one thing for another' (Smith 1979: 117). Every man 'lives by exchanging, or becomes in some measure a merchant, and the society itself grows to be what is properly a commercial society' (ibid.: 126). Thus when two members of society communicate, they do so according to the formula: 'Give me that which I want, and you shall have this which you want' (ibid.: 118). This idea, says Smith, is the basis of all exchange.

> It is not from the benevolence of the butcher, the brewer, or the baker that we expect our dinner, but from their regard to their own interest. We address ourselves, not to their humanity but to their self-love, and never talk to them of our own necessities but of their advantages. (Smith 1979: 119)

Smith, no doubt, has great faith in the possibilities of harnessing this prime mover of commercial society, this essential human propensity to exchange one thing for another, to the general good, in the service of universal opulence. In the following section I will briefly investigate Smith's grand civilising project, his moral vision of a commercial humanism, trying to find out how it works.

Let us start in the middle, where things begin, in the midst of two seemingly contradictory Smithian statements concerning human nature, in-between egoistic self-love and altruistic benevolence.

> Every man is, no doubt, by nature first and principally recommended to his own care; and as he is fitter to take care of himself than of any other person, it is fit and right that it should be so. Every man, therefore, is much more deeply interested in whatever immediately concerns himself, than in what concerns any other man. (Smith 2000: 119)

> How selfish soever man may be supposed, there are evidently some principles in his nature, which interest him in the fortune of others, and render their happiness necessary to him, though he derives nothing from it, except the pleasure of seeing it. (Smith 2000: 3)

Smith's problem, since man is a weak and imperfect creature, is how to thwart people from being completely taken over by their 'mutinous and turbulent passions' (ibid.: 386), to prevent their natural selfishness, their unruly egoistic appetites from bringing about a complete dissolution of society. What he needs is a ground firm enough to serve as the basis for a social institution or contract. Thoroughly conversant with the debate that had lasted for almost two centuries about whether destructive passions could be controlled by being subordinated to reason, or whether they should rather be counteracted and tamed by other, more benevolent passions, Smith follows the example of his close friend David Hume, who was undoubtedly his most important source of inspiration, and chooses self-interest, a potentially benign passion for wealth, a profound 'desire for bettering our condition, a desire which, though generally calm and dispassionate, comes with us from the womb, and never leaves us till we go into the grave' (Smith 1979: 441). The crucial idea here is that, whereas people agitated by riotous passions are changeable and inconstant and hence more or less unforeseeable, people preoccupied with their own material well-being become considerably more docile, predictable and governable. It is for this reason that Smith emphasises the importance of social institutions like the market, its tendency to channel human passions into morally laudable and socially beneficent forms of behaviour. In other words, commerce, the exchange of goods in search of self-interest that is cultivated and directed through the market into more virtuous forms of behaviour not only restrains egoism and makes men moral, it creates social stability as well, constancy. That is, it affords 'predictability in its most elementary form . . . and it is this quality that was perhaps the most important ground for welcoming a world governed by interest' (Hirschman 1977: 52). The institution of the market, by leading us to control ourselves, to restrain our passions, to adapt our behaviour to the needs and expectations of our fellows, to cooperate, has a disciplining effect upon society.

This market-oriented self-command, however, is far from unproblematic and, though important, is only one aspect of Smith's moral vision, his commercial humanism. Even if the market promotes some degree of benevolence – inferior virtues associated with the prudent pursuit of self-interest, individual wealth – that habituates people to develop decent behaviour towards others, it seems to harbour forces within itself that threaten the very virtues upon which it depends: for example, the potentially corrupting experience of making money too quickly and too easily. Since the market seems incapable of producing a higher conception of virtue, of inculcating 'pure and disinterested benevolence' (Smith 2000: 442) or truly altruistic action on behalf of others, Smith is sceptical about its ability to provide a sufficient degree of self-command, a circumstance that has serious consequences for the possibility of realising his moral vision. Smith's way of handling these market deficiencies is to invoke a benevolence principle, based on another passion, namely, sympathy. Sympathy, for Smith, is a natural, God-given desire for attention and praise, a propensity to seek the approval of others in and through social interaction; it is a feeling of fellowship, a human passion for approbation, for being in harmony with the emotions of others who observe our conduct; it is assuredly a selfish passion, but nonetheless an innate element of human nature that leads us all, and even the greatest ruffian, to concern ourselves with the happiness and misery of our fellows. Rather than loving our neighbour as we love ourselves, we should 'love ourselves only as we love our neighbour, or, what comes to the same thing, as our neighbour is capable of loving us' (Smith 2000: 28).

We gain pleasure from observing a feeling of fellowship with our own sentiments in others, and in order to be able to enjoy this pleasure we are willing to do everything in our power to attune ourselves to their feelings, so that they can approve of our level of emotions. We do this by projecting ourselves into the position of others, thereby learning to contemplate our own feelings and actions through their eyes. Despite the fact that we are naturally disposed to prefer our own interest to the interests of others, our egoism is curtailed to the extent that we learn to judge our actions as they must appear to people who do not share our selfish partiality towards ourselves.

> The all-wise Author of Nature has, in this manner, taught man to respect the sentiments and judgements of his brethren; to be more or less pleased when they approve of his conduct, and to be more or less hurt when they disapprove of it. He has made man, if I may say so, the immediate judge of mankind; and has in this respect, as in many others, created him after his own image, and appointed him his vicegerent upon earth, to superintend the behaviour of his brethren . . . But though man has, in this manner, been rendered the immediate judge of mankind, he has been rendered so only in the first instance; and an appeal lies from his sentence to a much higher tribunal, to the tribunal of their own consciences, to that of the supposed impartial and well-informed spectator, to that of the man within the breast, the great judge and arbiter of their conduct. (Smith 2000: 185)

Hence it is this external standard, this little outsider within, who passes judgement, always with an eye on higher grounds, in the constantly reopened controversy between reason and the calm, virtuous aspects of the prudent pursuit of self-interest on one side and the more violent and potentially destructive features of self-love on the other.

The problem to which this internalised normalising standard, this 'great inmate of the breast' (ibid.: 385), provides the solution concerns two interconnected issues. Firstly, because our beneficent passions are very limited and decline in strength in proportion to the increasing distance from family to friends to neighbours to compatriots, they form an inadequate basis to motivate proper conduct towards the many people outside the range of our benevolent feelings. Our sympathetic partiality must therefore be supported by a set of general rules of morality and conduct, 'the commands and laws of the Deity, promulgated by those vicegerents which he has thus set up within us' (ibid.: 234). Upon 'the tolerable observance of these duties, depends the very existence of human society, which would crumble into nothing if mankind were not generally impressed with a reverence for those important rules of conduct' (ibid.: 231–2). Putting it differently, we can say that our partial sympathy must be transcended, must be subjected to moral law, to an external principle independent of the sympathetic sentiments themselves. Only under this tutelage will they serve their purpose.

Second, in our search for praise, for the sympathetic approval of others, we might be tempted to act in such a way as to obtain the praise of others by unfair means, without actually having earned it. But if we instead act dutifully, that is, according to the principles of 'the man within' (ibid.: 186), we can rest assured that we will not simply be praised for our actions, but that we are truly worthy of the praise we receive, that we really are the praiseworthy characters we appear to be to others. Thus, altruistic behaviour is motivated less by the benevolent love of our neighbour than by the inclination to act in a way we know to be praiseworthy. The love of praise is hence replaced by a desire for praiseworthiness, a love of virtue for its own sake. For the wise man, the man who obeys 'reason, principle, conscience, the inhabitant of the breast, the man within, the great judge and arbiter of our conduct' (ibid.: 193–4), virtue is its own reward. Moral perfection is the name of the game.

To sum up, commercial society fosters self-control, or perhaps better, the freedom to command our own selfish passions. The two points to which it appears to be firmly fixed are sympathy, through which the individual transcends the limits of his own individuality; and 'the demigod within the breast' (ibid.: 187), the metaphysical tribunal through which human kind rises from the mere expediency of seeking praise to the genuine morality of seeking to be praiseworthy. Commercial society aspires to turn our natural benevolent sentiments for others into a social institution – the market – capable of constraining, channelling, cultivating, dampening, moderating and redirecting our self-interest, the ultimate goal being not simply the improvement of our character, but 'the perfection of human nature' (ibid.: 27). But more importantly, Smith, the social philosopher who has had, and perhaps still has, an unsurpassed influence on our understanding of the way social, cultural and economic forces combine to make up society as we know it, does not believe in this world as it is, has no confidence in life, in our capacities for being affected, but rather finds it necessary to anchor his civilising project in an external authority, an otherworldly principle, from where, in turn, our potentially unruly passions may be curbed.

Deleuze's reading of Hume, although in some respects quite similar to Smith's, differs on one critical point: the concept of self-interest. Smith regards it as an egotism to be limited; Deleuze as a partiality to be extended.

> One of Hume's simplest but most important ideas is this: human beings are much less egoistic than they are *partial* . . . It is precisely because the essence of passion or the essence of the particular interest is partiality rather than egoism that sympathy, for its part, does not transcend the particular interest or passion . . . Sympathy is no less opposed to society than egoism is. (Deleuze 1991: 38)

Both Smith and Deleuze see egoism and sympathy for what they are: passions; but while Smith, in order to limit egoism and transcend the partiality of sympathy, constructs a set of general rules secured by a metaphysical authority, Deleuze asserts that since we are partial and sympathetic rather than egoistic according to our nature, and egoism thereby becomes negligible, there is nothing to transcend and hence no need for otherworldly principles. However,

> even if society finds *as much* of an obstacle in sympathy as in the purest egoism, what changes absolutely is the sense or the structure of society itself, depending on whether we consider it from the point of view of egoism or sympathy. Egoisms would only have to be limited, but sympathies are another matter, for they must be integrated inside a positive totality. What Hume criticizes in contractarian theories is precisely that they present us with an abstract and false image of society, that they define society only in a negative way; they see in it a set of limitations of egoism and interests instead of understanding society as a positive system of invented endeavours. That is why it is so important to be reminded that the natural human being is not egoist; our entire notion of society depends on it. (Ibid.: 39)

Rather than finding ways of circumscribing egoism, the problem is how to expand and generalise our natural sympathy so that it embraces as many people as possible:

> how to go beyond partialities, how to pass from a 'limited sympathy' to an 'extended generosity,' how to stretch passions and give them an extension they don't have on their own. Society is thus no longer seen as a system of

legal and contractual limitations but as an institutional invention. (Deleuze 2001: 46–7)

The practical problem is that of how to invent institutions that force passions to go beyond their partialities and that will allow us to satisfy our natural sympathies. Thus, 'the essence of society is not the law but rather the institution' (Deleuze 1991: 45); that is, *nomos* – society as experiment rather than contract.

Nomos is the law or convention, the boundary or the very crisis of Smith's economy, his commercial society. It is the thin line traversing the *oikos*, which not only divides but breaks it open, opens it up towards further economic futures. It is an immanent place of creation and becoming where the nomic continuously forges new assemblages, where the forces of economy attempt to capture life in its essence, where the economic intervenes in human life itself. Hence this is where a certain economy of life is instituted, where human life is turned into an economic form of life, where the possibilities of living are contracted, economised. It is, in other words, a site in which the 'nomy' of economy, the rule of economic conduct, is turned into the general, that is, Smithian rule of life, the one and only way to live. Thus to live now means simply: living economically. But *nomos* is not merely a place where human life is constrained by Smithian laws, where man learns to obey the universal law of exchange. It is a place which is at one and the same time not in its place; it is a plays, a place in play, a field of intensity and transmutation where one has the opportunity to transform the economy of one's self, to find a way out that offers, if not an escape from the house of economy, then at least a modicum of hospitality.

In an ethological sense, economy is the tension between savings and expenditure, investment and consumption; or, in more general terms, it is the tension between containment and dissipation. This unhoused tension or intensity is precisely what I call *nomos* – pure economic force or energy, a sheer play of forces. On the one hand, the active forces of production: continuously expanding exceeding dispersing proliferating multiplying human experience – force unseparated from what it can do. On the other, the reactive forces of limitation: incessantly imposing laws, codes, restrictions restraints, and constraints upon human experience – force separated from what it can do. The productive forces work on the virtual plane of composition, where unformed experience emerges. The forces of limitation operate on the plane of organisation, surrounding production, forming it; experience which is separated from its mode of production by being defined according to a recognised code or convention, identified as a certain type of experience. The former forces are experimental and creative deterritorialising forces; the latter are curbing and contractive reterritorialising forces. It is in this sense, I suggest, that the concept of economy becomes the most productive, as an image of thought, a conceptual assemblage constituted by and consisting of these two incompatible forces. Hence the importance of conceptual personae for exploring the workings of economic thinking, since their role is 'to show thought's territories, its absolute deterritorialisations and reterritorialisations' (Deleuze and Guattari 1994: 69).

In the etymological sense, *nomos* signifies not only the law, *nómos*, but a *nomós* very different from the law, designating a distribution: *nómos* AND *nomós*. No doubt, Deleuze and Guattari assent, *nomos* later on came to designate the law, 'but that was originally because it was distribution, a mode of distribution. It is a very special kind of distribution, one without division into shares, in a space without border or enclosure' (1987: 380). It thus appears as if a lawless *nomós* potentially transgresses, or, rather, displaces the law of *nómos*. But how does this work?

> The root of *nomos* is *nem* and seems to have meant originally 'to bend'. These origins become most clearly visible in the meaning of the verb *nemō* which very frequently appears in Homer: to deal out, to dispense. A second meaning of *nemō* refers to the life of herdsmen: to pasture, to graze the flocks, to drive them to pasture, feeding them, and it is from this sphere that the word seems to have acquired the connotation: 'to spread on' and 'to dwell in a habitat'. Like many ancient words *nemō* has thus two opposite meanings . . . one meaning pointing to limitations imposed by acts of appropriation and apportioning, the other to expansion. (Singer 1958: 37–8)

Deleuze and Guattari further qualify this etymology:

> The root 'Nem' indicates distribution, not allocation, even when the two are linked. In the pastoral sense, the distribution of animals is effected in a non-limited space and implies no parcelling out of land . . . *To take to pasture* (nemō) refers not to a parcelling out but to a scattering, to a repartition of animals. It was only after Solon that *nomos* came to be identified with the laws themselves. (Deleuze and Guattari 1987: 557)

Obviously, *nomós*, the economy's way out, its creative line of flight, somehow bends the law, *nómos*, producing an opening, a turbulence of transformative movements, an inventive battlefield in the midst of economic practice itself. On the one hand, the passive, formative forces of *nómos*; on the other, the active, form-breaking forces of *nomós*. This warlike play of difference, this encounter between limitation and extension, is a composition of forces, a mode of intensity, an individuation without subject, an economic difference – economy. While *homo oeconomicus*, the man with limited resources, is dominated by the force of *nōmos*, moral law, rules of duty, social contract(ion)s that limit his passions, living economically means living as a degree of power, a variable of intensity, living according to the economy of one's body, *nōmos* AND *nomōs* — 'norms of power . . . norms of life' (Deleuze 1992: 268).

So, what can this economic body do? What is it capable of? The power of a body corresponds to its *nomōs*, its capacity to be affected, and the more ways a body can be affected, the more power it has. There are two kinds of affections:

> *actions*, which are explained by the nature of the affected individual, and which spring from the individual's essence; and *passions*, which are explained by something else, and which originate outside the individual. Hence the capacity for being affected is manifested as a *power of acting* insofar as it is assumed to be filled by active affections, but as a power of being acted upon insofar as it is filled by passions. (Deleuze 1988a: 27)

When our body encounters and comes into relation with another body, this produces in us a passive affection that changes our body's economy or composition of expansive and contractive forces. If we combine with another body whose relation is incompatible with our own, which disagrees with our nature, the encounter is bad or poisonous and hence limits our *nomos*. 'The idea of such an affection is a feeling of sadness, a sad passion corresponding to a reduction of [our] power of action' (Deleuze 1992: 241). Thus sadness turns our force of existence into a purely reactive force. If on the other hand, the forces of the body with which we come into contact enter into composition with our own forces, if the encounter is useful to us and expands our power of action, our *nomos*, it is a good encounter. But since the affection is explained by the external body, the affection is passive, and the idea of the affection is a passive feeling. Nevertheless it is a feeling of joy, because it is produced by the idea of something that is good for us.

> Any passion does of course keep us cut off from our power of action, but this to a greater or lesser extent. As long as we are affected by passions we have not come into full possession of our power of action. But joyful passions lead us closer to this power, that is, increase or help it; sad passions distance us from it, that is, diminish or hinder it. (Deleuze 1992: 273)

How, then, do we come into full possession of our force of existence, that is, how do we become truly active? First of all we must try to organise useful or good encounters, attempt to unite with what agrees with our nature, with what extends our *nomos*, strive to be affected by or experience a maximum of joyful passions that in turn makes us capable of resisting and extricating ourselves from sadness, the passions that embody the lowest degree of our power, the instant when we are most detached from our power of action, most estranged from this world as it is. We may then use these joyful passions to form a clear and distinct notion of what is common between the forces of the body we encounter and our own. By forming common notions, an understanding of this intensive community of forces, we turn the joyful passions into active affections; that is, we are put in possession of our power to act.

Living economically 'consists precisely in denouncing all that separates us from life, all these transcendent values that are turned against life . . . all the values in the name of which we disparage life' (Deleuze 1988a: 26). Living economically is doing all we can, is living according to *nomos*, the economy of our powers of action: *nōmos* AND *nomōs* – the forces that compose us. An economy of forces dominated by *nōmos*, dependent for its existence upon an exterior instance, a supplementary transcendent dimension, stifles life with laws, duties and properties, hence disabling itself, reducing itself to impotence, cutting itself off from its power to act. Its (re)actions are limited to imposing social restraints or contracts, metaphysical fences whereby it can free itself from the necessity of the passions affecting it. An economic body imbued with a maximum of intensity or *nomōs*, on the other hand, articulates a raw nomic force, an unformed, passionate experience capable of generating its own limitations, as products of its own activities. An economy limited by nothing beyond itself produces *nōmos* as an after-effect of its own affirmative generosity, its immanent productive power. *Nōmos*, in other words, is an effect of the creative fatigue of the economy itself, ensuing from a diminishing capacity to be affected by the passions it encounters.

It is to the potentiality of the generative force or generosity of the *nomōs* that we now turn our attention, to see whether or not this economic genopractice is capable of tracing new economic lines of experimentation, new economic modes of existing. We can let Deleuze pose the question.

> To do all we can amounts to two things: How exercise our capacity to be affected in such a way that our power of action increases? And how increase this power to the point where, finally, we produce active affections? There are weak men and strong, slaves and free men. There is no Good and Evil in Nature, there is no moral opposition, but there is an ethical difference. The difference lies in the immanent existing modes involved in what we feel, do and think. (Deleuze 1992: 269)

So, what do we – the weak, economised human creatures that we have become – feel, do and think when encountering a beggar? We could, like

Zarathustra, dejectedly exclaim: 'Beggars should be entirely abolished! Truly, it is annoying to give to them and annoying not to give to them' (Nietzsche 1969: 113). Or would it rather, as an alternative, be possible to use this encounter to try augmenting our power to be affected?

> Talk with prudence to a beggar
> Of 'Potosi' and the mines!
> Reverently to the hungry
> Of your viands and your wines!
>
> Cautious, hint to any captive
> You have passed enfranchised feet!
> Anecdotes of air in dungeons
> Have sometimes proved deadly sweet!

(Dickinson 1924: 36)

Why this prudence, this cautiousness? Whose dungeon? Who are the captives, the slaves? Who are the light-footed free men? Who needs to be safeguarded, the beggar? You? Me? And for whom does the fresh air turn out to be virulently poisonous? In other words, why do we find a begging encounter so disquieting? Is it because unsolicited, unilateral transfers threaten the very idea of commercial society? And why do we so readily turn beggars into salespersons, for instance newsvendors, selling street newspapers like the *Big Issue*? The answer is as obvious as it is Smithian: to prevent an encounter, an ardent and potentially revolutionary encounter – a far too passionate exchange.

Hence it seems as if the economy harbours something within itself, which it cannot comprehend, something radically unfamiliar in its most intimate familiarity; something which apparently cannot find any room in an economy of exchange and equivalence, but which would still be real and trans-active. The possibility of a non-transactional exchange on the outside of economy: an exchange without return, where nothing returns except the inevitability of the vagabond beggar himself returning, a return which has not been pre-fixed, an exchange which is not already morally decided for us. In this encounter with a purely receptive beggar lies, passively, an extremely creative potential which could, perhaps, be the gift of economy, the economic gift *par excellence*. This would necessarily be a possibility conditioned by its own impossibility, the impossibility of being incorporated into an economy of reciprocity and exchange – an economy, in other words, ambiguous enough to integrate its own outside. And perhaps this economy 'is an economy which has a more supple relation to property, which can stand separation and detachment, which signifies that it can also stand freedom – for instance, the other's freedom' (Cixous and

Clément 1986: 87). By allowing for separation, for trans-actions beyond transaction, for exchanges without contractual returns, that is, for pure, unbound gifts, 'we break with the return-to-self, with the specular relations ruling the coherence, the identification, of the individual' (Cixous 1981: 53). This would be an economy of interactive connections between people; an economy in which reappropriation can be deferred, perhaps infinitely, in exchange for the continued circulation of giving; an economy consisting of a people to come, a people of gift givers, a people capable of losing parts of themselves without losing their integrity, a people with a tolerance for the movements of the other, able to exist in a 'relationship to the other in which the gift doesn't calculate its influence' (Cixous and Clément 1986: 92).

We seem to have lost the ability to give, to give without expecting something in return. And if there is any pertinence at all in Nietzsche's words that 'the highest virtue is a bestowing virtue' (Nietzsche 1969: 100), a gift-giving virtue, then perhaps we must learn the art of giving, how to give a gift. This we can learn from a beggar, because a beggar knows not only the art of receiving, the art of being truly and passively receptive, of receiving without giving something in return (for there is no gift if there is no one there to refuse it or being unable to return it), a beggar is also a great gift-giver. The gift a beggar presents to us is an opportunity to think differently, to live otherwise. It is a chance to think and live economically. Whether this present turns out to be a gift of life or is poisoned; whether it promotes or inhibits what we are capable of thinking, feeling and doing; whether it increases or decreases our power to act depends upon our capacities for being affected. In other words, a begging encounter involves the risk of an event, a problem which forces us to think, and a potential change in our manner of existence. It is not the begging encounter as such that is at issue here but rather the encounter as a source of events. We might learn to see in the face of a beggar the expression of a possible economic world – where giving rather than having is the primary mode of being.

He held on his knees a big black bag, like a midwife's I imagine. It was full of glittering phials . . . He took one and held it out to me, saying, One and six. What did he want? To sell it to me? Proceeding on this hypothesis I told him I had no money. No money! he cried. All of a sudden his hand came down on the back of my neck, his sinewy fingers closed and with a jerk and a twist he had me up against him. But instead of dispatching me he began to murmur words so sweet that I went limp and my head fell forward in his lap. Between the caressing voice and the fingers rowelling my neck the contrast was striking. But gradually the two things merged in a devastating hope, if I dare say so, and I dare . . . He suddenly shoved me away and showed me the phial again . . . Want it? he said. No, but I said yes, so as not to vex him. He proposed an exchange. Give me your hat, he said. I refused. What vehemence! he said. I haven't a thing, I said . . . Long silence. And if you gave me a kiss, he said finally. I knew there were kisses in the air . . . He must have seen from my face that all passion was not quite spent. (Beckett 1967: 41–3)

Perhaps we can imagine an exchange that is no longer an exchange in the economic sense, no longer an exchange of something for something else, but 'a pure exchange where nothing is exchanged, where there is nothing real except the movement of exchange, which is nothing' (Blanchot 1982: 39). An exchange where we are given the opportunity to become something different from what we are, without knowing exactly who or what. And such becomings, such passionate trans-actions, by definition, occur only in this world as it is. It would demand 'a zone of indistinction, of indiscernibility, or of ambiguity' (Deleuze 1997: 78), a 'zone of exchange between [a house-holding man and an unhoused man] in which something of one passes into the other . . . and it is this double becoming that constitutes the people to come and the new earth' (Deleuze and Guattari 1994: 109). The concept by which I try to seize this becoming: living economically – an *ethos*, a manner of being, a mode of existence in which the forces of *nomōs* and *nōmos* incessantly encounter each other, producing, in and through the intensity of their exchanges, a belief in this economic world as it is, an economy of the gift, a trust in the economic subjects we may always yet become. This exchange is a generous exchange, an economic exchange, which exchanges that which cannot be exchanged, and in which *nomōs* 'surges forth as the highest power of the unexchangeable' (Deleuze 1990: 288), producing a generous world, an unhoused economy, an economy of gift-givers, giving without return and never receiving, a hospitable economy still in touch with *oikoumēne*, its plane of composition.

References

Aristotle (1991), *The Nicomachean Ethics*, trans. M. Pakaluk, Oxford: Oxford University Press.

Artaud, A. (1988), *Antonin Artaud: Selected Writings*, trans. H. Weaver, Berkeley and Los Angeles: University of California Press.

Beckett, S. (1967), 'The Calmative', in *Stories and Texts For Nothing*, New York: Grove Press.

Blanchot, M. (1982), *The Space of Literature*, trans. A. Smock, Lincoln: Nebraska Press.

Cixous, H. (1981), 'Castration or Decapitation?', *Signs: Journal of Women in Culture and Society*, 7: 1.

Cixous, H. and Clément, C. (1986), *The Newly Born Woman*, trans. B. Wing, Minneapolis: University of Minnesota Press.

Deleuze, G. (1988a), *Spinoza: Practical Philosophy*, trans. R. Hurley, San Francisco: City Lights Books.

Deleuze, G. (1988b), *Foucault*, trans. S. Hand, Minneapolis: University of Minnesota Press.

Deleuze, G. (1989), *Cinema 2: The Time-Image*, trans. H. Tomlinson, Minneapolis: University of Minnesota Press.

Deleuze, G. (1990), *The Logic of Sense*, trans. M. Lester and C. Stivale, New York: Columbia University Press.

Deleuze, G. (1991), *Empiricism and Subjectivity: An Essay on Hume's Theory of Human Nature*, trans. C. V. Boundas, New York: Columbia University Press.

Deleuze, G. (1992), *Expressionism in Philosophy: Spinoza*, trans. M. Joughin, New York: Zone Books.

Deleuze, G. (1997), *Essays Critical and Clinical*, trans. D. W. Smith and M. A. Greco, Minneapolis: University of Minnesota Press.

Deleuze, G. (2001), *Pure Immanence: Essays on a Life*, trans. A. Boyman, New York: Zone Books.

Deleuze, G. and Guattari, F. (1987), *A Thousand Plateaus: Capitalism and Schizophrenia*, trans. B. Massumi, Minneapolis: University of Minnesota Press.

Deleuze, G. and Guattari, F. (1994), *What is Philosophy?*, trans. H. Tomlinson and G. Burchell, London: Verso.

Deleuze, G. and Parnet, C. (1987), *Dialogues*, trans. H. Tomlinson and B. Habberjam, New York: Columbia University Press.

Dickinson, E. (1924), *The Complete Poems of Emily Dickinson*, Boston: Little, Brown, and Company.

Foucault, M. (1991), *Remarks on Marx: Conversations with Duccio Trombadori*, trans. J. Goldstein and J. Cascaito, New York: Semiotext(e).

Hirschman, A. O. (1977), *The Passions and the Interests: Political Arguments for Capitalism before its Triumph*, Princeton: Princeton University Press.

Nietzsche, F. (1967), *On the Genealogy of Morals*, trans. W. Kaufmann, New York: Vintage Books.

Nietzsche, F. (1969), *Thus Spoke Zarathustra*, trans. W. Kaufmann, London: Penguin Books.

Singer, K. (1958), 'Oikonomia: An Inquiry into Beginnings of Economic Thought and Language', *Kyklos*, 11.

Smith, A. (1979), *The Wealth of Nations*, Books I–III, London: Penguin Books.

Smith, A. (2000), *The Theory of Moral Sentiments*, New York: Prometheus Books.

Chapter 6

Becoming-Cyborg:
Changing the Subject of the Social?

Chris Land

Human monsters are embryos that were retarded at a certain degree of development, the human in them is only a straitjacket for inhuman forms and substances.

Deleuze and Guattari, *A Thousand Plateaus*

This is the space-age, and we are here to go.

William Burroughs, *Dead City Radio*

The main thing about them is *not* that they wish to go 'back,' but that they wish to get – *away*. A little *more* strength, flight, courage, and artistic power, and they would want to *rise* – not return.

Friedrich Nietzsche, *Beyond Good and Evil*

In 1960 Manfred E. Clynes and Nathan S. Kline coined the term cyborg to refer to (nothing less than) an 'exogenously extended organisational complex functioning as an integrated homeostatic system unconsciously' (Clynes and Kline 1995 [1960]: 30–1). In so doing, they simultaneously heralded at least four decades of speculation on the post-human, and sought to close down this potentiality to effectuate a homeostatic-repetition of Homo sapiens. The exogenous extension of which Clynes and Kline spoke was the technological extension of a biological organism to enable its continued survival in the hostile environ of space. Whilst their first experiments involved the ubiquitous lab-rat, Clynes and Kline's ultimate goal was the merging of high technology and a human body to produce the ultimate astronaut. Whilst apparently radical, insofar as it broached the boundaries of the human body and took technics out of humans' conscious control, at its core Clynes and Kline's work was conservative. It sought to *conserve* the essence of the human intact and untouched thereby reproducing Homo sapiens. This move was both literally conservative and politically conservative.

As Londa Schiebinger has noted, Homo sapiens was the name chosen

for 'mankind' as separate from other animals, even those otherwise
included in the same taxonomic classification: *Mammalia*. Where
humans were deemed closest to the animal kingdom, Linnaeus broke
with zoological tradition and devised a term that highlighted the singu-
larly female trait of lactating glands. Where he sought to divide and separate mankind from the animals, he chose the term Homo sapiens,
emphasising the rational mind, traditionally associated with the male of
the species, as opposed to any merely physical features (Schiebinger
2000). When, just over 200 years later, Clynes and Kline sought to send
man into space, and protect him from the ravages of such a hostile environment, what they wanted to protect was precisely this faculty of
reason: the mind. In contrast they saw the body as a mere housing for
this faculty, as something that could be surgically, chemically and
mechanically modified without damaging the essence of man.
Perpetuating the Cartesian schism that had informed Linnaeus, the body
itself was seen as a mere prosthesis. No wonder then, that they felt quite
able to suggest its wholesale prosthetic modification.

Clynes and Kline's early formation of a logic of prosthesis has been
carried into contemporary debates on cyborgs and the post-human. In the
work of modern-day cyberneticians like Hans Morovec and Kevin
Warwick, the human race is in an evolutionary battle with its own products, and the machines are winning (Moravec 1990; Warwick 1997; Dery
1996). The only way to stay ahead of this Darwinian/capitalist battle for
supremacy is to transcend our merely mortal condition and become
cyborgs, downloading our consciousness into robot bodies, or computer
networks where they can travel freely, unhindered by the vagaries of the
flesh and its resistance to even sub-light speed acceleration. Such a model,
however, remains wedded to a logic of 'cosmic evolutionism' (Deleuze and
Guattari 1987: 49) where Man is the telos of creation, albeit in a cyber-
netically modified livery. Evolution is seen as an anthropomorphic force,
actively seeking a combination of increasing complexity and efficiency.
The particular model of evolution that underpins the idea of the post-
human is itself all too human (Ansell Pearson 1997a).

This chapter seeks an escape from this impasse by delineating the conditions of possibility for a trans-human becoming that neither collapses
back into the humanist conceit of an enhanced anthropomorphism
(the post-human), nor simply negates this figure, thereby remaining
caught in a binary bind of opposition (the anti-human). Rather, following Keith Ansell Pearson (1997a and 1997b), the paper suggests a trans-
human becoming in which technology plays a role that is decidedly
non-prosthetic. By entering into heterogeneous relations of becoming,

the human is always already other than itself, but the deterritorialisations enveloped in these becomings can either be reterritorialised upon the image of the human (demonstrating the limits of a politics based on representation), or can open up new lines of becoming apocalyptic deterritorialisations in a constant process of de-individualisation (Foucault 1983: xiv). Distinguishing the trans-human from various dehumanising process in this way enables us to evaluate again the openings offered by new becomings-technology, where these becomings translate and transform both parties in the relationship. Indeed, following a Deleuze and Guattarian ontology of flow and connection that some have referred to as 'cyborganization' (Parker and Cooper 1998) we could say that there is no human essence independent of, or prior to, its becomings and connections, in which case man has always been a cyborg. But this does not mean that there are not different becomings, even becomings-technology. Where Clynes and Kline sought to fix the face of the human through technological innovation, others have sought to reject all technics in a return to a 'pure' human form, itself impossible to conceive without a techno-scientific other to articulate itself against. But, if the human is *ontologically* a cyborg-becoming, rather than *empirically* becoming a cyborg then both of these positions are untenable. Rather than retreating from the fascism of the human face, into a romanticised primitive body, or remaining fixed upon the face of an always imperialist human cast in the image of God (Deleuze and Guattari 1987: 178), the alternative it to peel away this all-too-human face, and transform it into a probe-head (Deleuze and Guattari 1987: 191). Of course, this raises the whole question of what this trans-human probe-head might be, and whether it can be represented. As this paper will argue, this question of representation goes right to the heart of the problem of overcoming the human. At best, as examples from William Burroughs, Nick Land and Deleuze and Guattari suggest, when such points are reached, the limits of representation suggest that a text can only point outside itself, one reason for the difficulties faced by textual responses to the question of technology (Land, forthcoming). The (in)conclusions of the paper then, like those of the two plateaus discussed in it, offer a series of departures from the text, rather than an ending, though each of these departures point to the end of what has thus far been legislated as *the* human subject.

Man and Technics

[A]fter Napoleon the machine-technics of western Europe grew gigantic and, with its manufacturing towns, its railways, its steamships, it has forced us in the end to face the problem squarely and seriously. What is the significance of technics? What meaning within history, what value within life, does it possess, where – socially and meta-physically – does it stand? (Spengler 1932: 4)

Faced with this question of technics, Oswald Spengler asks, 'What does it mean? What does it signify?' The question of technics is immediately reinscribed as a question of meaning, something that needs to be interpreted. And from whence should such an interpretation issue? Significant to whom? To Man.

We might say the same of most contemporary theories of technology and social change. Perusing the shelves of any bookshop today will reveal a wealth of texts dealing with the incredible rate of technologically induced change that is currently afflicting society, like a terminal case of retro futuristic chrono-semiitis (Land and Jones 2001). Authors as diverse as Daniel Bell (1974, 1980), Alvin Toffler (1970), Marshall McLuhan (1964) and Bill Gates (2000) all offer a vision of radical social change driven by a virtual engine of technological transformation. All are concerned to delineate the implication and meaning of these technological changes for human society: to interpret the meaning of technics.

For Spengler there are two possible responses to this question. First there is an Aristotelian heritage, sieved through the nets of the humanists, notably Humboldt and Goethe, to produce an idealism that denigrates the economics and technics of production as mere material concerns, beneath the threshold of serious thought. For these idealists, humankind's energies should be focused on the achievements of culture. At best, technics are there to free people to get on with what is of real value, literary, artistic, political achievements, and if a sub-class of machines, slaves or workers needs to be kept subordinate so that an elite can produce such cultural achievements, then so be it. The irony of this version of humanism is that humans are all too easily expendable in the pursuit of humanity's striving towards greatness. Opposed to this idealist response is the materialism of Marx, Bentham and Mill. Whilst at first glance, given the vitriolic bile that Marx regularly poured upon the Utilitarians, it seems absurd to group these three thinkers together, Spengler's point is similar to Anthony's when he recognises a shared 'ideology of work' that unites such seemingly politically opposed foes (Anthony 1976). For these materialists, economics and technics provide the material base of all society. They determine its form and dynamics, its evolution. Culture, from this view, and all that is valued by the idealists, is merely ideological superstructure.

What both of the responses outlined by Spengler share is a drive to evaluate technics in terms of a pre-given human subject. Whether this is the labouring, value-producing human body that provides the foundation of a Marxist theory of value (Marx 1976; Elson 1979) or the eternal human subject at the heart of the humanities, the terms upon which valuation should occur are given. These responses to the challenge of technology are still repeated today. When faced with managerial discourses on information systems and knowledge management, critical scholars accuse theorists and practitioners alike of technocentrism, of ignoring the really crucial human factors at play in organised social settings: leadership, culture and commitment (Land and Corbett 2001: 153). In such critical responses to technological determinism, the privileging of technical objects is inverted to replace the human subject at the centre of all social analysis.

More subtly a collection of approaches that we can gather together under the idea of a 'textual turn' develops a particular stream of social constructivism to suggest that the only way to rid ourselves of the delusions of positivism, and eliminate any elements of 'residual technicism' from our analyses of technology, is to conceive of technology as a text (Grint and Woolgar 1997; Joerges and Czarniawska 1998). Like the critics of technocentrism, however, these theorists are so keen to obliterate any evidence of objectivism that they fail to reflect sufficiently upon the subject of interpretation. If technology is textual, then we must pay attention to its interpretation. All well and good, but what is it that performs this interpretation? If the answer is simply a human subject, then we would be well advised to heed Nietzsche's note of warning, addressed to an earlier generation of critics of positivism:

> Against positivism, which halts at phenomena – 'There are only *facts*' – I would say: No, facts is precisely what there is not, only interpretations. We cannot establish any fact 'in itself': perhaps it is folly to want to do such a thing.
> 'Everything is subjective,' you say; but even this is interpretation. The 'subject' is not something given, it is something added and invented and projected behind what there is – Finally, is it necessary to posit an interpreter behind the interpretation? Even this is invention, hypothesis. (Nietzsche 1968: 267)

When faced with the question of technology, then, the trick is to avoid any kind of essentialism, even an essentialism of the subject. To put it another way, the subject does not organise interpretation, uniting it into a complete whole. The subject is not behind or above interpretation, but alongside; a product of interpretation. But where does this leave the question of technology and its significance for the human?

After the Human 1

In '10,000 BC: The Geology of Morals (Who Does the Earth Think It Is?)' Deleuze and Guattari go after the figure of the human in hot pursuit across the anthropomorphic stratum. Caught in a series of double-articulated straitjackets, this elusive human monster suffers the judgements of a lobster-god working on a mineral timescale (Deleuze and Guattari 1987: 46). Fortunately, Leroi-Gourhan finds geological traces of change out on the steppe:

> What some call the properties of human beings – technology and language, tool and symbol, free hand and supple larynx, 'gesture and speech' – are in fact properties of [a] new distribution [of form and content]. It would be difficult to maintain that the emergence of human beings marked the absolute origin of this distribution. Leroi-Gourhan's analyses give us an understanding of how contents came to be linked with the hand–tool couple and expressions with the face–language couple. (Deleuze and Guattari 1987: 60)

Instead of proposing an essentialist definition of *the* human, Deleuze and Guattari recognise the formation of an anthropomorphic stratum, formed by folding and sorting processes not entirely unlike the formation of geological strata (ibid.: 58–61). Those features recognised by the philosophers as distinctive of the human – language (for example, Searle 1984; Fellows 1995) and tool use (Ansell Pearson 1997a; Bergson 1998) – are not so much essential attributes as processes of de- and reterritorialisation. Human evolution has been the result of complementary changes in the mouth and the hands that have enabled tool use and language to emerge in parallel. When bodies begin to move in a more upright position, the hands are freed from their locomotive functioning (deterritorialisation) to take on other functions, such as making and using tools (reterritorialisation). With hands and tools, the mouth is freed from those functions where it has to act on the external world, for example to carry things, or to tear and grind food. This deterritorialisation of the mouth frees it up for other purposes, such as language (another reterritorialisation) (Bogue 1989: 128–9). These stratifications are double articulations producing forms and contents, to use a materialist rendering of Hjelmslevian semiotics. The hand is produced as a form of content, with its corresponding tools as a substance of content; language as a form of expression, with the face (supple-larynx, mouth and lips) as its respective substance of expression. Spiralling out, we recognise that these shifts can only occur within a relatively deterritorialised milieu: the steppe with its spaces open for upright movement. The anthropomorphic stratum is a distribution that can only be mapped: 'Maps should be made of these things, organic, ecological, and technological maps one can lay out on the plane of consistency' (Deleuze and Guattari 1987: 61). Such an approach is quite distinct from Spengler's response to the question of technics. Rather than seeking the meaning of technics within human history, or its significance for human-being – both reductions of technology to language and signification – Deleuze and Guattari do not ask what it means, but what it does, and how its movements can be mapped, not subservient to the human but as a constituent form of content within the anthropomorphic stratum. Whilst the textual turn seeks to reduce all material existence to questions of meaning, signification and interpretation, '[t]he end result of Deleuze and Guattari's analysis of the content and expression of the strata of reality is not to convert the world into signs, but to situate material signs within a substrate of matter' (Bogue 1989: 126).

Language and the Subject

> The elementary unit of language – the statement – is the order-word. Rather than common sense, a faculty for the centralization of information, we must define an abominable faculty consisting in emitting, receiving, and transmitting order-words. Language is made not to be believed but to be obeyed, and to compel obedience. (Deleuze and Guattari 1987: 76)

> My general theory since 1971 has been that the Word is literally a virus, and that it has not been recognized as such because it has achieved a state of relatively stable symbiosis with its human host. (Burroughs 1986: 47)

Deleuze and Guattari suggest that the elementary unit of language is the order-word. As well as playing upon the sense of *mot d'ordre* as a password (Deleuze and Guattari 1987: 523, translator's note) so that the statement becomes the repetition of an access code, saying the right thing at the right time, this idea of ordering operates on two registers. Also reflecting its military connotations, there is the giving of orders. In this sense, language and control are entirely implicated in one another, a co-implication that is reflected in the way that cyberneticians have employed the term 'communication' (Wiener 1961; Hayles 1999). On the other hand, there is the idea of linguistic ordering as a mode of organisation particularly concerned with hierarchical relations of dualism. As they put it in relation to the teaching of language in school:

> The compulsory education machine does not communicate information; it imposes upon the child semiotic coordinates possessing all of the dual foundations of grammar (masculine–feminine, singular–plural, noun–verb, subject of the statement–subject of enunciation, etc.). (Deleuze and Guattari 1987: 75–6)

In this sense, language itself is fundamental to the production of the subjects it presumes, in particular the subject of enunciation assumed by the subject of statements in the first person. This point has been made quite forcefully by Nietzsche in his critique of the Cartesian cogito. Giving the example of the statement 'lightning strikes' Nietzsche points to the absurd anthropomorphism implied by these two words: a subject ('lightning') who 'strikes' (Nietzsche 1994: 28). The same point applies to Descartes' 'Cogito ergo sum' (Descartes 1986: 17, 68): there is no logical necessity of a subject who thinks. Even to say 'it thinks' is too far for Nietzsche as the very supposition of a subject is to infer according to 'the grammatical habit: "Thinking is an activity; every activity requires an agent; consequently" ' (Nietzsche 1989: 24).

But if language and thought are not products of a pre-existent human subject, but producing and positioning the subject in a semiotically structured social field then attention must be paid to the materiality of discourse. Language is not a simple reflection or representation of internal subjective states but an external objective material force.

William S. Burroughs' thesis that the word is a virus is not metaphorical, but literal, or at least metonymic (Lydenberg 1987). Language is not a simple product of the subject, nor a neutral tool of representation. Rather it is something simultaneously external to and constitutive of 'the human' (Burroughs 1986: 47). Passed from one body to another, language produces the effect of subjectification precisely as a symptom of viral infection. That this virus has achieved a degree of symbiosis with its host does nothing to alter this fact, but merely conceals it. Deleuze and Guattari also recognise the viral nature of language, which they claim has nothing to do with the simple representation of information from one party to another:

> Language is not content to go from a first party to a second party, from one who has seen to one who has not, but necessarily goes from a second party to a third party, neither of whom has seen. It is in this sense that language is the transmission of the word as an order-word, not the communication of a sign as information. (Deleuze and Guattari 1987: 77)

Discourse is always indirect and communication is all too communicable.

Pause

Returning briefly to the anthropomorphic stratum, before finally taking our leave, whilst language begins as a form of expression linked to the face, and associated with the hand–tool couple as content, it soon spreads beyond this narrow remit. The anthropomorphic stratum sees the formation of machines, such that technology and language exceed themselves. Expression is a semiotic collective machine that constitutes a regime of signs, including, but much more than, the face–language couple, just as content is a technical social machine that pre-exists the hand–tool couple, constituting it through a formation of power. In *Dialogues*, Deleuze and Parnet illustrate this latter with reference to Lynn White Jr's study of feudal technology:

> The history of technology shows that a tool is nothing without the variable machine assemblage which gives it a certain relationship of vicinity with man, animals and things: . . . the stirrup is a different tool depending upon whether it is related to a nomadic war machine, or whether, on the contrary, it has been taken up in the context of the feudal machine. It is the machine that makes the tool and not vice versa. (Deleuze and Parnet 1987: 104–5)

Today we might say the same of the internet. Whilst it is a commonplace that the internet was developed in the depths of the US state-military machine as a means of keeping missile systems active in the event of nuclear attack, this origin has been problematic for many of the theorists concerned with delineating the net's rhizomatic, even emancipatory potential (Stivale 1998). But the question of origins is not important here so much as what variable machine assemblage gathers it into its organisation (cf. Deleuze 1988: 3–4). De- and reterritorialised on to the *socius* of capital the net looks quite different from its ARPANET military origins, just as it is quite distinct from its association with academic research tools. Alternatively it can also be taken up by a nomadic war machine, as when the internet is employed by anti-capitalist protestors to disseminate information on events around the meetings of the World Economic Forum, or G8 for example, or is taken up by the Zapatistas in the Chiapas region of Mexico (Cockburn et al. 2000: 66).

These two machines – the technical social machine of content and the semiotic collective machine of expression – whilst being fully a part of the anthropomorphic stratum, 'at the same time rise up and stretch their pincers out in all directions at the other strata' (Deleuze and Guattari 1987: 63). Language is not only viral, but imperialist. The semiotic collective machine appears to colonise the other strata; to translate them into language; 'to unfold, to stand to full height, producing an illusion exceeding all strata, even though the machine itself still belongs to a determinate stratum' (ibid.: 63). But what is this translation? It is 'the ability of language, with its own givens on its own stratum, to represent all the other strata and thus achieve a scientific conception of the world' (ibid.: 62). It is this illusion that is 'constitutive of man', an illusion that 'derives from the overcoding immanent to language itself' (ibid.: 63). As Burroughs would put it, the human is a virus (Burroughs 1982: 36). Man assumes that he can interpret even non-linguistic systems in terms of language; it is from this that his apparent power over, and separation from the other strata appears. It is in this that he is most like a god, stretching his pincers out across the strata in judgement.

After the Human 2

But if man's linguistic god-complex is constitutive of Man (alongside his machines) then what are we to make of the supposedly profound changes affecting us at the close of the mechanical age (Stone 1995)? We are now told that advances in information and communication technologies are heralding a new era, not only in the social organisation of the network society (Castells 2000), the information society (Webster 1995) or the post-industrial or postmodern society (Kumar 1995), but also in the very formation of the human, traditionally conceived as the building block of social organisation (Badmington 2000; Pepperell 1997; Davis 1998; Bukatman 1993). Bringing together linguistic communication and technology, these new machines seem to hold open the prospect for a deterritorialisation of the anthropomorphic stratum. The Oedipal, straitjacketed figure of the human is still evolving and the story of Man is not at an end. Not yet: 'What is animal at dawn, a human at noon, and a cyborg at dusk, passing through (base four) genetic wetware, (binary) techno-cultural software, and into the tertiary schizomachine program?' (Land 1995: 198).

As Professor Challenger nears the (in)conclusion of his lecture on the evolution of the anthropomorphic stratum and its distributions of form and content in plateau 3, he 'slowly hurries' towards the plane of consistency, performing a destratification of the human.

> Disarticulated, deterritorialized, Challenger muttered that he was taking the Earth with him, that he was leaving for the mysterious world, his poison garden. He whispered something else: it is by headlong flight that things progress and signs proliferate. Panic is creation. (Deleuze and Guattari 1987: 73)

Here then we have a vision of the end of the human, suggestive of a deterritorialisation of the anthropomorphic stratum, of the distributions of form and content that are constitutive of Man. As signs proliferate in the recesses of cyberspace the techno-cultural binary of words and things is disarticulated and comes apart at the seams but what is the line of flight thereby produced and can it escape recapture? To address this question some lines of distinction need to be drawn and worked through. On the one hand, there are the post-humanists, with their desire to escape the mortal world of flesh and fluid wet-ware into the clean and dry non-space of the matrix, thereby achieving immortality as information (Davis 1998). On the other hand, there are those driven by Thanatos towards the death of 'the human' in the full recognition that 'it is impossible to die one time, to die *once* and *for all*' (Ansell Pearson 1997a: 65) and who seek annihilation as a means of overcoming the human (Land 1995; Land 1993). Both are seeking an escape from the human, but are they equivalent?

Post-humanism

> Time to get off this stinking, cop-ridden planet.
> (Burroughs 2002: back cover)

In his study of US techno-culture at the end of the twentieth century, Mark Dery characterises the technophilic excesses of the post-humanists as a 'theology of the ejector seat' (Dery 1996). Taking Burroughs' oft-cited 'This is the space age, and we are here to go' (Burroughs 1990) as emblematic of this new religion, Dery, like Eric Davis (1998), points to the suggestive links between post-humanism and the ascetic ideal of Gnosticism where the body is a prison to be escaped and denied in favour of the immaterial and eternal life of the soul. Converted to pure information, the profane world of matter can be left behind and transcendence is assured. This take on the post-human is quite clearly anthropomorphic. It offers transcendence, permanence and an unchanging ever-after. Rather than heralding change, this is the end of evolution as Baudrillard characterises it in *The Vital Illusion* (2001). The end of the human is embraced as the end of becoming, the end of death and the end of all change in favour of an eternity of the same – pure being. Anything but a transformation, the post-human is the perfection of human being and an end to change. This figure of the post-human is surprisingly like the ideal liberal–humanist subject. Completely disembodied and obscenely rational, it is a pure will that has finally cut itself free from its puppet strings to become a self-contained master. Of course one paradox of this transcendence and liberation is that it is entirely dependent upon a massive social and technical infrastructure.

A second problem with this conception is the version of evolution that provides its justification. Based in a neo-Darwinism that anthropomorphically deifies 'evolution' as seeking either 'the fittest' or more recently 'the most complex' (Ansell Pearson 1997a), evolution for the post-humanists is a competition in which the human is threatened by more complex and efficient technologies. This human essence is then what needs to be defended against this perceived threat, however much this involves mutation and cyborging (Warwick 1997). Not only is the western neo-liberal model of capitalism taken as the model for this neo-Darwinian evolution, but it is then reinserted as the goal of social evolution. Machines are more efficient at producing goods and processing information (a quantitative evaluation); therefore they will and should displace humans.

Trans-humanism

An alternative to post-humanism then seems to lie in a recognition that 'we have never been human', to paraphrase Latour (1993; cf. Davis 1998: 10). As *Challenger*'s lesson teaches us, there is no human essence just assemblage so the dream of post-human transcendence is just that: a dream, or perhaps better, a nightmare (Ansell Pearson 2002). In contrast to this, and following Deleuze, another reading of the 'beyond' of the human condition is possible. After Nietzsche we can look to the idea of the overman as that which may come out of the human as an immanent potential, but also that which overcomes the human as a limited straitjacket: as that which destratifies the anthropomorphic stratum and releases its constitutive flows. In reading the trans-human as a cyborganic becoming through an anti-Oedipal journey up river that improvises on a science-fictional reworking of *Apocalypse Now*, Nick Land rejects the limits of theatrical representation to see what might be produced in the shadows of hypercapitalism: the cyborg gravediggers whose birth is immanent to the deterritorialising flows of capital. This cyborganic subject is quite distinct from the Marxian return of the repressed proletarian subject, however (Land 1995). It is not privileged because it is replication, simulation and forgery, without origin (Murphy 1997). It is for this reason that Land suggests that the revolutionary figure *par excellence* is the replicant (Land 1993) with no father left to kill and no mother to love:

> The Willard skin is coming away in ragged scraps, exposing something beyond masculinity, beyond humanity, beyond life. Patches of mottled technoderm woven with electronics are emerging. Daddy and mummy means nothing anymore. You scrape away your face and step into the dark . . .
> (Land 1995: 204)

Oh, Christ . . . Year Zero

In the seventh of their *Thousand Plateus*, *Year Zero: Faciality*, Deleuze and Guattari consider the importance of the face to the idea of the human. When discussing the human we have spoken of the mind/body dualism, but to speak correctly, the human doesn't have a body. Recalling the face of God in the clouds, or the shadows on the Turin shroud (Deleuze and Guattari 1987: 167), it is this face of the father that over-codes primitive heads and bodies to become faces:

> The head, even the human head, is not necessarily a face. The face is produced only when the head ceases to be a part of the body, when it ceases to be coded by the body, when it ceases to have a multidimensional, polyvocal corporeal code – when the body, head included, has been decoded and has to be *over-coded* by something we shall call the Face. (Deleuze and Guattari 1987: 170)

So what is the human face-to-face, the authenticity of unmediated communication or communion, between faces that a humanist romanticism harks back to and sees contaminated by the new technologies of communication? 'I too would like to know the warm heart beating at the centre of all human activity . . . I want to have my finger on its pulse, its hand in mine and our eyes meeting' (Parker 2000: 84). Certainly, 'the face is produced in humanity', and yet:

> The inhuman in human beings: that is what the face is from the start. It is by nature a close-up with its inanimate white surfaces, its shining black holes, its emptiness and boredom. Bunker-face. To the point that if human beings have a destiny, it is rather to escape the face, to dismantle the face and facializations. (Deleuze and Guattari 1987: 171)

Whilst a centrepoint of humanist sentimentality, the face, and what ten Bos and Kaulingfreks (2002) have called the 'interfacial hothouse' (the heat between faces of an authentic human encounter like the idealised one alluded to by Parker), cannot help but point to an inhuman in the human. Like the stony face and impenetrable gaze of a Nazi prison camp administrator (Finkielkraut 2001: 1), the overcoding of the human face is always colonial. It measures and compares to a transcendent model of humanity and, in judging, finds wanting. The face of the human has the inhuman, the horrors of the Inquisition and the Holocaust as its counterpoint. It is Janus faced and, like a mask, inanimate. Fixed by ideals and the purity of separation, it has no movement, just a fixed gaze staring blankly.

But even with this overcoding, the human is already departing from the anthropomorphic stratum. Whilst the hand was a relative deterritorialisation of the locomotive paw, in association with a tool (for example a club as a deterritorialised branch), the face is an absolute deterritorialisation that rises up along with language and signifiance, to connect to all of the other strata:

> the face represents a far more intense, if slower, deterritorialisation. We could say that it is an *absolute* deterritorialisation: it is no longer relative because it removes the head from the stratum of the organism, human or animal, and connects it to other strata, such as signifiance and subjectification. (Deleuze and Guattari 1987: 172)

Of course, it is not just technology, but language which is central to these overcodings and deterritorialisations (cf. Sørensen, 2006). The mouth is emptied of food and, in a bulimic movement, fills itself with words to vomit out. In this sense the movement of faciality and the blackhole of the mouth has always already departed from the organic or anthropomorphic stratum. There is no purity and language spreads out to effectuate codings (genetic, technical, linguistic) on the other strata. Man is constituted by an illusion, by the purity of separation, but the abstract machine producing that illusion, and by extension Man, is not illusory. The distributions of content and expression really are changing, and reaching out *across* the strata: Man has always been trans-human.

Pause

So where does this leave us? One on hand it seems as though the post-human is a reterritorialisation back on to the human. On the other we are forced into a recognition that the human, as faciality, always had in it something of the inhuman as a fascistic deterritorialisation. So what might it mean to overcome the human when its face is already spreading out across the strata? Here there is no contradiction. The human is fascistic and imperial. It colonises all Others into its representation and judges them as more or less deviant from its norm, more or less civilised precisely insofar as it is caught up in its faciality. In contrast Deleuze and Guattari suggest something else, a movement that escapes the fascism of faciality and refuses a return to the more thoroughly territorialised, pre-facial body: becoming probe-head.

> Beyond the face lies an altogether different inhumanity: no longer that of the primitive head, but of 'probe-heads'; here, cutting edges of deterritorialization become operative and lines of deterritorialisation positive and absolute, forming strange new becomings, new polyvocalities. Become clandestine, make rhizome everywhere, for the wonder of a nonhuman life yet

to be created. *Face, my love*, you have finally become a probe-head . . .
(Deleuze and Guattari 1987: 190–1)

Here then is Willard scraping away his face and stepping into an unknown
dark, revealing a 'mottled technoderm' beneath that is decidedly non-
human and yet escapes the inhuman reterritorialisation of faciality. In
both cases we are left with an ending and an inconclusion. As an air strike
is called into the jungle the battle between bodies and faces ends in death
and a return of something quite different. For Deleuze and Guattari the
ending is left hanging with probe-heads reaching out and multiplying. In
neither case there is a clear image of the post-human. It is quite simply
beyond representation. But far from being a limitation, this is a crucial
feature of change. Becoming is not simple mimesis, a hylomorphic stamp-
ing of the face of the future on to that of the (human) past. It is itself a
tenuous probing of becoming as mutation and multiplication: the capture
of a segment of code by all means, but always to bring it into another
assemblage, to make it do something.

Robo-cop: Cyborg Fascism

We should be wary then of calls to a return to human values where they
seek to arrest change and development, returning to a facial and fascistic
overcoding in the name of the father. Just as Linnaeus' taxonomy separated hu/men/minds from women/animal/bodies, a separation overcoded
by racial anatomy in the nineteenth century (Schiebinger 2000), so contemporary discourse calls for a return of the (same) privilege of the imperial white male's face:

> Why the lament for a lost humanity which since the evolutionary epics of
> the Enlightenment has been habitually defined in the male term to the exclu-
> sion of all others? All that is lost is what we could refer to as the western
> White Male will. Any pretentious eulogy for its timely death is merely a call
> for more negation, more misogyny, more racism, an exterior to dominate:
> the revivalist frenzy of fascism, for the dead end of humanism. (Metcalf
> 1998: 114)

In this sense a deterritorialisation of the human is an explicitly political
move in two ways: rejecting the Othering process that enables the domination and overcoding of faciality on the human side; resisting the
apparent depoliticisation of technological progress and post-humanism
on the other. In the face of a homogenising globalisation operating often
in the name of 'universal' human rights to spread liberalism's twin faces
of representative democracy and free-markets, the trans-human cyborg

is a figure of resistance. As Deleuze and Guattari write, prefiguring the fallout of the terrorist attacks on the USA on 11 September by over twenty years:

> Doubtless, the present situation is highly discouraging. We have watched the war machine grow steadily stronger and stronger, as in a science fiction story; we have seen it assign as its objective a peace still more terrifying than fascist death; we have seen it maintain or instigate the most terrible of local wars as parts of itself; we have seen it set its sights on a new type of enemy, no longer another State, or even another regime, but the 'unspecified enemy'; we have seen it put its counterguerrilla elements into place, so that it can be caught by surprise once, but not twice. (Deleuze and Guattari 1987: 422)

In the face of this apparent totalisation of power and control, it is unsurprising that more conventional humanist scholars, however radical, have trouble conceptualising resistance (Thompson and Ackroyd 1995; Ackroyd and Thompson 1999). But rather than calling for a return to human values from some position external to the technical evolution of the anthropomorphic stratum, the suggestion from Deleuze and Guattari is to recognise that there is no position outside technics or outside power. Any attempt to legislate such a position necessarily involves a return to the fascism of the linguistic universal God-complex. As Klaus Theweleit puts it:

> The more terrible mistake of the nineteenth century: the abandonment of creation theory was based on a biological rather than a technical-artificial foundation. We are the children of the consequences of this mistake. Instead of technical practices, we inherited the master race as our God-function. As good children of the master-race elders, 'we' believe (*green* as we are) – still – that we can protect ourselves against fascism with 'nature' (instead of realizing that only technics can abolish fascism).(Theweleit 1992: 260)

In the absence of a transcendent human/nature, it is artifice and technics that hold out the key to the non-fascist life. Not a reterritorialisation back on to the face of Man, but rather a deterritorialised, becoming probe-head of the trans-human replicant. In this respect the technics of late capitalism produces its gravediggers not as a dialectical contradiction but because of the spaces and cracks that open up in between.

> [T]he very conditions that make the state or World war machine possible, in other words, constant capital (resources and equipment) and human variable capital, continually recreate unexpected possibilities for counterattack, unforeseen initiatives determining revolutionary, popular, minority, mutant machines. (Deleuze and Guattari 1987: 422)

Or in more science-fictional terms:

> With all prospects of moderate reform buried forever, true revolution brews up in the biotech-mutant underclass. Viruses are getting creepier, and no one really knows what cyberspace is up to. WELCOME TO KAPITAL UTOPIA aerosoled on the dead heart of the near future. (Land 1995: 201)

This is a long way from the all-too-human, hypermasculine cyborgs of contemporary Hollywood cinema (see Rushing and Frentz 1995) with their Freikorps imagery, impenetrable steel surfaces and relentless, emotionless determination (Parker and Cooper 1998). It is also a long way from suggesting that all technological change should be unquestioningly embraced. What it does mean, however, is that power is far from absolute and we should be wary of tales of complete technological domination (Weiss 1999). It also means that we should be careful of a pre-emptive Luddism, however. As the human has its roots in an originary technics, so we should be wary of fascistic discourses of purification that seek to hold life in a straitjacket. This is precisely the response of humanist approaches to the question of technology, whether in the form of a Marxist humanist rejection of new technology as deskilling (Braverman 1974; Noble 1999) or in terms of human-centred design. In two senses then, this trans-human position is distinct from post-humanism. It doesn't return (eternally the same) to the idea(l) of Homo sapiens. Nor does it reinscribe a Judeo-Christian theology of transcendence on to the mechanosphere.

> The trans-human condition is not about the transcendence of the human being, but concerns its non-teleological becoming in an immanent process of 'anthropological deregulation'. (Ansell Pearson 1997a: 163)

Indeed, according to Deleuze the issue is not achieving escape velocity at all:

> Not leaving Earth, at all – but becoming all the more earthly by inventing laws of liquids and gases on which the Earth depends. (Deleuze 1992: 293)

References

Ackroyd, S. and Thompson, P. (1999), *Organizational Misbehaviour*, London: Sage.
Ansell Pearson, K. (1997a), *Viroid Life: Perspectives on Nietzsche and the Transhuman Condition*, London: Routledge.
Ansell Pearson, K. (1997b), 'Life Becoming Body: On the "Meaning" of Post Human Evolution', *Cultural Values*, 1: 2.
Ansell Pearson, K. (2002), 'A Post Human Hell', in J. Baggini and J. Stangroom (eds), *New British Philosophy: The Interviews*, London: Routledge.
Anthony, P. D. (1976), *The Ideology of Work*, London: Tavistock Publications.
Badmington, N. (ed.) (2000), *Posthumanism*, Houndmills: Palgrave.
Baudrillard, J. (2001), *The Vital Illusion*, New York: Columbia University Press.

Bell, D. (1974), *The Coming of the Post-Industrial Society*, London: Heinemann.
Bell, D. (1980), 'The Social Framework of the Information Society', in T. Forester (ed.), *The Microelectronics Revolution*, Oxford: Basil Blackwell.
Bergson, H. (1998), *Creative Evolution*, trans. A. Mitchell, New York: Dover Publications.
Bogue, R. (1989), *Deleuze and Guattari*, London: Routledge.
Braverman, H. (1974), *Labor and Monopoly Capital: The Degradation of Work in the Twentieth Century*, New York: Monthly Review Press.
Bukatman, S. (1993), *Terminal Identity: The Virtual Subject in Post-Modern Science Fiction*, Durham: Duke University Press.
Burroughs, W. S. (1982), *Cities of the Red Night*, London: Picador.
Burroughs, W. S. (1986), *The Adding Machine: Selected Essays*, New York: Arcade.
Burroughs, W. S. (1990), *Dead City Radio* (CD), New York: Island Records.
Burroughs, W. S. (2002), *Burroughs Live*, ed. S. Lotringer, New York: Semiotext(e).
Castells, M. (2000), *The Rise of the Network Society (The Information Age)*, Oxford: Blackwell.
Clynes, M. and Kline, N. (1995 [1960]), 'Cyborgs and Space', in C. H. Gray (ed.), *The Cyborg Handbook*, London: Routledge.
Cockburn, A., St Clair, J. and Sekula, A. (2000), *5 Days that Shook the World: Seattle and Beyond*, London: Verso.
Davis, E. (1998), *Techgnosis: Myth, Magic and Mysticism in the Age of Information*, London: Serpent's Tail.
Deleuze, G. (1988), *Foucault*, trans. S. Hand, Minneapolis: University of Minnesota Press.
Deleuze, G. (1992), 'Mediators', in J. Crary and S. Kwinter (eds), *Incorporations*, New York: Zone Books.
Deleuze, G. and Guattari, F. (1987), *A Thousand Plateaus: Capitalism and Schizophrenia*, trans. B. Massumi, Minneapolis: University of Minnesota Press.
Deleuze, G. and Parnet, C. (1987), *Dialogues*, trans. H. Tomlinson and B. Habberjam, London: The Athlone Press.
Dery, M. (1996), *Escape Velocity: Cyberculture at the End of the Century*, New York: Grove Press.
Descartes, R. (1986), *Meditations on First Philosophy: With Selections from the Objections and Replies*, trans. J. Cottingham, Cambridge: Cambridge University Press.
Elson, D. (1979), 'The Value Theory of Labour', in D. Elson (ed.) *Value: The Representation of Labour in Capitalism*, London: CSE Books.
Fellows, R. (1995), 'Welcome to Wales: Searle on the Computational Theory of Mind', in R. Fellows (ed.), *Philosophy and Technology*, Cambridge: Cambridge University Press.
Finkielkraut, A. (2001), *In the Name of Humanity: Reflections of the Twentieth Century*, London: Pimlico.
Foucault, M. (1983), 'Preface' to Deleuze and Guattari (1983), *Anti-Oedipus: Capitalism and Schizophrenia*, trans. R. Hurley, M. Seem and H. R. Lane, Minneapolis: University of Minnesota Press.
Gates, B. (2000), Business @ *the Speed of Thought: Succeeding in the Digital Age*, London: Penguin Books.
Grint, K. and Woolgar, S. (1997), *The Machine at Work: Technology, Work and Organization*, Oxford: Polity Press.
Hayles, N. K. (1999), *How We Became Posthuman: Virtual Bodies in Cybernetics, Literature, and Informatics*, Chicago: University of Chicago Press.
Joerges, B. and Czarniawska, B. (1998), 'The Question of Technology, or How Organizations Inscribe the World', *Organization Studies*, 19: 3.

Kumar, K. (1995), *From Post-Industrial to Post-Modern Society*, Oxford: Blackwell.
Land, C. (forthcoming), 'Text, Technology, Subject', *Tamara: Journal of Critical Postmodern Organization Science*.
Land, C. and Corbett, J. M. (2001), 'From the Borgias to the Borg (and Back Again): Rethinking Organizational Futures', in W. Smith, M. Higgins, M. Parker and G. Lightfoot (eds), *Science Fiction and Organization*, London: Routledge.
Land, C. and Jones, C. (2001), 'O cursèd spite', *ephemera. theory and politics in organization*, 1: 2.
Land, N. (1993), 'Machinic Desire', *Textual Practice*, 7: 3.
Land, N. (1995), 'Meat (or how to kill Oedipus in Cyberspace)', in M. Featherstone and R. Burrows (eds), *Cyberspace, Cyberbodies, Cyberpunk: Cultures of Technological Embodiment*, London: Sage.
Latour, B. (1993), *We Have Never Been Modern*, trans. C. Porter, Hemel Hempstead: Harvester Wheatsheaf.
Lydenberg, R. (1987), *Word Cultures: Radical Theory and Practice in William S. Burroughs' Fiction*, Urbana: University of Illinois Press.
Marx, K. (1976), *Capital: Volume 1*, trans. B. Fowkes, London: Penguin Books.
McLuhan, M. (1964), *Understanding Media: The Extensions of Man*, London: Routledge.
Metcalf, S. (1998), 'Autogeddon', in J. Broadhurst-Dixon and E. J. Cassidy (eds), *Virtual Futures: Cyberotics, Technology and Post-human Pragmatism*, London: Routledge.
Moravec, H. (1990), *Mind Children: The Future of Robot and Human Intelligence*, Cambridge: Harvard University Press.
Murphy, T. (1997), *Wising Up The Marks: The Amodern William Burroughs*, Berkeley: University of California Press.
Nietzsche, F. (1968), *The Will to Power*, trans. W. Kaufman and R. J. Hollingdale, New York: Vintage.
Nietzsche, F. (1989), *Beyond Good and Evil: Prelude to a Philosophy of the Future*, trans. W. Kaufmann, New York: Vintage Books.
Nietzsche, F. (1994), *On the Genealogy of Morality*, ed. K. Ansell Pearson, trans. C. Diethe, Cambridge: Cambridge University Press.
Noble, D. (1999), 'Social Choice in Machine-design: The Case of Automatically Controlled Machine Tools', in D. MacKenzie and J. Wajcman (eds), *The Social Shaping of Technology*, Buckingham: Open University Press.
Parker, M. (2000),'Manufacturing Bodies: Flesh, Organization, Cyborgs', in J. Hassard, R. Holliday and H. Willmott (eds), *Body and Organization*, London: Sage.
Parker, M. and Cooper, R. (1998), 'Cyborgisation: Cinema as Nervous System', in J. Hassard and R. Holliday (eds), *Organization/Representation: Work and Organization in Popular Culture*, London: Sage.
Pepperell, R. (1997), *The Post-Human Condition*, Exeter: Intellect.
Rushing, J. and Frentz, T. (1995), *Projecting the Shadow: The Cyborg Hero in American Film*, Chicago: University of Chicago Press.
Schiebinger, L. (2000), 'Taxonomy for Human Beings', in G. Kirkup, L. Janes, K. Woodward and F. Hovenden (eds), *The Gendered Cyborg: A Reader*, London: Routledge, in association with the Open University Press.
Searle, J. (1984), *Minds, Brains and Science*, London: Penguin Books.
Sørensen, B. M. (2006), 'Defacing the Corporate Body. Or, Why HRM Needs a Kick in the Teeth', *Tamara: Journal of Critical Postmodern Organization Science*.
Spengler, O. (1932), *Man and Technics*, London: George Allen and Unwin Ltd.
Stivale, C. (1998), *The Two-Fold Thought of Deleuze and Guattari: Intersections and Animations*, New York: The Guilford Press.

Stone, A. R. (1995), *The War on Desire and Technology at the Close of the Mechanical Age*, Cambridge: MIT Press.
ten Bos, R. and Kaulingfreks, R. (2002), 'Life Between Faces', *ephemera. theory and politics in organization*, 2: 1.
Theweleit, K. (1992), 'Circles, Lines and Bits', in J. Crary and S. Kwinter (eds), *Incorporations*, New York: Zone Books.
Thompson, P. and Ackroyd, S. (1995), 'All Quiet on the Workplace Front? A Critique of Recent Trends in British Industrial Sociology', *Sociology*, 29: 4.
Toffler, A. (1970), *Future Shock*, London: Pan Books.
Warwick, K. (1997), *March of the Machines: Why the New Race of Robots will Rule the World*, London: Century Books.
Webster, F. (1995), *Theories of the Information Society*, London: Routledge.
Weiss, G. (1999), 'The Durée of the Techno-Body', in E. Grosz (ed.), *Becomings: Explorations in Time, Memory and Futures*, New York: Cornell University Press.
Wiener, N. (1961), *Cybernetics: Or Control and Communication in the Animal and the Machine*, Cambridge: MIT Press.

Part III

Art and the Outside

Chapter 7

Practical Deleuzism and Postmodern Space

Ian Buchanan

'We pay a heavy price for capitalising on our basic animal mobility' writes Edward Casey and that price is 'the loss of places that can serve as lasting scenes of experience and reflection and memory' (Casey 1993: xiii). This loss is usually blamed on the proliferation of generic spaces – or, 'non-places', to use Marc Augé's (1995) phrase – like malls, airports, freeways, office parks, and so forth, which prioritise cost and function over look and feel. Even so, Casey still wants to argue that transitory spaces like airports retain a certain 'placial' quality that gives meaning to contemporary existence. In contrast, writers like Augé (he is by no means alone – Augé himself attributes the key elements of his idea of non-place to de Certeau and Foucault) have in much recent writing on space sought to elucidate this new type of generic space's distinct lack of placiality. These two positions are, however, simply two sides of the same conceptual coin – Augé does not conceive of a new type of place, he uses a traditional model of place to decry the seemingly soulless transformations to the built environment he witnesses everywhere in the developed world. By the same token, Casey acknowledges that these new spaces appear placeless, but that is only because one isn't looking at them in the right way. His work then seeks to restore their seemingly lost placiality. The interest of bringing Deleuze and Guattari into this debate resides in the fact that they do not hold that the idea of place continues to be relevant. Taking this as my starting point, I want to advance three propositions relating to the analysis of contemporary space. These three propositions will not by any means exhaust what can be said about this subject, but my hope is that they will inflect discussion about it in a useful way.

1. Alfred Hitchcock's cinema anticipated the affect of postmodern space – a kind of anxious mourning for the loss of place.

2. The suburban shopping mall was the harbinger of postmodern space – it is the form of content proper to postmodernism as form of expression.
3. The transformations that have made postmodern space what it is can be understood in terms of deterritorialisation.

I   Body without Organs

'The modern fact,' as Deleuze puts it, 'is that we no longer believe in this world. We do not even believe in the events which happen to us, love, death, as if they only half concerned us. It is not we who make cinema; it is the world which looks to us like a bad film' (Deleuze 1989: 171). The world Deleuze is speaking of is post-war Europe, a world of rubble, housing shortages, refugees and bold reconstructions. He is also speaking of the cinematic or virtual worlds created in this period, signalling their radical difference in construction and operation from the cinema that preceded this moment. Pre-war cinema was a cinema of belief, or better, a cinema that could be believed in; in the post-war period this was no longer true, the cinema had to confront a world that exceeded what cinema up to that point could contrive to present, it went beyond its limits. 'Why is the Second World War taken as a break? The fact is that, in Europe, the post-war period has greatly increased the situations which we no longer know how to react to, in spaces which we no longer know how to describe. These were "any spaces whatever", deserted but uninhabited, disused warehouses, waste ground, cities in the course of demolition or reconstruction. And in these any-spaces-whatever a new race of characters was stirring, a kind of mutant: they saw rather than acted, they were seers' (Deleuze 1989: xi). It is a world that has been emptied out, a world in which the people are missing. A world of any-space-whatever not place.

What Deleuze is attempting to describe here is something he would in other works call the body without organs. So what is the body without organs? It is well known that the phrase itself is lifted from a poem by Antonin Artaud, but it is in vain that we look there for an explanation of the concept. Instead we must look to two quite distinct sources: Marx and Lacan. The first accounts for how the body without organs (BwO) functions, while the latter explains how it is possible for it to function that way. In *Anti-Oedipus*, Deleuze and Guattari say if we want to have some idea of the forces exerted by the BwO then we must first establish a parallel between desiring-production and social production. Forms of social production, like those of desiring-production, involve, they argue, 'an unengendered nonproductive attitude' or what they call a 'full body' which functions as a *socius*. 'This *socius* may be the body of the earth, that of the tyrant, or capital. This is the body that Marx is referring to when he says that it is not the product of labour, but rather appears as its natural or divine presupposition' (Deleuze and Guattari 1983: 10). This is the body without organs. It is an active form of presupposition that inserts itself into a given context and in so doing smothers its origins so that it always appears as naturally occurring. It falls back on (*il se rabat sur*) all production, constituting a surface over which the forces and agents of production are distributed, thereby appropriating for itself all surplus production and arrogating to itself both the whole and the parts of the process, which now seem to emanate from it as a quasi cause (Deleuze and Guattari 1983: 10). It defines not what we think and feel about something, but the unthought set of presuppositions we utilise to compose our thoughts and feelings without them ever being intelligible to us.

I want to suggest that the body without organs of postmodern space is precisely the unintelligible fear that we have that it is placeless. Cinema's attraction, I would further suggest, stems from the fact that it is able to make this body without organs tangible. While it is true American cinema did not go down the same pathway as European cinema, it nevertheless ended up confronting its own kind of placelessness, or rather it generated its modulation of the same anxiety: that place had been destroyed. At this point in his history of cinema, Deleuze gives centre stage to the European directors. But even if Deleuze's implication is true that no new aesthetic developments were occurring in Hollywood at this point, that doesn't mean that nothing of interest was happening. Indeed, it is widely agreed that the films Hitchcock made in this period are among his best, to which judgement I want to add that these films are also films about a very different kind of landscape. As Joan Didion put it:

> It was a peculiar and visionary time, those years after World War II to which the Malls and Towns and even Dales stand as climate-controlled monuments [. . .] The frontier had been reinvented, and its shape was the subdivision, the new free land on which all the settlers could recast their lives *tabula rasa*. (Didion 1979: 180–1)

Hitchcock's cinema helped to shape the unsettling feeling tone of this new unhomely era by perfecting what Deleuze calls a cinema of the 'mental image', that is, a cinema of the closed universe of the monad and the bunker (Deleuze 1986: 198). The worlds Hitchcock constructs in his films, especially the later ones, do look like 'bad films', but in that precise sense they anticipate the postmodern landscape of glitzy but standardised façades. It is a cinema of a 'global style' that could be anywhere and, as Rem Koolhaas puts it, has spread everywhere like a virus.[1]

Hitchcock's films operate within highly contrived and closely observed buildings: the apartment block, the motel, the mansion, the terrace house at the end of the street (the ensuing claustrophobic atmosphere of constant surveillance is doubtless the element of his work that retains the most potent resonance in contemporary society). Hitchcock's famous preference for sound stages over locations, back-projections and mattes instead of the 'real' thing created a cinema of what (after Eco and Baudrillard) and in contrast to Rossellini's neo-realism might be termed hyperrealism.[2] The outside world in Hitchcock is literally a simulacra of a simulacrum. Hitchcock's disdain for actors (he notoriously used to fall asleep during the actual filming of scenes), which Deleuze charitably describes in terms of an opposition to the Actor's Studio, is clearly of a piece with this (Deleuze 1986: 201). If one must speak of a break between Hitchcock and Rossellini it is because Hitchcock could not reconnect the severed link between humankind and the world; his characters persist 'in the world as if in a pure optical and sound situation' (Deleuze 1989: 172). His worlds, like shopping malls, are interiors whose aim is to eliminate the desire for the outside by reproducing it in facsimile: everything within is related at the price of their being no relations without (Deleuze 1986: 204).

This closed-off world is difficult to sustain and, as Deleuze argues, some of Hitchcock's best films give us a glimpse of the ways in which the mental image would be pushed into a crisis.

> *Vertigo* [1958] communicates a genuine image to us; and, certainly, what is vertiginous, is, in the heroine's heart, the relation of the Same with the Same which passes through all the variations of its relations with others (the dead woman, the husband, the inspector). But we cannot forget the other, more ordinary, vertigo – that of the inspector who is incapable of climbing the bell-tower staircase, living in a strange state of contemplation which is communicated to the whole film and which is rare in Hitchcock. (Deleuze 1986: 204–5)

The Bates' motel is a relic of an older 'placial' mode of spatiality, one that is nostalgically filled with all the qualities supposedly lost to us now that motels belong to freeways not towns, now that they are part of a spatial network, which may span the globe, rather than places in their own right. Chain motels like Howard Johnson's began to take a hold of the American landscape in this period, too, precisely by promising an end to particularity, to place-specific motels with idiosyncratic characteristics. The new chain motel guaranteed an end to the variations in motel fittings and fit-out that old-style travellers like Humbert Humbert speak of, at once knowingly and ironically.

> We came to know – *nous connûmes*, to use a Flaubertian intonation – the stone cottages under enormous Chateaubriandesque trees, the brick unit, the adobe unit, the stucco court, on what the Tour Book of the Automobile Association describes as 'shaded' or 'spacious' or 'landscaped' grounds. The log kind, finished in knotty pine, reminded Lo, by its golden-brown glaze, or fried-chicken bones. We held in contempt the plain whitewashed clapboard Kabins, with their faint sewerish smell or some other gloomy self-conscious stench and nothing to boast of (except 'good beds'), and unsmiling landlady always prepared to have her gift ('. . . well, I could give you . . .') turned down. (Nabokov 1995: 145–6)

Lolita (1955) is, among other things, an ironic paean to a rapidly disappearing kind of place, namely the kind of place the Bates' motel is, a spatial native, a highly localised, albeit still generic, species of place.[3] At least part of the thrill of *Psycho* is the familiar fear it evokes of the unexpected that dominated travel in the age before chain motels. It confirms the suspicion 'we moderns' have been taught to harbour that such unbranded places are at best uncongenial and at worst unsafe. Humbert is in this respect perfectly modern: he is not the least sentimental about the out of the way places he goes to, although he is occasionally moved to regret not really remembering where exactly he'd been to, nor what he'd seen: 'We had been everywhere. We had really seen nothing' (Nabokov 1995: 175). He is not a tourist as such, but a nomad moving ceaselessly in order to stay put in the smooth any-space-whatever of the cloistered motel room. Like Norman Bates, he has a horror of the family home because he knows full well his particular fantasy cannot be enacted there. Not surprisingly, Humbert expresses a strong preference for the streamlined spaces that were even then replacing the eccentric places described above. 'To any other type of tourist accommodation I soon grew to prefer the Functional Motel – clean, neat, safe nooks, ideal places for sleep, argument, reconciliation, insatiable illicit love' (Nabokov 1995: 145). What he looked for were spaces where the idiosyncrasies of lived place (noises, smells and assorted other discomforts and distractions) did not intrude on his designs.

As Deleuze narrates it, then, what emerges in the years following the Second World War are two separate but dialectically connected cinematic traditions: a European tradition of any-spaces-whatever and (by implication) a Hollywood tradition of non-places; or, to put it another way, a neo-realism of the bombed-out city and a hyperrealism of suburban monoculture. This hyperrealism should not be read as a kind of intensified verisimilitude or cinematic equivalent of photorealism. I'm not suggesting that Hitchcock's cinema captures the truth of postmodern space in a representational sense. On the contrary, I'm suggesting his cinema has helped create the unthought recording surface on which much writing about, and indeed film-making in response to, postmodern space takes place – it was his cinema that taught us to think of the motel, the suburban family home and so on as places of anxiety; and he did so precisely by showing us that these places aren't as homely as we'd like to assume. Of course, Hitchcock didn't act alone, but we find encapsulated in his work the potent feeling that place isn't placial anymore: it is unsettling, unhomely, fearful, empty, lacking human dimension.

II Abstract Machine

At least part of the shock of Fredric Jameson's programme essay on postmodernism stemmed from its willingness to pronounce this new space of hotels and malls uninhabitable.[4] His entire argument can be understood as an attempt to describe a new kind of space that puts the old, or received spatial sense in question, leaving us unsure of how to act or feel in the face of such radical transformations in the built environment as the Bonaventure Hotel appeared to betoken. While much of his discussion of this space centres on its architectural attributes, which are to him in equal parts striking and banal, it is the emergence of a total space of shopping that he is at most pains to document.[5] The Bonaventure Hotel, which sits on top of a six-storey shopping mall, plus ubiquitous foodcourt, offers a telling example of the way in which the built environment follows the postmodern dictate that all aspects of everyday life can and should be made to generate surplus value. Every aspect of life – eating, sleeping, shitting, fucking and so on – can take place within its confines for a price. As Sharon Zukin argues in her history of this transformation of the American landscape, although no one had eyes to see it at the time, the spread of the suburban shopping mall previewed the post-boom landscape inasmuch that – as we now know – spaces of consumption (rather than manufacturing, growing, or indeed simply living) would dominate and indeed determine our sense of place (Zukin 1991: 20).

In Deleuze's terms, the mall is an abstract machine – it is an ideal form that is actualised in a variety of formats. Central to the abstract machine is the distinction between form of content and form of expression that Deleuze and Guattari draw from Hjelmslev. Deleuze and Guattari refer us to Foucault's analysis of the prison for an example of how this kind of analysis works.[6] The prison is a form of content and is related to other forms of content (schools, barracks, hospital, factories and so on). But this form does not refer to the word 'prison' for its sense, but to an entirely different set of statements to do with the discourse of 'delinquency'. Delinquency is a form of expression articulating a new way of translating, classifying, stating and ultimately even committing criminal acts. The form of expression cannot be reduced to words – it refers to statements arising in the social field (the realm canvassed by Deleuze and Guattari's concept of the regime of signs). By the same token, the form of content is not reducible to a thing, or set of things; it refers to an assemblage (rather than to a state of affairs) comprising architecture, discipline and so on. Ultimately, we can say that there are two constantly intersecting fields here, one, a discursive multiplicity of expression, and the other, a non-discursive multiplicity of content. But, 'it is even more complex than that' because these two terms each have their own microhistories, but also they make other kinds of connections to other kinds of formalisations. At most, Deleuze and Guattari say, they share an implied state of the abstract machine (Deleuze and Guattari 1987: 67).

Writing about postmodernism has tended to concentrate on the form of expression – the very word 'postmodernism' is an example *par excellence* of a form of expression. Expression refers to the production of what Deleuze and Guattari call (following Foucault) statements. Theorists as diverse as Meaghan Morris, John Fiske, Rob Shields, Anne Friedberg, as well as many others, have tended to focus the debate around the question of what is the proper statement for the mall – banality, resistance, panopticism, and so on. What makes Jameson's approach different is that he not only discusses the form of expression, he also attempts to isolate the form of content of the mall, namely the creation of a new total space of consumerism that not only seeks to incorporate everything under one roof, but actively seeks to exclude or denigrate the world beyond its walls. The mall is a supreme example of what Rebecca Solnit has aptly described as the propagation of monoculture (Solnit and Schwartzenberg 2000: 153–72). Her analogy is derived from agriculture and essentially depicts a situation in which a single 'cash' crop is grown to the exclusion of all other crops and ruthlessly defended using every available means. All the available evidence now suggests that in spite of its appearance of high productivity the monocultural approach is not only ecologically disastrous it is also commercially disastrous too since it is overly prone to bacterial and insect infestation and therefore too reliant on increasingly expensive pesticides. As a form, the mall promotes a single objective: the sale of consumer goods and services. Unlike the city, the mall is not a shared space – it has a single governing body reporting to a corporation which in turn reports to shareholders; unlike the city it is not a mix-use space – it is a

single-use space, shopping and not-shopping are simply opposite sides of
the same coin; unlike the city, the mall has no residents – it is a space for
customers and employees only; unlike the city, the mall does not command
our love and pride, it only wants our business. It is the proliferation of this
form that I am suggesting has been a primary shaping force with respect
to the shape and feel of contemporary space.

Despite the naïve celebrations of the 'pleasures' afforded ordinary citi-
zenry by shopping malls and the still more naïve accounts of the possibilities of resistance to be found within their windowless walls, the reality is
that their triumph came at the expense of previous models of coherent connection between population and place. They are not the organic product
of economic growth in a community, but transplants from afar that settle
into an area with no more care for the local than any foreign invader has.

The regional shopping centre looks in retrospect like the inevitable
outcome of mass automobile ownership and suburban growth, but its
emergence in the 1950s was a dramatic event. Newspapers wrote glow-
ingly about the advantages of 'markets in the meadows': places totally
planned for the consumer that made more sense than the helter-skelter
competition of the average Main Street (Frieden and Sagalyn 1991: 62).

As Baudrillard astutely observed, the mall-form functions as a nucleus
around which the new, still to be built, suburb eventually settles like so
much kipple (Baudrillard 1994: 77). Wal-Mart, currently the largest corporation in the world (its 2003 net worth was a staggering $US258
billion, its revenues amounting to 2 per cent of US GDP), took this strategy a step further in the 1950s and concentrated on towns with populations under 5,000, effectively turning them into satellites of its superstores
(Head 2004: 80). With no other competition in sight, these stores effectively sucked the life out of the town's commercial districts, as small and
fragile as they were, and refocused the flow of traffic and funds in the
direction of an ugly bunker situated in an airfield-sized car park at the
outer edge of the town.[7]

The advent of the freeway system brought an end to point to point
travel, journeys no longer plotted a route from town to town, but instead
pursued a transversal line of pure speed. The mall was an integral part of
this system, displacing the town centre almost completely within a few
years. Main Street America reappeared in fantasy form in Walt Disney's
homage to a nostalgically remembered America of his childhood that had
by then all but disappeared, Disneyland. Malls occupy those spaces in the
city where the factors we associate with place have either ceased to operate,
or (more usually) are vulnerable to predatory reinterpretation. The mall
took the beating heart of the city – the crowds, the big variety stores, the

small specialty stores, and the eclectic eateries – and transplanted it in greenfield sites sure in the knowledge that the people would come. But not all people, since one of its most potent attractions was and continues to be its promise of social homogenisation. As a privately owned space, the mall is, in contrast to the city, selective about who it permits to use its space. So although its use may appear public in character, the mall is not given to the public to use; it is rather 'open' to the public, providing they agree to abide its rules – no skating, no chewing gum, no smoking, no drinking, no loitering, and so on. Its commercial success is built on a series of what Zukin calls 'abstractions'. She has in mind both architectural abstractions – visual adumbrations of the city's iconography – and what might be thought of as abstractions of some, at least, of its more typical sensual pleasures, particularly those of the palate. I specified the visual here because the mall's real breakthroughs in architectural terms lay elsewhere.[8] The mall's success as an apparatus of consumption hinges to a large degree on the canny way in which it has created a form that can be decorated in such a way as to recollect the city minus its actual grittiness, smells, noise, in short, any of its typical characteristics. In this sense, it is perhaps more precise to say it recollects a movie of a city, rather than an actual city, and doubtless part of its appeal lies in the fact that to walk through a mall is like walking through not a movie set as such, but the virtual world the movie projects as a necessary condition to its cognition. The mall is the after-image of the city.

Abstraction, of the type Zukin talks about, can be seen in the Trafford Centre mall John Urry discusses in *The Tourist Gaze*. As can clearly be seen in the image he reproduces, it encases within its featureless walls a facsimile New Orleans streetscape replete with iron balustrades, French windows, gas lamps and ivy cascading from balcony planter boxes, but without the litter, horse dung, stale urine, drunks passed out in doorways, panhandling bums and prostitutes of the real French Quarter. One cannot help but note in Urry's photo the ubiquitous presence of Starbucks, also very much at home in the real New Orleans (Urry 2002: 112). If one were to revive an outmoded critical discourse and ask which of the two spaces – the mall or the city – is the more authentic, the answer wouldn't be as easy to determine as one might expect. The French Quarter, today, although it continues to exude many of the same smells as it did when it was playground to the thousands of boilermakers and stevedores labouring in its shipyards and wharves, is nevertheless a Disneyfied facsimile of itself – an 'adults only' theme park. Indeed, these days Jackson's Brewery is literally a shopping mall. The waterfront has been converted into a bicycle path and the eateries in the Quarter have gone so far upmarket none but the middle class can afford an 'authentic' poughboy. Now that the Quarter is girded by the postmodern equivalent of the Maginot line, a vast grey curtain of dour concrete superbunkers variously kitted out as a convention centre, casino, this or that chain hotel, and last but not least the superdome, the only people who visit the Quarter these days are middle-class tourists of that peculiarly American kind: conventioneers, sports fans and salesmen. In this sense, New Orleans represents the apotheosis of the logic of the mall.[9]

III Deterritorialisation

How does an entire city become monocultural? How do malls work in other words? What follows is an attempt to show how the terms 'deterritorialisation' and 'reterritorialisation' might be used to understand, for example, that what makes the Bonaventure a postmodern building is precisely the fact that it was built as part of an earnest programme to transform Los Angles into a business centre to rival San Francisco and not simply its architecture.[10]

While it is customary to celebrate the architects for their creative work, it is not the architects, but the city-planners (the regulators who make and police zoning laws, land taxes and so on), and behind them the financiers who reap value from these laws, who are the real visionaries, the true mechanics of space, for they are the ones who create the context in which the new structure will work.

In spite of what many people (Deleuzians among them) seem to think, reterritorialisation and deterritorialisation are not a binary pair: reterritorialisation is not the opposite of deterritorialisation. As such, one must be wary of shorthand attempts to define them with reference to either a logic of opening and closing or detachment and reattachment because intended or not this cannot but instil the idea that they are a binary pair after all (Holland 1999: 20). It is true Deleuze and Guattari do say that every deterritorialisation is followed by an accompanying reterritorialisation, but the one (deterritorialisation) does not spontaneously give rise to the other (reterritorialisation) as Keith Ansell Pearson (1999: 1777) implies. To suggest that one kind of process can give rise to another is tantamount to smuggling dialectics back into a philosophy that is famously anti-dialectical. Even more wrongheaded, though, is to suggest, as Charles Stivale (1998: 22–3) does, that territory, deterritorialisation and reterritorialisation form a ternary structure. If this were indeed the case, then we would be compelled to concede that Deleuze and Guattari do indeed practise dialectics. Also to be resisted, even though it is in fact very close to the spirit of Deleuze and Guattari's intent, is Jameson's claim that 'its first and as it were foundational meaning lies in' the emergence of capitalism itself; this was, he continues, 'the first and the most fateful deterritorialisation' (Jameson 1998: 152). This definition hypostatises deterritorialisation as a one-shot event, when in fact it is an ongoing, continuous process, or constant force (to use the not unrelated Lacanian language of the drives); deterritorialisation is not something that can be caused: one can unleash it, accelerate it, decelerate and contain it, but never engender it.[11]

What Deleuze and Guattari actually say is that capitalism is 'the thing, the unnameable, the generalised decoding of flows that reveals *a contrario* the secret of all [social] formations' (1983: 153) that stands at the end of history enabling us to read history retrospectively in its light. It is not the first deterritorialisation, but the last. The first was in fact the coming of the state form, but in one respect Jameson is right in saying capitalism was the first because, as Deleuze and Guattari put it, it 'cannot be said that the previous formations did not foresee this Thing that only came from without by rising from within, and that at all costs had to be prevented from rising' (Deleuze and Guattari 1983: 153). Before Derrida (1994) coined the word 'hauntology', the concept was already – albeit namelessly – operating in Deleuze and Guattari's work.[12] Capitalism is synonymous with the breakdown of the social conceived as a 'territorial machine' which connects a people to an earth (BwO) by means of inscription, but not the actual cause. Capitalism was able to come into being because of the propensity for deterritorialisation inherent in every social system: it is in effect the product not the cause of deterritorialisation. 'In a sense, capitalism has haunted all forms of society, but it haunts them as a terrifying nightmare, it is the dread they feel of a flow that eludes their code' (Deleuze and Guattari 1983: 140). In this respect, Jameson is also correct to describe it as fateful, for in its dissolute, decoded state, it is the end primitive societies feared and worked consciously to avoid. The coding of desire and the fear of decoded desire 'is the business of the socius' (ibid.: 139). The 'essential thing is to mark and be marked', Deleuze and Guattari say, and what they mean by this is that all 'organs' (anything capable of producing or interrupting a flow – signs, status, women, children, herds, seeds, sperm, shit and menstrual blood can all be conceived as 'flows') must be subject to a collective investment that 'plugs desire into the *socius* and assembles social production and desiring-production into a whole on the earth' (ibid.: 142).

It should be clear enough from the foregoing that deterritorialisation cannot be understood independently of territoriality, what is perhaps less clear is that territoriality (or territory, these terms are used interchangeably) is not a 'placial' concept. Deleuze and Guattari quite explicitly rule this out. If territoriality 'is taken to mean a principle of residence or of geographic distribution, it is obvious that the primitive social machine is not territorial' (ibid.: 145). The territorial machine does not divide land, it divides people, 'but does so on an indivisible earth where the connective, disjunctive, and conjunctive relations of each section are inscribed' (ibid.: 145). The earth, a great, immanent, unengendered unity, is the space where our soul (in Foucault's sense of the term) circulates; it is the thing to which we pledge allegiance and attach ourselves and more especially our organs by means of ritual and bodily marks; but it also appears to us as our origin, where we came from, our mother, our memory. 'These are the two aspects of the full body: an enchanted surface of inscription, the fantastic law, or the apparent objective movement; but also a magical agent or fetish, the quasi cause' (ibid.: 145).

Let me try, then, to give deterritorialisation and reterritorialisation a more concrete meaning: land value and ground rent create a powerful, contradictory motor for urban development. Zoning laws are designed to protect land values, but their efficacy is dependent upon ground rent, which is where the problem lies. If ground rent is a form of value mortgaged on the future surplus value of the labour performed on that site, it is essentially a highly coded form of value dependent upon a structure of equivalence that in an era of such rapid technological change as we are in now is a very uncertain proposition indeed. Futurists are constantly predicting that most or all of the jobs we'll be performing two or three decades from now have yet to be invented. But if that isn't risky enough, ground rent also faces competition from land value itself, which isn't tied to labour in any determinate fashion and may rise or fall according to its own inner logic. It is, in this sense, the classic example of a deterritorialising force – if it is allowed to run free it can literally destroy a city, whereas ground rent is a steady engine of growth (ibid.: 145). The shopping mall is the example *par excellence* of this, and for this very reason its rapid rise to prominence as a new cultural form was largely financed by pension funds in search of stable, non-speculative investments (Crawford 1992: 8).

Capitalism has at its disposal two means (axioms) of 'overcoding' the free flow of ground rent: (1) zoning laws; and (2) land tax. Zoning laws exert pressure on land value by regulating the supply (increasing the residency rating of a suburb increases the number of houses or dwellings that may be located there – the effect of this on price varies because in a poor suburb it may provoke the view that it is tending towards a slum, whereas in a middle-class suburb it will increase the value of the land because it enables 'development'), while land taxes exerts pressure on land value by regulating demand (reducing the taxes generally increases demand, while raising taxes will tend to slow demand). These two instruments are used in combination by city governors to at least preserve value, but more importantly to maintain structural equilibrium. If production is profitable and property values fall, this can be a serious problem if the production process is underwritten by loans guaranteed against the land value of the factory site itself. By the same token, if land values appreciate too much the economics of production itself ceases to make sense – if the land turns a profit without producing anything, why continue to produce? In both instances, the company involved may choose to exit the city, which if the company is big enough or it occurs on a sector-wide scale can be disastrous for the city.

The point I want to make here is that deterritorialisation isn't a placial concept, but rather an inherent property of the notion of value itself. But more importantly, the example above brings to our attention the essential matrix of Deleuze and Guattari's thinking: on the one hand, property value in isolation is an intensity, it moves up and down a sliding scale seemingly of its own accord; but on the other hand, when viewed in the context of a city as a whole, its effects are felt in extension, even though it remains an intensity. Supply and demand are tensors of value, not creators of value. Value is like wind velocity, air pressure, temperature and so on, indivisible: if a bucket of water is 40 degrees Celsius and you tip half out, you'll have half a bucket of water left, but it will still be 40 degrees Celsius. Or, to give a different example, if you take a five dollar note and tear it in half you won't get two times two fifty; indeed, if you set fire to it, you don't necessarily end up with zero either. The value of money is an intensity. This doesn't mean, however, that intensities are not subject to change or somehow protected from the effects of their environment. Water can obviously be heated up and cooled down by a variety of means and likewise one can heat up an economy and thereby affect the value of money. Hot water in an airtight container isn't dangerous, but spilled on unprotected flesh it can scald and even kill; money in a closed economy (such as China used to have) is similarly benign, but when placed in an international exchange context it becomes vulnerable to fluctuation and in turn jeopardises the livelihoods of the people who rely on it – if the value falls too far or worse too fast, it leads to impossible trade deficits and debt burdens; yet if it rises too far or too fast it can cripple exports and trigger an import bonanza.

IV Schizoanalysis and the City

We are still a long way from being able to say what a Deleuzian analysis – that is, schizoanalysis – of space might, much less should look like. There are literally dozens of books on Deleuze and Guattari, but not one of them can tell you how to read a text in a manner that is recognisably Deleuzian. Even if one accepts Deleuze and Guattari's injunction against interpretation, it should nonetheless still be possible to identify reliably a body without organs and distinguish that from an abstract machine and so on. Otherwise, Deleuze's famous toolbox is useless to us in much the same way as surgical instruments are useless to the non-surgeon. And yet, given the wide differences in definitions to be found in the secondary literature, one can safely say we have not yet reached that stage. As cultural critics we are the poorer for this because it means the rich critical language Deleuze left us is not being utilised to its fullest extent. We need to return to Deleuze in the Lacanian sense, that is, return to the analytic situation itself. This gesture is not at all foreign to Deleuze. His frequent insistence that we should start with problems, that philosophers must be allowed to ask their own questions, and so on, means nothing other than this: the analytic situation of the philosopher is precisely the creation of problems and their associated concepts. The parallel with Lacan can be made more forcefully. In his book on Bacon, Deleuze writes of the clinical underpinnings of concepts, thus nudging us in the direction of the analytic situation as Lacan conceives it. Is this not what Guattari brought to the collaboration? Many readers of Deleuze object to the very idea that some kind of analytic programme of action might be elaborated in his name. While I am sympathetic to the anarchic spirit underpinning this view of Deleuze, it is not supported in Deleuze's own work. He is quite explicit in saying that he wanted to create a practical, useful form of philosophy. This is what he meant when he said *Anti-Oedipus* is an experiment in writing Pop Philosophy.

References

Ansell Pearson, K. (1999), *Germinal Life: The Difference and Repetition of Deleuze*, London: Routledge.

Augé, M. (1995), *Non-Places: Introduction to an Anthropology of Supermodernity*, trans. J. Howe, London: Verso.

Baudrillard, J. (1994), *Simulacra and Simulation*, trans. S. Faria Glaser, Ann Arbor: The University of Michigan Press.

Buchanan, I. (2000), *Deleuzism: A Metacommentary*, Edinburgh: Edinburgh University Press.

Buchanan, I. (2005), 'Space in the Age of Non-Place', in Buchanan and Lambert (eds), *Deleuze and Space*, Edinburgh: Edinburgh University Press.

Casey, E. (1993), *Getting Back into Place: Toward a Renewed Understanding of the Place-World*, Bloomington and Indianapolis: Indiana University Press.

Cook, C. (2004), *Diet for Dead Planet: How the Food Industry is Killing Us*, New York: The New Press.

Crawford, M. (1992), 'The World in a Shopping Mall', in M. Sorkin (ed.), *Variations on a Theme Park: The New American City and the End of Public Space*, New York: Hill and Wang.

Deleuze, G. (1986 [1983]), *Cinema 1: The Movement-Image*, trans. H. Tomlinson and B. Habberjam, Minneapolis: University of Minnesota Press.

Deleuze, G. (1989 [1985]), *Cinema 2: The Time-Image*, trans. H. Tomlinson and R. Galeta, London: Athlone.

Deleuze, G. and Guattari, F. (1983), *Anti-Oedipus: Capitalism and Schizophrenia*, trans. R. Hurley, M. Seem and H. R. Lane, Minneapolis: University of Minnesota Press.

Deleuze, G. and Guattari, F. (1987), *A Thousand Plateaus: Capitalism and Schizophrenia*, trans. B. Massumi, Minneapolis: University of Minnesota Press.

Derrida, J. (1994), *Spectres of Marx: The State of Debt, the Work of Mourning, and the New International*, trans. P. Kamuf, London: Routledge.

Didion, J. (1979), *The White Album*, New York: Farrar, Straus and Giroux.

Eco, U. (1986), *Travels in Hyperreality*, trans. W. Weaver, London: Picador.

Foucault, M. (1977 [1975]), *Discipline and Punish*, trans. A. Sheridan, Middlesex: Penguin Books.

Frieden, B. and Sagalyn, L. (1991) *Downtown, Inc. How America Rebuilds Cities*, Cambridge, MA: The MIT Press.

Head, S. (2004), 'Inside the Leviathan', *The New York Review of Books*, 51: 20.

Holland, E. (1999), *Deleuze and Guattari's 'Anti-Oedipus': Introduction to Schizoanalysis*, London: Routledge.

Jameson, F. (1991), *Postmodernism, or, the Cultural Logic of Late Capitalism*, London: Verso.

Jameson, F. (1998), *The Cultural turn: Selected Writings on the Postmodern, 1983–1998*, London: Verso.

Jameson, F. (2003), 'Future City', *New Left Review*, 2: 21.

Nabokov, V. (1995 [1955]), *Lolita*, Harmondsworth: Penguin.

Solnit, R. and Schwartzenberg, S. (2000), *Hollow City: The Siege of San Francisco and the Crisis of American Urbanism*, London: Verso.

Spoto, D. (1983), *The Dark Side of Genius: The Life of Alfred Hitchcock*, London: Plexus.

Stivale, C. (1998), *The Two-Fold Thought of Deleuze and Guattari: Intersections and Animations*, New York: The Guildford Press.

Urry, J. (2002), *The Tourist Gaze*, 2nd edn, London: Sage.

Zukin, S. (1991), *Landscapes of Power: From Detroit to Disney World*, Berkeley: University of California Press.

Notes

1. 'The virus ascribed to junkspace is in fact the virus of shopping itself; which, like Disneyfication, gradually spreads like a toxic moss across the known universe' (Jameson 2003: 77).

2. See Eco 1986; Baudrillard 1994. Hyperrealism is an aesthetic of the 'realer than the real'. There are any number of examples one could point to, but one of the more ironic (because of its 'ruse of history' undertone) is the filming of *The Trouble with Harry* (1955) – according to biographer Donald Spoto (1983: 355), Hitchcock deliberately set it in Vermont to capture the striking autumn colours. However, when he got to East Craftsbury in October 1954 to photograph it, he found he had been preceded by a storm and had to film indoors in a converted school-gym prepared in case of inclement weather. The finishing

touches were done on a sound stage in Hollywood using East Craftsbury leaves hand-pasted on to plaster trees.

3. This is perhaps the moment to rue the lost opportunity of a Nabokov/Hitchcock collaboration. In 1970, on the back of a couple of terrible films – *Torn Curtain* (1966) and *Topaz* (1969) – Hitchcock thought to revive his fortunes by calling in a writer of high quality. Having seen the treatment of *Lolita*, he thought Nabokov might be just the writer he needed, but alas it was never to be (see Spoto 1983: 508).

4. 'Postmodernism, or, the Cultural Logic of Late Capitalism' was first given as a lecture at the Whitney Museum in 1982 and appeared in *New Left Review* two years later. The definitive version is to be found in the book of the same name (see Jameson 1991).

5. For further discussion of Jameson's account of the Bonaventure see Buchanan 2000: 143–74; Buchanan 2005: 16–35.

6. It is perhaps worth noting here that *Discipline and Punish* is Foucault's most explicitly Deleuzian book. In the notes, Foucault (1977: 309) says: 'I could give no notion by references or quotations what this book owes to Gilles Deleuze and the work he is undertaking with Félix Guattari.'

7. More indirectly, but no less tangibly, its effect on agriculture – understood as a 'small' business – is similarly egregious as Christopher Cook (2004: 19–20) argues. As a major contributor to the price-suppression of commodities, Wal-Mart contributes powerfully to creating a business environment in which the family-owned and run farm, once the lifeblood of small-town America, cannot survive.

8. Koolhaas (see Jameson 2003) claims the mall as apparatus hinges on three innovations for its efficacy: air-conditioning; the escalator; the automatic fire-sprinkler. To which one may add the bar-code and the brand, which, although not architectural in themselves, have had an enormous impact on the architecture of the mall. The bar-code revolutionised inventory control, while the brand means products display themselves – the old idea of the department store, modelled on the museum, was that spaces had to be created to display goods in an attractive light. The buildings themselves had to be magnificent to compensate the shabby mercantilist dealings within (e.g., Harrods in London, Magasin du Nord in Copenhagen). This is patently not the way of postmodern supermarkets which stack products floor to ceiling. Their display occurs in the virtual space of TV and billboards, their branding functioning then as a synedoche of these images.

9. This was written before the tragic events of hurricane Katrina.

10. In other words, one shouldn't read Davis against Jameson, but rather read them together. Although Jameson doesn't put it this way himself, his later reading (through the angry filter of Robert Fitch's *The Assassination of New York*) of the transformation of New York City, particularly the waterfront (i.e., where the Twin Towers once stood), makes essentially this argument: it is not the buildings, finally, that are postmodern; what is postmodern is the willingness to transform a city (to creatively destroy it) as a whole in order to revitalise it as a source of surplus value (Jameson 1998: 183–5).

11. On the connection between territoriality and the Lacanian drive see Deleuze and Guattari 1983: 35.

12. It is tempting to think that Derrida was directed to this aspect of Marx's work precisely because of Deleuze and Guattari's work, but I cannot find any evidence to support this speculation save for the fact that 'haunting' is central to their reading of Marx too. It remains an idea to be cherished alongside the dream that one day Deleuze's fabled book on Marx will appear in print.

Chapter 8

Anti-Oedipus – Thirty Years On (Between Art and Politics)

Éric Alliez

A kind of entrance into politics took place for me in May 68 . . .
Gilles Deleuze, Negotiations

One must not look for a 'philosophy' amid the extraordinary profusion of new notions and surprise concepts: *Anti-Oedipus* is not a flashy Hegel. I think that *Anti-Oedipus* can best be read as an 'art'. [. . .] Questions that are less concerned with *why* this or that than with *how* to proceed. How does one introduce desire into thought, into discourse, into action? [. . .] *Anti-Oedipus* is a book of ethics . . .
Michel Foucault, Preface to Anti-Oedipus

1

The title of this chapter was suggested to me some time ago by my best enemy – or my best fiend, to paraphrase Werner Herzog – who also happens to be a very good friend: Alain Badiou. The idea was to use the occasion to pursue our dispute – or *chicane*, to use a favourite expression of his – a dispute instigated by the publication in 1997 of Badiou's *Deleuze: The Clamor of Being* (1999).

Let it be noted in passing that this dispute prolonged a problematic that I had previously examined in a book-intervention entitled *Of the Impossibility of Phenomenology: On Contemporary French Philosophy*, published in 1995. With regard to the topic at hand, I argued that the philosophical field *with a grip on our present – in other words, contemporary philosophy as a political ontology of the present* – could be, and must be, thought starting from the idea of a maximal ontological tension between Deleuze and Badiou. In my view, Deleuze and Badiou constitute the extreme polarities, not only of the contemporary domain of French philosophy, but perhaps of the real of thought as such – to the extent that thought, in accordance with the plurality of all its modalities, has no other choice today than to counter the pseudo-democracy of Empire with a materialist necessity that can no longer be elaborated except in terms of singularities and multiplicities. These are notions that our two philosophers entrust with absolutely antagonistic missions, renegotiating the theoretical and practical sense of the very idea of materialism.

Badiou's invitation could not but engender a stark and cutting quarrel, which the publication of Slavoj Žižek's recent book, *Organs without Bodies: On Deleuze and Consequences* (2004), prompts me to reconsider here, modifying its initial trajectory in order to extract some of its 'aesthetic' stakes.

Žižek's 'Lacanian book on Deleuze' – because the Organ without Body is the Phallus as signifier of castration – this Lacano-Leninist book which borrows its dialectic from the French philosopher (its compulsive *motto* is 'As Alain Badiou puts it . . .') has, in my view, the merit of focusing its argument on the 'Body without Organs' by reversing and combating the movement that presided over the emergence of this notion in

> the inner tension of Deleuze's thought between *Anti-Oedipus* [Deleuze's worst book, È.A.] and *The Logic of Sense*, between the [Guattarised, È.A.] Deleuze who celebrated the productive multitude of Becoming against the reified order of being and the Deleuze of the sterility of the incorporeal becoming of the Sense-Event. (Žižek 2003: xi)

This is a movement I tried to track in my essay 'The BwO Condition, or, The Politics of Sensation' (2003). In that piece I could not refrain from recalling the way in which the Body without Organs ex-pulsed by Artaud dis-organ-ises the philosophical surface *structurally* defined by the *incorporeal univocity of Being and Language*, leading the *Logic of Sense* into a veritable *breakdown*. The *breakdown* of structure as a 'machine for the production of incorporeal sense' is followed, in *Anti-Oedipus* (we will return to this at length), by the *breakthrough* of the incorporation of a machinic constructivism into a desire that commands becomings . . .

On the contrary, as you know, Badiou in his book erects an image of Deleuze as a metaphysician of the One, whose essential *monotony – in itself indifferent to differences*, subtracted as it is from the 'inexhaustible variety of the concrete' and from the anarchic confusion of the world – can and must cause us to dismiss the works co-authored with Félix Guattari, beginning with *Anti-Oedipus*. It is only after having carried out this operation that one will be able to re-establish the philosophical truth of Deleuze-Thought against the ambient image ('radical chic', as Žižek puts it) of Deleuze as the proponent of a liberation of the anarchic multiplicity of desires that would invariably turn him – as Žižek once again notes – into the 'ideologist of today's "digital capitalism"'. But it is also, and inevitably, only once Deleuze has been reduced to the monotony of the One – and/or once this pole will have been extricated from the vitalism with which it *impossibly* coexists (Žižek) – that it will be possible to oppose this 'truth' to the *Nouvelle Alliance Deleuze–Guattari*, to paraphrase the original French title of Prigogine and Stengers' *Order Out of Chaos* (1984). Or again, in accordance with Žižek's specious interrogation: 'Therefore, was Deleuze not pushed toward Guattari because Guattari presented an alibi, an easy escape from the deadlock of his previous position?' (Žižek 2003, subsequent quotes are all drawn from this text). A position that consists in the 'opposition of the virtual as the site of the productive Becoming [from the BwO] and the virtual as the site of sterile Sense-Event [= pure affect of the OwB, a grin without a cat]' . . .

Badiou's operation – the 'truth' of the Žižekian remake – cannot but pose a serious problem, on two levels whose difference is entirely relative. First, at the level of Deleuze's trajectory, given that Deleuze himself presents his encounter with Guattari – in a horizon of life and thought opened up by '68, what he called 'an irruption, of becoming in its pure state' (Deleuze 1995: 171) – as the reality condition for the constitution of *his own* philosophy (whence the necessity of returning to what happens in *Logic of Sense*, in which we end up reading that 'we would not give a page of Artaud for all of Carroll', and between *Logic of Sense* (1969) and *Anti-Oedipus* (1972), when Lewis Carroll, this putative father of the (structuralist) series of the logic of sense, is no longer anything but 'the coward of belles-lettres' (Deleuze and Guattari 1983: 135) – and to what happens to *philosophy* when the question is no longer 'to *describe* a certain exercise of thought' but rather to *exert* a 'thought without image' (Deleuze and Parnet 1987: 19ff) by investing these micropolitical conditions of enunciation in the *in between* (*entre-deux*) of Deleuze *and* Guattari, without which it would be impossible to respond to these 'concrete questions' (Foucault, in the preface to the American edition of *Anti-Oedipus*)).

Second, at the strictly speaking *political* level, whose essential ambiguity in Deleuze is condemned by Badiou. In Badiou's eyes, this ambiguity is corroborated by the fact that Deleuze does not endow politics with any kind of theoretical autonomy, thus leading to the permanent threat of a spontaneous deviation or drift (*dérive*), embodied by what he calls the '*anarcho-désirants*'. This is what Lenin long ago branded with the name of 'leftism' and which tends here to reduce Deleuze's declared vitalism to the latest incarnation of Romanticism (after Phenomenology) – in other words, into a natural mysticism of the vitalist expression of the world, as Badiou affirmed in his review of *The Fold* from 1989 (Eng. trans. 1994). (This idea is taken up and developed by Žižek, painting Deleuze's portrait as a 'new Bogdanov': 'Lacan *versus* Deleuze: again, materialism *versus* empirio-criticism?') But in this case, it is the very unity and identity/alterity of Deleuzean thought that finds itself gravely compromised *after Anti-Oedipus*, precisely to the extent that the latter was, as Deleuze remarked, 'from beginning to end a book of political philosophy' (1995: 170). What's more, it is hard to fathom how the biomachinic conception of desire in the *Anti-Oedipus* – which depicts desire as co-extensive with the lines of flight of the *socius* – could ever translate anti-humanism into, as Badiou writes, 'the infinite and inhuman resource of the One', in which 'everything is always "already-there"' (1999: 12). (Because he projects *at the source*, in Deleuze 'himself', the terms of the *subtraction* carried out by Badiou, Žižek's book can be read as a response to this problem.) Unless, of course, we wish to argue that Deleuzean leftism was nothing but a pure opportunism and that 'Mitterandism' revealed the underlying truth of this 'soft rebellion' – to speak like Guy Lardreau in his anti-Deleuzean pamphlet, a text thoroughly inspired by Badiou's decisionism . . . 'It is crucial to note – Žižek observes in turn – that *not a single one* of Deleuze's own texts is in any way directly political; Deleuze "in himself" is [. . .] indifferent toward politics' (Lardreau 1999).

In an article reacting to a set of objections that his own book did not fail to provoke, Badiou makes the following remark.

> How is it that politics, for Deleuze, is not an autonomous form of thought, a singular section of chaos, unlike art, science and philosophy? This point alone testifies to our divergence, and everything could be seen to follow from it. (2000: 196)

It might be interesting therefore to prolong the dispute, taking our cue from the manner in which it was carried on by Badiou in the two books of politics that follow his *Deleuze*, books in which what is at stake is investing singularity qua operator of universalism (in other words, to address the question: 'What precisely is a universal singularity valid for everyone?'). These two books are *Saint Paul: The Foundation of Universalism* (Badiou 2003) and *On Metapolitics* (Badiou 2005) – a *metapolitics* of the dethronement of difference which is to be opposed to the *micropolitical* principle that presides over the question of 'becoming-revolutionary' in Deleuze–Guattari, following *Anti-Oedipus*. Having said that, it is imperative to remark straight away that what Badiou's Paulinian allegiance rejects is precisely the anti-oedipal affirmation of

*desiring production as the social power of difference within a becoming-
minoritarian*, as well as the way in which this desiring production rejects,
de jure and *de facto*, the principle of a separate sphere for politics (this
is the *disidentification* of politics as a means of integration into identity
and unity). It is no wonder then that Badiou's *Saint Paul* advocates 'love'
as that of which militant faith is capable of, when it seeks to extricate
itself from the 'living autonomy of desire' . . . By the same token, the
theorem of the militant amounts to a subjective fidelity to the event of
the separation from the world, sustained by the universal communication of a subtractive foundation which can conceive of desire only as a
Lack of the Law, in order to impose upon the subject, by way of a process
of subjectivation, the universal grace of Signifier. Let us recall, in this
regard, Saint Paul's famous pronouncement, from Romans 7: 7–23: 'I
have known sin only through the Law'. Whence the following theorem:
Lacanian psychoanalysis is the symptom of the refoundation of universalism when philosophy puts itself under the metapolitical condition of
creating the event of Nothing addressed to All.

What is of most importance here is less the predictable, strict alternative with respect to Deleuze and Deleuzo–Guattarianism (immediately
collapsed into one another, as is to be expected, within the dispute) than
the prescriptive character of this universalism of the Subject-of-Truth
declared by Badiou *for all, and for everyone* who seeks the elimination
of the *leftism of the party of desire* (to speak like Guy Lardreau, who is
wholly faithful to the other party, the party, I quote, 'of lack, of the One,
of knowledge, of war' (Lardreau 1999: 84)). I say prescriptive *because
the universal is as such the truth of the subject who declares the Void of
Being* – from which Badiou knows how to draw *immanently* all the necessary consequences (including its 'inaesthetic' necessity, to use the term
proposed by Badiou in a book that complemented his *Metapolitics*
(2005): the *Handbook of Inaesthetics* (2004a)). After his *Deleuze*, it is
to be expected that the militant objective of Badiou's *Saint Paul* is to
unfold the logic of the break with the movement of vitalist affirmation
*by demonstrating the inconsistency of becoming with respect to the
excess of the Real over reality*. This can only be grasped via a Lacan who
posits the Real in the predication of the no (*non*) and of the name (*nom*)
as subject-intervention.

As the founder of the figure of the militant, 'Paul's unprecedented
gesture is to subtract truth from the clutches of communitarianism'
(Badiou 2003, subsequent quotes are all drawn from this text). How
extraordinarily contemporary! By involving the 'for all', the break of universal singularity with regard to the *identitarian particularity* of a closed

sub-set is bereft of an alternative, given *its* description of the present state of the 'communitarianisation' of a public space fragmented into closed identities which deliver so many new territories over to the market. And Badiou – more resourceful and crafty than Žižek in this regard – cannot write these lines without also inviting Deleuze to this wedding between capitalist logic and identitarian logic, a wedding whose stakes are precisely to refuse emancipatory reality to any kind of *becoming-minoritarian*: 'Deleuze put it perfectly' – Badiou says – 'capitalist deterritorialisation requires a constant reterritorialisation' (2003: 10). The perfection to which Badiou refers is entirely nominal, and ultimately represents a complete misunderstanding of Deleuze, since the reterritorialisation of capitalism is no longer practised upon the *absolute* form of deterritorialisation, without any assignable limit, whether external or internal, a form of deterritorialisation that capitalism can only put to work by subjecting it to the expanded reproduction of its own immanent limits. Furthermore, *becoming* is no longer related to flows of desire that flee, flows that *can* limit the process of capitalist valorisation itself when they turn against it the power of invention of other possible worlds – for Badiou becoming turns out to be purely and simply the occasion for the 'mercantile investments' it gives rise to . . . This ultimately leads Badiou to accept *de facto* the point of view of Capital – while we know that *desire reduced to the primitive accumulation of identitarian reterritorialisations* under the name of 'communitarianism' is no longer Capitalism and Schizophrenia – it's Capitalism and Paranoia . . . *The minoritarian is frozen into the identitarian.* I quote, from the same page in *Saint Paul*:

> What *inexhaustible potential* [*devenir*] for mercantile investments in this upsurge – taking the form of communities demanding recognition and *so-called cultural singularities* – of women, homosexuals, the disabled, Arabs! (Badiou 2003: 10, emphasis added)

Before examining the (in)aesthetic translation of this *freezing* ('timeless coldness' is a value Badiou lays claim to, but it is also the defining mark of his writing), recall that Deleuze and Guattari's question is that of a *political ontology of becomings* which never ceases to undo the sedimentation of identities ('the primacy of lines of flight' – which has not failed to stir up furious clashes in the field of *gender studies*) and to produce 'strikes', sudden variations that affect every system by not allowing it to become homogeneous, variations as unpredictable to the sociologist as they are to the militant. Thus, as Deleuze remarks in *Dialogues*, there also exists 'a becoming-revolutionary which is not the same thing as the future of the revolution, and which does not necessarily need to go through militants'. *This is because the constructions of the militant tend to cut themselves off from the creative 'socio-cultural' expressions of the world and from the propagation of the molecular becomings of real multiplicities* – which as such are denied by Badiou under the postmodern rubric of the 'total exposure of particularisms' itemised into 'ethnic and communitarian products, including their sexual sub-category, and egoic products' (Badiou 2004b: 81, subsequent quotes are all drawn from this text).

It is to this 'compound of mysticism and pornography' – which Lenin had earlier denounced as the 'sad arrogance of imperialisms [. . .] in those periods when critical and revolutionary political activity is very weak' – to this 'abolition of the universal' tied to the 'idea of the *expressive value* of the *body*' (emphasis added), that Badiou opposes

> an axiomatic that sets itself the following task: at the dawn of a new century, we must return artistic will to its incorporeal rigour, to its anti-romantic coldness, to the subtractive operations whereby it holds itself as close as possible to this real without image which is the sole cause of art. A subtraction through which, by addressing the real to all, it annuls any hold that may be exerted by particularity.

In so doing, Badiou denounces a romanticism degraded into 'the pornographic stupidity of performances'. Following the great tradition of *modernist purification*,[2] Badiou thereby affirms this 'dynamic of abstraction' which has not ceased, in 'the great 20th century', to counter the naturalist and romantic vitalism whose contemporary formula would subject art to 'the radiant and suffering exposure of the Flesh' . . .

Against which we will *affirm* here that the *Anti-Oedipus* – such as it mobilises, under the name of 'Body without Organs', the *politics of sensation* to which Artaud had devoted his convulsive constructions – grows out of all the movements which, in the art of the twentieth century, ever since Jarry and Matisse the Hyper-fauvist, knew how to free vitalism from the romantic expressiveness of the subject (therefore Dada rather than Surrealism; fauvism, a permanent fauvism, that of Matisse, as the rigorous alternative to Cubism and to the Spiritual in abstract Art).

In so doing, to borrow Foucault's remark, *Anti-Oedipus* works as an 'art' – an *art of the self*. 'I shall reconstruct the man that I am' (Deleuze 1990: 342), Artaud affirms in this passage which Deleuze quotes in order to introduce us to this other world ('We are in another world . . .'), which is that of the insurrection of the *breath-words* of the 'body without organs' of Artaud-the-Schizo against the language and surface effects of Carrollian structuralism:

Pas de bouche Pas de langue Pas de dents Pas de larynx Pas d'œsophage Pas d'estomac Pas de ventre Pas d'anus Je reconstruirai l'homme que je suis

[No teeth No larynx No esophagus No stomach No intestine No anus I shall reconstruct the man that I am.] (quoted in Deleuze 1969: 108; Eng. trans. Deleuze 1990: 82)

To reconstruct man, this *machine which breathes*, from that starting point, from a *multiplicity of fusion*, with 'the fusibility as infinite zero, plane of consistency' conquered on the primary order of schizophrenia, in the night of a pathological creation affecting bodies (the 'body of the abyss', Artaud writes in order to speak pure intensity, the a-signifying violence of 'life' precipitated against the signifying violence of the transcendence at work in immanence) . . .

To restart from there, then: not from a 'real without image' attained in the formalism of art by subtraction from the world (Badiou), but from a *'body without image'* (pro-voked by the 'rupture of the *principium individuationis*' – Nietzsche invoked with Artaud in the first chapter of *Anti-Oedipus*). For we need a *'body without image'*, that is to say, an Anti-Flesh, in order to replace every 'image of the body' ('the latest avatar of the soul', according to Deleuze and Guattari) and attain 'the infinite of the decomposition of the socius' on the basis of which one will be able to *affirm* 'the coextension of the social field and desire' (see the whole first chapter of *Anti-Oedipus*) and *deny* (deconstruct, destroy) the dominant, majoritarian structures, through a chaosmic immersion in the matters of sensation that these structures repress, and which will be put to work in the composition of mutant percepts and affects. *What the Body costs* the art that bears its name – *Body Art*, the art which has turned away from the stage (recall the anti-theatrical spirit of Nietzsche and Artaud) – a cost which it manifests in the unworldly squalor (*l'immonde*) and the unruly dance of organs, *or not* ('*un corps neuf / où vous ne pourrez / plus jamais / m'oublier*', 'a new body / in which you will never again / be able / to forget me', Artaud announces in Sontag 2005: 660), so that it may be able to produce *Events* capable of *exceeding* the 'democratic' reformism of so-called 'relational aesthetics' (fill in the fissures in the social bond, etc.) by functioning as a fulcrum for a processual relaunch, between art and life. To cross, once again, Artaud with Guattari (a Guattari not 'recuperated' by Bourriaud and his ilk): the '*dynamic investigation* of the Universe', endorsed by Artaud in his *Revolutionary Messages* (1971), and the 'going outside' (beginning with this outside of language which structures every *logic of sense*) are inseparable from a *critical investigation* of the 'Universes of reference' that imprison life and *demand that war be carried into the body itself* (Guattari 1995) (in *Anti-Oedipus*, the Body Without Organs is the essential component in this *dispositif* that aims at extirpating the *deus in machina*) . . . There is here an extreme and permanent danger – do we even need to recall it? – of falling into an empty theatralisation of the 'behavioural' and/or 'drive' type (a falling back into *representation* – even if its inspiration is 'Dionysian', as in the case of Hermann Nitsch, who capitalised on his forty years of Actionism in order *to bring the butcher out into the open air* in his latest 'mystery'). What is referred to, somewhat superficially, as Otto Muehl's 'return to painting', would deserve a serious re-examination in terms of his 'Konzept der aktionistischen Malerei' (Alliez 2004c). So, for instance, isn't the disqualification of painting, to which some have wanted to juxtapose Performance – in an explicit and phenomenologically affirmed anti-modernism (the *lived body*) – specularly derivative of the despised modernism, by way of the primacy of the medium that such a disqualification assumes even when it seeks to reverse its course . . .? Let us not forget that it is with regard to Action Painting, to the action on the canvas, that Harold Rosenberg evokes an artist who 'organizes his emotional and intellectual energy as if he were in a *living situation*' because this 'new painting has broken down every distinction between art and life', marking in space a vital movement which is *performance* – '*not an image but an event*' (Rosenberg 1952: 23–39). To close this parenthesis, opened with Muehl: doesn't he lead us today to reread Deleuze's *The Logic of Sense* with an eye on Guattari's *Chaosmosis* and its proposal of a 'New aesthetic paradigm'? *And inversely*, since we are dealing here with two expressions of this *politics of sensation* which had led to the surpassing of the *Logic of Sense*, when 'du sens, subsiste seulement de quoi diriger les lignes de fuite' (Of sense there remains only enough to direct the lines of flight) (Deleuze and Guattari 1986: 21).

2

We will not develop here, for their own sake, the questions inevitably raised by the 'New aesthetic paradigm' that Guattari lays claim to into *Chaosmosis* (1995), this book-intervention (like all the books published by Guattari 'alone' – but how could they fail to *also* stem from the *in-between* (*entre-deux*) with Deleuze?), this book written in order to 'go outside', reading which we cannot ignore that it was *assembled* (*monté*) by drawing on this 'toolbox' (an expression of Foucault *stolen* from Guattari) from whence the two volumes of *Capitalism and Schizophrenia*

emerged. Except in order to register, as a simple clue, that the paradigmatic importance accorded to performance is not without reviving, as its
plane of consistency (of the book *and* of performance), Dewey's motif of
Art as Experience (Dewey, 1980, originally published in 1934) – to the
extent that this motif, through a vitalism renewed by its will *to disclose*
the art that had been *subtracted from life* (a subtraction that by the same
token reduces aesthetic experience to a *formal and formalist purification*
(*épuration*), what Dewey calls the 'museal conception of art', 'art as the
beauty parlour of civilization'), entails *Experience as art*. For if, on the
one hand, 'esthetic experience is pure experience', 'experience freed from
the forces that impede and confuse its development as experience', on the
other, 'esthetic experience is always more than esthetic', 'the material of
esthetic experience [qua experience] is social' (ibid.: 274, 324). The fundamental point here, for us, is that this *social challenge* issued to art, and
to the philosophy of art, which commands the 'new aesthetic paradigm'
(Dewey's influence on Kaprow, for instance, has been acknowledged for
some time) does not go without a *Challenge to Philosophy* (according to
the very title of the twelfth chapter of *Art as Experience*). I would like to
suggest here that it is to this kind of *social challenge* issued to philosophy that *Anti-Oedipus responds*. Foucault perceived this perfectly when
he spoke of an 'art', an art which he expounds in three *transitive* (and
communicating) forms, which serve here to fill in the cuts that I introduced in the epigraph, bringing it to a close: *Ars erotica, ars theoretica,
ars politica*.

A *return to Anti-Oedipus*, therefore, and to the constant *vis-à-vis* and
versus Deleuze advocated by Badiou as the defining trait of his metapolitics and inaesthetics. One will remark in Badiou a total *denegation* of
the Deleuzo-Guattarian thesis about desire, the thesis that 'desire only
exists when assembled or machined [*machiné*]' (Deleuze and Parnet
1987; 70ff, 96ff; subsequent quotes are all drawn from this text) and that
one cannot 'grasp or conceive of a desire outside a determinate assemblage, on a plane which is not pre-existent but which must itself be constructed', in a process of liberation *which never unifies parts into a Whole*
(even from the most closed of sets, *some thing* always escapes). Here we
must quote the lines with which Deleuze introduces this *statement*. He
writes:

> it is objected that by releasing desire from lack and law, the only thing we
> have left to refer to is a state of nature, a desire which would be natural and
> spontaneous reality. We say quite the opposite: *desire only exists when
> assembled or machined*.

Whence the conclusion that desire '*is constructivist, not at all spontaneist*', and the question: 'How can the assemblage be refused the name it deserves, "desire"?'[3] (Allow me to recall that the concept of 'desiring machines' will turn into that of 'assemblages' pure and simple after the *Kafka* book, which can be regarded as the bridge between *Anti-Oedipus* and *A Thousand Plateaus*.) This is the key thesis of the *Anti-Oedipus*, according to which, from a materialist point of view, there can be no Expression (of the 'full body' of the world) without Construction of assemblages of desire or 'desiring machines' that free Life in the *processual (i.e. non-totalising) and performative* identity between production and product. This *non-romantic* identity is precisely opposed to:

1. The 'natural mysticism' initially denounced by Badiou under the name of Deleuze, which ignores the fact that Deleuze himself will only evoke a 'plane of Nature' to better convey the point that we are dealing with 'a nature which must be constructed with all the fabrications of the plane of immanence' (in other words, the irrelevance of the nature/artifice distinction undermines any naturalist expressionism, cf. Deleuze and Parnet 1987: 98).
2. The 're-accentuated Platonism' into which Badiou wishes to merge Deleuze by registering the production of differences under the heading of simulacra (in other words, a constructivism deprived of ontological reality).

But reciprocally, and this time against the grain of Badiou's mathematical ontology, which declares the indifference of truth to the flow of the world, that 'mathematics of being' through which politics and aesthetic production can be made 'equivalent': Construction without Expression is *void* of any real becoming, of any *real-desire* whatsoever. If 'the objective being of desire is the Real in and of itself', then 'desiring production is one and the same thing as social production' (Deleuze and Guattari 1983: 26–7, 30), by virtue of the biopolitical identity between Expression and Construction, an identity that gives body to the theory of machinic desire and the affirmation of a *universal contingency*, according to which:

> In desiring machines everything functions at the same time, but amid hiatuses and ruptures, breakdowns and failures, stalling and short circuits, distances and fragmentations, within a sum that never succeeds in bringing its various parts together so as to form a whole. (Deleuze and Guattari 1983: 42)

This biopolitical identity between Expression and Construction also gives body to the new aesthetic paradigm. 'New' with regard to the very three schemata outlined by Badiou at the outset of his *Handbook of Inaesthetics* (2004a) – the didactic schema, the classical schema, the romantic schema – and to the synthetic 'didactico-romantic' schema into which he seeks to *merge* the avant-gardes; 'new' with regard to a *romantic formalism* that we do not think can serve to define contemporary art, but which, in and from contemporary art, has *missed* (*raté*) the politics of sensation opened up by the *modern and anti-modernist* identity of Expression and Construction. This explains why the aforementioned *romantic formalism* says and reads *upside down* (*à l'envers*) the *constructivist expressionism* that we oppose to it. This constructivist expressionism is deployed in contrast with the History and Philosophy of art because these two notions *do not* mean here what they are taken to mean in these disciplines. And it's no wonder, I would argue, if the artists who have appropriated the practical principle of their experimental identity have produced so many alterations of the 'standard' opposition between 'expressionism' and 'constructivism', 'romanticism' and 'formalism' – since Construction is no longer that of an Object subtracted from the world 'in the timeless coldness of its invented form' (Badiou), and Expression is no longer that of a Subject or of a Nature saturating the artistic gesture of a double-entry romanticism (that is why 'expressionism' and 'impressionism', in their ordinary sense, are ideally complementary).

Thus, it is due to its very constructivist alteration that *Anti-Oedipus* adamantly affirms: 'we cannot accept the idealist category of "expression"' (Deleuze and Guattari 1983: 6). After all, production as process overflows (the romantic origin of) its notion by relating to desire qua immanent principle, not the principle of a given/giver of flows which it would *naturally or spontaneously express*, but rather of a *flow-cut system that desire engineers, in such a way that the cut implies what it cuts, as a universal continuity which is expressed* from *an artificial 'Nature'* towards *schizophrenic productivity*. Lacking this continuum, this *real* implication of the world singularised and *machinically engineered* in each of its cuts-flows, the cut would count as a section (*découpe*), which is to say a separation (from 'common' reality),[4] in accordance with the principle of a post-existential *decision* (*decidere* = to separate) constantly put forward by the Lacanising philosopher (the Real as the indifference of the pure event). As Deleuze and Guattari write, 'It is not at all a question of the cut considered as a separation from reality.' With *Anti-Oedipus*, the ontological monism of Deleuzean biophilosophy becomes the biopolitical fact of the machinic system of cuts and flows, relating the univocal plane of the living to desire as a 'universal' process of production. We thereby move from biophilosophical expressionism, such as it implies (after Spinoza) production qua affective affirmation in immanence, and (with Bergson) the creative affirmation of the full differentiating reality of the virtual, to biopolitical constructivism, which allows one *in the present* to invest the created from the point of view of creation – it is this passage which makes it possible to comprehend Deleuze's assertion, in the interview on *Anti-Oedipus* (reprinted in *Negotiations*), according to which up to that point he had only worked 'with concepts, rather timidly in fact. Félix had talked to me about what he was already calling "desiring machines" [. . .]. So I myself thought that it was he who was in advance of me . . .' (Deleuze 1995, trans. modified). In this phrase the very *advance* of *Anti-Oedipus* is played out, the advance of a machinic ontology over the transcendental, as the latter is developed into a structuralism (of the kind that is experimented with in *Difference and Repetition* and *Logic of Sense*).[5] The machine will be defined on the basis of the cut-flow system which introduces production into desire by guaranteeing its real (and non-'symbolic') primacy qua immanent constitutive process. Unparalleled, except perhaps by the first chapter of *Matter and Memory*, it is the masterful opening chapter of *Anti-Oedipus* which links the philosophy of multiplicity – employed as a vital substantive that 'goes beyond the multiple just as much as the one' (contrary to the kind of reading that will be offered by Badiou) – to the politics of desiring production, a politics that can be understood as the anoedipal reality condition of philosophy, between capitalism and schizophrenia. This all comes down to *schizophrenising philosophy by treating writing as the machinic expression of constitutive desire, an expression which takes the real to the point at which it is effectively produced in bodies that are both biological and collective, and which imply the constitution of a field of immanence or 'body without organs' defined by zones of intensity, thresholds, gradients, flows, and so on.* (The BwO is to be considered as the very body of desire, as its purest Expression, so absolutely inseparable from what it can do that it relates back to an unliveable power, a social anti-production which is as such the precondition of every real experience of desire, driven by the necessity of Constructions that cut the BwO *in and from itself.*) Whence the 'generational' effect of this immense provocation – which no longer dissociates ontological production from the being of the micropolitical expression-construction of singularities – upon the way of thinking of a 'life style' (Foucault's expression) from which the intellectual left and the political left and extreme-left have yet to recover (see their embarrassment when confronted with the real multiplicities of the anti-capitalist movement, its collective assemblages or *coordinations* and their difference of style and action with regard to the mandatory forms of political 'organisations': the resistance against power and the deployment of heterogeneous forms of subjectivation are in a relation of reciprocal presupposition[6]). The project laid out in *Anti-Oedipus* will begin by subverting the Freudo-Marxism fashionable at the time, by confronting structuralism head on (lines of flight are primary qua process, contrary to structure, conceived as the static genesis of the unconscious and the *socius*, and implying a complete determination of singular points), before moving on to critique the philosophies of 'resistance' by establishing the biopolitical primacy of desire qua 'conjugation and dissociation of flows' against the Foucauldian thesis of a biopower whose *dispositifs* would in some sense be constitutive (coming first, as they do, 'lines of flight [. . .] are not phenomena of resistance or counterattack in an assemblage, but cutting edges of creation and deterritorialisation [*pointes de création et de deterritorialisation*]' (Deleuze and Guattari 1987: 530–1, note 39[7]). Moving beyond its Foucauldian sense, biopolitics is thereby affirmed as the infinite tension that affects a process of constitution launched against all the strata of organisation that block becomings, by causing them to fall back on an anti-production that functions from the inside out (the psychoanalytic Oedipus, a State which turns into the Entrepreneurial State of the society of control) – and all this, not in the name of any kind of spontaneism or marginalism, but, *on the contrary*, by virtue of the dynamic of real multiplicities, such as it is determined by the plane of immanence of desire qua social and intellectual power of production-creation (it was Gabriel Tarde who conceived the power of invention of the 'cooperation between brains' as the principle of sociology, cf. Alliez 2004b). In this respect, and in accordance with the principle of a universal history revisited in 'Savages, Barbarians, Civilized Men' (the longest chapter in *Anti-Oedipus*), it is legitimate 'to retrospectively understand all history in the light of capitalism' (Deleuze and Guattari 1983: 140), a capitalism that does not put to work the decoded and deterritorialised flows it organises and axiomatises without, by the same token, liberating the forces of desire that animate it, forces that it must counteract by reintroducing the most merciless transcendence into the immanence of a person who has been rendered 'private' (*privé*, which is to say 'deprived') in order to keep these forces in a bound state. It follows that a fantastic death instinct always threatens to transform the Oedipal triangle – which invests the social re-territorialisation of 'democratic' capitalism into an 'intimate' territoriality of the paranoiac type – into a 'micro-fascism'.

Here lies the greatness of the Vienna Action Group, which will have proven itself to be by far the most radical movement of the sixties by having *shown* this (it was not in vain that Muehl and Brus read Reich – a central reference, as you know, for *Anti-Oedipus*).

But the Greatness of Deleuze, too, when he indicates the 'turn' of *Anti-Oedipus* as the moment of the constitution of a philosophy – his own, caught up and freed by the New Alliance with Guattari – *that does not work through concepts alone*, but moves beyond the pure form of the determinable 'in thought', to finally become capable of *physicalising* the concept (the *physicality* of the concept – as a 'centre of vibrations' – is developed as such in *What is Philosophy?*, Deleuze *and* Guattari's testament-book), and to *incorporate* it in the non-organic life of the world. 'The idea of a non-organic life,' Deleuze tells us in an interview from 1980, 'is constant in *A Thousand Plateaus*. It's precisely *the life of the concept*.'

Anti-Oedipus is the response to what the philosopher christened the *ridiculousness of the abstract thinker* in the *Logic of Sense*, when it was a matter of attaining 'this *politics*, this complete and utter *guerilla*' required by the schizoid irruption of the Body without Organs which came to 'tear the structuralist surface' of the 'psychoanalysis of sense', throwing it into a 'progressive and creative disorganisation' inscribed 'in the physical presence of bodies' (Deleuze 1990, trans. modified).

This is also what *Anti-Oedipus* still tells us thirty years on: that we cannot oppose the will to resist the Empire of Digital Capitalism which finds expression in the Hyperstructuralism of a Badiou with any kind of 'weak' (*debole*) and belated Poststructuralism that would make room for a spontaneous democracy of desire and its pop-philosophical flights of fancy. Rather, we must counter it with a transversalist Biopolitics, 'always to be conquered through a pragmatics of existence' (as Guattari never ceased repeating), a Biopolitics generative of a heterogeneity whose socially constitutive character is the ontological creativity that sustains the constructivism of desire by subordinating the claim to equality to the politics of difference.[8] The constructivism of desire prohibits, *in vivo*, any projection of these questions into a 'philosophical eternity', into a 'politics of Grace' under the guidance of the militant, or into an 'inaesthetics' which is supposed to produce, 'through the finite means of a material subtraction', 'an infinite subjective series' (Badiou 2004b: 97).

In guise of a Post-scriptum. – The investment of 'the transverse multiplicities that convey desire as a molecular phenomenon' (Deleuze and Guattari 1983: 280), a phenomenon that constitutes the subjective-machinic essence of production, is affirmed in the *flight* and *secession* from the order of *representation* that organises representation into an exterior and an interior (into social reproduction and political representation, on the one hand, and infinite subjective representation, on the other). 'Leaving, fleeing, but by causing more flights . . . [*Partir, fuir, mais en faisant fuir . . .*]' (ibid.: 315, trans. modified) through a pragmatics of collective assemblages which overturns the apparatuses of blockage and control, imposing upon them schizzes which turn against capitalist antiproduction and undermine the State's forms of sovereignty. The fact that this schizoid investment of the non-separated ensemble of the social field is tantamount to a re-opening of historicity in the production of new, common modes of life, in the real constitution of a post-socialist and post-communist multiplicity, points to the caesura vis-à-vis any utopian communitarian project, and highlights the difference between the 'schizo' and 'becoming-revolutionary': a difference between 'the one who flees' and 'the one who knows how to make what he is fleeing flee' – for, as Deleuze–Guattari declare, 'the schizo is not revolutionary, but the schizophrenic process – in terms of which the schizo is merely the interruption, or the continuation in the void – is the potential for revolution' (ibid.: 341, trans. modified). A potential which is just as much Anti-State as Anti-Party, as is obvious when *Anti-Oedipus* schizophrenises the Marx who was fascinated by the machinic economy of deterritorialised flows, overflowing any 'structural' form of Marxism in order to instigate the flight of capitalist machinery on the basis of a *rupture of causality* which is also a *passage to the limit* expressing the ontological event of the desire-that-produces (in) a *de-individualising* subjective mutation. It is this reversal of power – tantamount to a re-opening of the possible, of the proliferation of possible worlds (becomings) – which is invariably accompanied by a 'collective exile' ('desire is an exile', say Deleuze and Guattari, ibid.: 377) that takes place within the very time in which one experiences the constitutive character of desiring production at the level of new social, intellectual and scientific forces, such as they define the machinic society of the *General Intellect* (in order to return to the key expression of the *Grundrisse*, where the wild 'Marxism' that Deleuze and Guattari lay claim to is played out, as well as their convergence, on this point, with Negri).

Translated by Alberto Toscano

References

Alliez, É. (1995), *De l'impossibilité de la phénoménologie: sur la philosophie française contemporaine*, Paris: J. Vrin.
Alliez, É. (2003), 'The Body without Organs' Condition or, The Politics of Sensation', in É. Alliez and E. Samsonow (eds), *Biographie des Organlosen Körpers*, Wienna: Turia + Kant; republished in J. de Blois, S. Houppermans and F.-W. Korsten (eds) (2004), *Discern(e)ments: Deleuzian Aesthetics/Esthétiques deleuziennes*, Amsterdam and New York: Editions Rodopi.
Alliez, É. (2004a), 'Anti-Oedipus – Thirty Years On', *Radical Philosophy*, 124, March/April.
Alliez, É. (2004b), 'The Difference and Repetition of Gabriel Tarde', *Distinktion. Scandinavian Journal of Social Theory*, 9.
Alliez, É. (2004c), '"You see Baby painting is out"', in *Otto Mühl, Leben / Kunst / Werk. Aktion Utopie Malerei 1960–2004*, Vienna: Verlag Walther König.
Artaud, A. (1971), *Messages revolutionaires*, Paris: Gallimard.
Badiou, A. (1994), 'Gilles Deleuze, *The Fold: Leibniz and the Baroque*', in C. V. Boundas and D. Olkowski (eds), *Gilles Deleuze and the Theater of Philosophy*, London: Routledge.
Badiou, A. (1999), *Deleuze: The Clamor of Being*, Minnesota: University of Minnesota Press.
Badiou, A. (2000), 'Un, multiple, multiplicité(s)', *multitudes*, 1; translation published as 'One, Multiple, Multiplicities', in R. Brassier and A. Toscano (eds) (2004), *Theoretical Writings*, London: Continuum.
Badiou, A. (2003), *Saint Paul: The Foundation of Universalism*, trans. R. Brassier, Stanford, CA: Stanford University Press.
Badiou, A. (2004a), *Handbook of Inaesthetics*, trans. A. Toscano, Stanford, CA: Stanford University Press.
Badiou, A. (2004b), 'Troisième esquisse d'un manifeste de l'affirmationnisme', *Circonstances*, 2.
Badiou, A. (2005), *Metapolitics*, trans. J. Barker, London: Verso Books.
Deleuze, G. (1969), *Logique du Sens*, Paris: Les Éditions de Minuit.
Deleuze, G. (1990), *The Logic of Sense*, trans. M. Lester and C. Stivale, New York: Columbia University Press.
Deleuze, G. (1994), *Difference and Repetition*, trans. P. Patton, London: The Athlone Press.
Deleuze, G. (1995), *Negotiations, 1972–1990*, trans. M. Joughin, New York: Columbia University Press.
Deleuze, G. (1997), 'Desire and Pleasure', in A. I. Davidson (ed.), *Foucault and his Interlocutors*, Chicago: University of Chicago Press.
Deleuze, G. (1998), 'How do we Recognize Structuralism?', in C. J. Stivale (ed.), *The Two-Fold Thought of Deleuze and Guattari: Intersections and Animations*, New York: Guilford Publications.
Deleuze, G. and Guattari, F. (1983), *Anti-Oedipus*, trans. R. Hurley, M. Seem and H. R. Lane, New York: Viking Press.
Deleuze, G. and Guattari, F. (1986), *Kafka, Toward a Minor Literature*, trans. D. Polan, Minneapolis: University of Minnesota Press.
Deleuze, G. and Guattari, F. (1987), *A Thousand Plateaus*, trans. B. Massumi, Minneapolis: University of Minnesota Press.
Deleuze, G. and Guattari, F. (1994), *What is Philosophy?*, trans. G. Burchell and H. Tomlinson, New Columbia: University Press.
Deleuze, G. and Parnet, C. (1987), *Dialogues*, trans. H. Tomlinson and B. Habberjam, New York: Columbia University Press.

Dewey, J. (1980), *Art as Experience*, New York: Perigee Books.

Guattari, F. (1995), *Chaosmosis: An Ethico-Aesthetic Paradigm*, trans. by P. Bains and J. Pefanis, Sydney: Power Institute.

Lardreau, G. (1999), *L'exercice différé de la philosophie. A l'occasion de Deleuze*, Lagrasse: Verdier.

Lazzarato, M. (2004), *Les révolutions du capitalisme*, Paris: Les Empêcheurs de Penser en Rond.

Prigogine, I. and Stengers, I. (1984), *Order out of Chaos: Man's New Dialogue with Nature*, Toronto: Bantam Books.

Rosenberg, H. (1952), 'The American Action Painters', *Art News*, 51: 8, reprinted in Harold Rosenberg (1994), *The Tradition of the New*, New York: Da Capo Press.

Sontag, S. (2005), *Antonin Artaud*, Los Angeles: University of California Press.

Žižek, S. (2004), *Organs without Bodies: On Deleuze and Consequences*, New York: Routledge.

Notes

1. **Editorial Note:** This chapter is the revised text of a lecture held by Alliez at the International Summer Academy in Frankfurt on 24 August 2004. The lecture was an expanded version of a paper originally published in the journal *Radical Philosophy* (Alliez 2003). It has been supplied with a postscript for this book.

2. The French *épuration* also possesses the political connotations of 'purging' or 'cleansing' in English.

3. *Dialogues*, pp. 96, 70. See also p. 103: 'Desire is always assembled and fabricated [*machiné*], on a plane of immanence or composition which must itself be constructed at the same time as desire assembles and fabricates.'

4. Deleuze and Guattari write unequivocally that 'these breaks should in no way be considered as a separation from reality' (1983: 36).

5. See Gilles Deleuze 1998, 'How do we recognize structuralism', originally written in 1967 and published in 1972, in which Deleuze writes: 'Structuralism cannot be separated from a new transcendental philosophy' (251ff).

6. On this 'French' *dispositif* of coordination, which has been omnipresent in the struggles of these past few years, see Lazzarato 2004: 213ff.

7. See the letter that Deleuze sent to Foucault in 1977, published in 1994 under the title 'Desire and Pleasure' (now reprinted in Deleuze 1997: 183–92). In this text he writes: 'if the *dispositifs* of power are in some sense constitutive, they can only be opposed by phenomena of resistance, etc.' Deleuze will oppose to this the primacy of lines of flight which imply 'no return to nature whatsoever, they are the points of deterritorialisation in the assemblages of desire'.

8. See Lazzarato (2004: 212): 'In the [separate, autonomous] political space of the Western tradition, one can only affirm identity and equality (we are women and we are equal to men). To be truly emancipatory, the claim to equality must be subordinated to a politics of difference, which is not the "bustle of democracy and capital", but the invention and effectuation of the multiplicity of worlds, the becoming other, conflictive, of subjectivities.' What is here put forward against Rancière applies *automatically* against Badiou.

Part IV

Capitalism and Resistance

Chapter 9

The Concepts of Life and the Living in the Societies of Control[1]

Maurizio Lazzarato

We have left behind the epoch of discipline to enter that of control. Gilles Deleuze described in a concise but effective way this passage from disciplinary societies to the societies of control (Deleuze 1990). He provided us with this historical reconstruction by setting out from the dynamics of difference and repetition, thereby generating new interpretations of the birth and development of capitalism. One of his most important theoretical innovations concerns the question of multiplicity: individuals and classes are nothing but the capture, integration and differentiation of multiplicity.

It is not only the phenomenological description of this evolution which interests me here, but the method employed. For Deleuze, the constitutive process of both capitalist institutions and multiplicity can be understood only by calling upon the concept of the virtual and its modalities of actualisation and effectuation. The passage from disciplinary societies to the societies of control cannot be understood by starting out from the transformations of capitalism. We must begin instead from the power of the multiplicity.

Marxists generally accept Foucault's description of disciplinary societies, provided that it is regarded merely as a complement to the Marxian analysis of the capitalist mode of production. But though Foucault acknowledged his debt to Marx (his theory of discipline was doubtless inspired by the Marxian description of the organisation of space and time in the factory), he understood the confinement of workers according to a very different logic.

For Foucault the factory is but one of the forms taken by the actualisation of the paradigm of confinement. The capital – labour relation is not the fundamental social relation on to which the ensemble of other social relations is aligned. The school, the prison and the hospital, along with law, science and knowledge – in short, everything that Foucault defines as what can be stated [*l'énonçable*] must be understood without entertaining a structure – superstructure relation to production.

Marxist theory concentrates exclusively on exploitation. Other power relations (men/women, doctors/patients, teachers/pupils and so on) and other modalities of the exercise of power (domination, subordination, enslavement) are neglected for reasons that pertain to the very ontology of the category of work. This category is endowed with a power of dialectical totalisation, both theoretical and political, which may be criticised precisely along the same lines that Tarde criticised Hegel: it is necessary to 'depolarise' dialectics with the help of the notion of multiplicity.

In capitalism, it is not a single drama – that of Spirit (Hegel) or Capital (Marx) – but a 'multiplicity of social dramas' which must be taken into account. To seize the dynamics of capitalism, we should not refer to the 'immense, external and superior' forces of the dialectic (capital/labour), but to the 'infinitely multiplied, infinitesimal and internal' forces (Tarde 1999: 112). The logic of contradiction, the motor of the 'single drama', is far too poor and reductive. This assertion, which Foucault will take up again after Tarde, is aimed directly at the Marxist conception of power, in which power is always dependent on a deeper economic structure.

The microphysics of power replaces the pyramidal aspect of the Marxist conceptualisation with an immanence wherein the various 'enclosures' (factory, school, hospital, etc.) and disciplinary techniques are articulated with one another. In relation to this, Deleuze points out that it is the economic structure and the factory which presuppose disciplinary mechanisms already acting on souls and bodies, not the other way round. Other forces and other dynamics may then be invoked to explain the expansion of capitalism. These forces and these dynamics obviously imply a relationship between capital and labour, but they cannot be reduced to it.

This is not to deny the relevance of the Marxian analysis of the capital–labour relation, but rather its claim to reduce society and the multiplicity of power relations that constitute it to the single relation of command and obedience exercised in the factory or in the economic relation. On the contrary, it is the latter which must be integrated within a broader framework, that of the disciplinary societies and their twofold techniques of power: discipline and biopower.

Likewise, the imposition of conducts and the subjection of bodies are not explicable by monetary constraints and economic imperatives alone. Regimes of signs, machines of expression and collective assemblages of enunciation (law, knowledges, languages, public opinion, etc.) act like the cogs of the assemblages, in the same way as machinic assemblages (factories, prisons, schools).

By concentrating on one dimension of the power relation alone (exploitation), Marxism is inevitably led to reduce the machine of expression to ideology. One of the objectives of Foucault's writings on disciplinary societies is to take leave from economism and the dialectical culture of dualisms, to expose the poverty of explaining dominations in terms of ideology.

The multiplicity of singularities, their power of creation and coproduction, and the modalities of their coming together were not born with post-Fordism, but instead traverse the entire history of modernity. The power of the disciplinary societies (whether we are dealing with techniques of confinement or so-called biopolitical techniques) acts, primarily and always, on a multiplicity. Accordingly, dialectical dualisms must be thought of as captures of multiplicity. For Foucault, disciplines transform the confused, useless or dangerous *multitudes* into ordered classes.

The techniques of confinement (disciplines) impose a nondescript [*quelconque*] task or conduct for the sake of producing useful effects, provided that the multiplicity is not great in number and the space well defined and limited (school, factory, hospital etc.). They consist in distributing the multiplicity across space (by gridding, confining, serialising), ordering it in time (by breaking up gestures, subdividing time, programming actions), and composing it in space-time so as to extract from it useful effects by augmenting the forces which constitute it.

The biopolitical techniques (public health, politics of the family and so on) are exercised as the management of the life of any multiplicity, no matter its provenance. Here, unlike in disciplinary institutions, the multiplicity is numerous (the population as a whole) and the space is open (the limits of the population are defined by the nation).

The Deleuzian interpretation of Foucault (independently of the issue of its faithfulness to Foucault's work) will be very useful for us in analysing the dynamics of difference and repetition (Deleuze 1984). Deleuze distinguishes between power relations and institutions. Power is a relation between forces, while institutions are agents of the integration and stratification of forces. Institutions fix forces and their relations into precise forms by according them a reproductive function. The state, capital and the various institutions are not the source of power relations, they derive from them. Thus Foucault, as interpreted by Deleuze, analyses *dispositifs* of power which deploy themselves according to the modalities of integration and differentiation, and not according to modalities that could be traced to the subject/work paradigm.

Power relations are virtual, unstable, non-localisable, non-stratified potentialities. They only define possibilities or probabilities of inter-action; they are differential relations that determine singularities. The actualisation of these differential relations and singularities by institu-tions (state, capital, etc.) that stabilise them, stratify them, and make them non-reversible, is simultaneously an integration (capture) and a dif-ferentiation.

To integrate means to connect singularities, to homogenise them and make them converge qua singularities towards a common goal. Integration is an operation that consists in tracing a general line of force which passes through forces and fixes them into forms. The integration does not function by abstraction, generalisation, fusional unification, or subsumption (to speak the Hegelian–Marxist language). The actualisation of power relations takes place gradually, 'stone by stone', as Gabriel Tarde thought. It is an ensemble of integrations, first local, then global. Deleuze describes integration as a procedure aimed at making the ensemble of net-works and patchworks, flows and aggregates, hold together.

Tarde too uses the term 'integration' to avoid understanding the consti-tution of social quantities and values (whether economic or otherwise) either as a totalisation or as a simple generalisation or abstraction. Social type or social quantity are understood as integrations of small differences, small variations, in accordance with the model of integral calculus.

But the actualisation of power relations is not only integration, it is also differentiation [différenciation]:[2] power relations are exercised to the extent that there is a difference between forces. In capitalism, this dif-ferentiation, instead of being a differentiation of difference, the unfold-ing of multiplicity, is a creation and reproduction of dualisms, of which the most important are the dualisms of class (proletarians/capitalists) and sex (men/women).

Binary groupings, like sexes and classes, must capture, codify and control virtualities, the possible variations of molecular assemblages, the probabilities of interaction of neo-monadological cooperation. Classes carry out the reduction of multiplicity to dualisms and to a collective whole which totalises and unifies irreducible singularities. The concept of working class designates a collective whole and not a distributive whole.

Dualisms of sex also function as a *dispositif* of capture and coding of the multiple combinations that bring into play not just the masculine and the feminine, but also a thousand tiny sexes, the thousand tiny possible becomings of sexuality. These thousand sexes must be disciplined and cod-ified in order to be related back to the men/women dualism. Social classes are literally carved out from the multiplicity of activities, crystallising possible interactions in the form of a dualism. In the same way, the opposition men/women is carved out from the becoming-possible of the thousand sexes, crystallising them in the dualism of the heterosexual norm.

The conversion of multiplicity into classes and of the thousand sexes into heterosexuality functions both as the constitution of types and the repression of multiplicity, as the constitution and coding of the norm and as the neutralisation of the virtualities of other becomings. The two modalities of the exercise of power (repression and constitution) are obviously far from being contradictory.[3]

To trace a possible way out from the economism and the dualisms of the labour movement, Foucault affirms that a society is not defined by its mode of production, but by the statements that express it and the visibilities that effectuate it.

Deleuze and Guattari assimilate the Foucauldian relation between the statable and the visible [*l'énonçable et le visible*] to the relation between machines of expression and corporeal assemblages which they themselves established. This relation between the statable and the visible, like the one between corporeal assemblages and machines of expression, is not reducible to the base–superstructure relation (Marxism), any more than to the signifier–signified relation (linguistics and structuralism).

The prison is a space of visibility which makes a mixture of bodies, a corporeal assemblage (prisoners), emerge and be seen. The penal code, as a machine of expression, defines a field of sayability (statements on delinquency) which carries out incorporeal transformations on the body. Thus the verdicts of the court instantaneously transform defendants into sentenced persons. The machinic assemblage of bodies has its form (the prison) and its substance (prisoners). The machine of expression also has its form (the penal code) and its substance (delinquency).

The relationship between the visible and the statable can be thought neither in the form of the structure and superstructure nor in the form of signifier and signified, since it is a non-relation that refers to an informal outside, a virtual, an event.

What is Confined is the Outside

Deleuze provides another very important indication to help us define disciplinary societies. We know that the school, the factory, the hospital and the barracks are *dispositifs* to confine multiplicity. But more fundamentally, Deleuze says, that which is confined is *the outside*. What is confined is the virtual, the power of metamorphosis, becoming. Disciplinary societies exercise their power by neutralising difference and repetition together with their power of variation (the difference that makes a difference), subordinating them to reproduction. The function of the training of bodies is to prevent any bifurcation, to eradicate any possibility of variation, any unpredictability, from action, conduct and behavior. In some magnificent pages, Foucault speaks about disciplines as a power which concerns 'the virtualities of conduct themselves', which intervenes 'at the moment when virtuality is becoming reality' (Foucault 2003: 53).

Without a doubt, disciplinary institutions are productive. They do not restrict themselves to repression: they constitute bodies, statements, sexes and so on. But at the same time it is necessary to recognise, beyond Foucault, that they contrive a more profound repression, not because they would deny an already present human nature, but because disciplines and biopower separate out the forces of the outside, of the virtual, because they separate out the forces belonging to the dynamics of the 'difference that makes a difference'.

Disciplines and biopower are modes of production of subjectivity, but only when the infinity of monstrosity virtually harboured by the soul (becoming-monster) is subjected to the reproduction of dualisms (men/women, master/worker, etc.).

To confine the outside, to confine the virtual, means neutralising the power of invention and codifying repetition so as to drain it of all power of variation, thereby reducing it to a simple reproduction. In disciplinary societies, institutions, which are either those of power or those of the labour movement, do not know becoming. They do indeed have a past (traditions), a present (administration of power relations in the here and now) and a future (progress), but they lack becomings, variations. The social sciences which legitimated the constitution and action of these institutions function by equilibrium (political economy), integration (Durkheim), reproduction (Bourdieu), contradiction (Marxism), struggle for survival (Darwinism) or competition, but they know nothing of becoming.

They organise and impose the temporality of the clock – chronological time – but neglect the temporality of the event, save as an exception to be neutralised, a danger to be avoided, an always exceptional occasion to be seized (revolution). The time of the event, the time of invention, the time of the creation of possibles must be curtailed and fenced in within rigorously established procedures and deadlines. Antonio Negri has shown how constituent power is an anomaly or an exception for political philosophy, to be subordinated to the procedures of constituted power. For his part, Tarde had already shown why economic and social sciences exclude any theory of invention and creation, and how they constitute themselves as theories of reproduction, as is still the case with the sociology of Bourdieu.

Let us take up again our hypothesis on the proliferation of possible worlds as the ontology of our present. Disciplinary societies operate like Leibniz's God. They allow only one world to pass into reality. From this point of view, they can be regarded as productive – they constitute the monads for the world of disciplinary societies and this world is included in each monad through the techniques of confinement and biopower. But they brutally prevent the infinity of other possible worlds from passing into reality. They block and control becoming and difference.

The theories of equilibrium (political economy and sociology) or the theories of contradiction (Hegelianism and Marxism), as well as the practices they authorise, have the same horizon in common: the idea that there is only one possible world. Reproduction of power and seizure of power, equilibrium and contradiction, respond paradoxically to the same problem: to live together in a single possible world.

In a truly astonishing way, these practices – which exclude both the outside and becoming – converged in the twentieth century in policies of planning, that is, in the neutralisation and control, at a social scale, of the logic of event, of the creation and production of the new. We could speak of the triumph of reproduction over difference, in capitalism as well as in socialism. But this triumph can only be short-lived. At the end of the nineteenth century, the sociology and philosophy of Tarde already announced the failure of this will to confine the outside, this will to make only one disciplined world among the infinity of possible worlds pass into existence. The Weberian 'iron cage' has been broken, the monads have fled from the disciplinary world by inventing incompossible worlds which are actualised within the same world.

The series constituted by the monads do not converge any longer towards the same disciplinary world, but diverge here and now. The world has really become difference, bifurcation of bifurcations, as in the tales of Borges where all possibles coexist.

Let us take up again the examples mentioned above: classes do not manage to contain multiplicity, in the same way that heterosexuality no longer normalises the thousand sexes. The monster as modality of sub-jectivation deploys itself in the here and now. Only then is the radical change in the forms of organisation of power and the modalities of its exercise produced.

For power, the problem no longer lies in the confinement of the outside and the disciplining of whatever subjectivities [*subjectivités quelconques*] (after having separated them from the virtual, from creation). Since the outside and the power of proliferation of difference have rent asunder the regime of confinement, they can be seized only through modulation. It is no longer a matter of disciplining them within a closed space, but of modulating them in an open space. Control is superimposed on to discipline.

The time of the event, of invention, of the creation of possibles, can no longer be regarded as an exception, but must instead be seen as what needs to be periodically regulated and captured. The assemblage of difference and repetition cannot be neutralised any more, but must be controlled as such.

It was around the events of 1968 that this new reality asserted itself, even if it had been there for a long time, manifesting itself in different ways throughout the century (in art, as well as in political and cultural movements).

But what is modulation as a modality of the exercise of power? What are the forces which modulation controls and captures?

The Deleuzian concept of 'modulation' (Deleuze 1990)[4] harbours considerable heuristic possibilities which I would like to examine here. Unlike what goes on in disciplinary societies, where one moves linearly and progressively from one 'enclosure' to another (from the school to the army, from the army to the factory), Deleuze shows that in the societies of control one is never done with anything. One moves from the school to the enterprise and from the enterprise one returns to school, and so on.

I would like to extend this sociological reflection on modulation as a diagram of the flexibility of production and subjectivity by seizing hold of the new concepts of life and of the living implied by this modality of the action of power. It is necessary then to start from the power exercised on life (biopower), which Foucault uses to define the disciplinary societies.

From Disciplinary Societies to the Societies of Control

Disciplinary societies are characterised by the assemblage of disciplinary power and biopolitical power. On this point Foucault is unequivocal: disciplinary techniques were born at the end of the seventeenth century and the biopolitical techniques some fifty years later, in second half of the eighteen century.

But what does Foucault mean by biopower? Biopower is a modality of action which, like disciplines, is aimed at a whatever multiplicity. Whereas disciplinary techniques transform bodies, biopolitical technologies are aimed at a multiplicity inasmuch as it constitutes a global mass, invested with overall processes that are specific to life – such as birth, death, production and illness. Disciplinary techniques only know the body and the individual, while biopower targets the population, man qua species and, at the limit, as Foucault says in one of his courses, man qua spirit or mind. Biopolitics 'installs bodies within overall biological processes'.

If we follow Foucault's descriptions, we can easily identify these technologies with the politics of the Welfare State. The object of biopower is the fertility of the species (politics of the family, birth control, etc.) but also the extent, duration and intensity of the dominant diseases within a given population (politics of health). With the development of industrialisation, new terrains of intervention appear: industrial accidents, risks related to the loss of employment (joblessness), to old age (retirement), and so on. A last domain of intervention mentioned by Foucault is that of the administration of territory: geographical and climatic effects, management of water resources, and so on.

According to Foucault, the problem was not that of inventing institutions of assistance which, generally speaking, existed already, but to set up different and more effective *dispositifs* than those guaranteed, primarily by the church, until the middle of the seventeenth century: insurance, individual and collective savings, social security.

The objective of biopower is indeed the management of life, but in the sense that it seeks to reproduce the conditions of existence of a population.

Both disciplinary and biopolitical techniques reach their highest level of development after the Second World War, with Taylorism and the Welfare State. This apogee corresponds to the reorganisation of the *dispositifs* of confinement and management of life, impelled by new forces and relations of power. Yet, ever since the end of the nineteenth century, new techniques of power, resembling neither disciplines nor biopower, have been in the process of gestation. How can we define the singularity of these relations, which Deleuze calls relations of control?

Gabriel Tarde might put us on the right path. At the end of the nineteenth century, when the societies of control begin to elaborate their own techniques and *dispositifs*, Tarde explains that the 'social group of the future' is neither the crowd, the class, nor the population, but the 'public' (or rather publics). By the public, Tarde understands the public of the media, the public of a newspaper: 'the public is a dispersed crowd in which the influence of minds [*esprits*] on one another has become an action at a distance' (Tarde 1989: 17).

At the end of the nineteenth century we enter the time of the publics, that is to say, the time in which the fundamental problem is how to hold together whatever subjectivities, which act on one another at a distance, in an open space. The subordination of space to time defines a space-time bloc which incarnates itself, according to Tarde, in the technologies of speed, transmission, contagion and propagation at a distance. Whereas the disciplinary techniques are fundamentally structured in space, the techniques of control and constitution of the public allow one to bring time and its virtualities to the foreground. The public is constituted through its presence in time.

Tarde grasped at their birth three phenomena which came to characterise the societies of control and their massive deployment, starting from the second half of the twentieth century onwards: (1) the emergence of the cooperation between brains and its functioning by flows and connections, network and patchwork; (2) the rise of the technological *dispositifs* of action at a distance, which duplicate and amplify the power of action at a distance of monads: telegraph, telephone, cinema, television, the internet; (3) the corresponding processes of subjectivation and subjection: the formation of publics, that is to say, the constitution of a being together that takes place in time.

The societies of control generate their own technologies and processes of subjectivation, which are noticeably different from the technologies and processes of subjectivation of disciplinary societies. The (social and technological) machine of expression not only cannot be reduced to ideology, as Marxism and political economy wish to do, but it becomes more and more the strategic locus for the control of the process of constitution of the social world. It is in it and through it that the event actualises itself in souls and effectuates itself in bodies.

The integration and differentiation of new forces, of new power relations, takes place through new institutions (public opinion, collective perception and collective intelligence) and new techniques (of action at a distance). In the societies of control, power relations come to be expressed through the action at a distance of one mind on another, through the brain's power to affect and become affected, which is mediatised and enriched by technology: 'The mechanical means designed to carry far and loud the suggestive action of the leader (words, writing, print) do not cease their progress' (Tarde 2003: 58).

The institutions of the societies of control are thus characterised by the use of the technologies of acting at a distance, rather than of mechanical technologies (societies of sovereignty) or thermodynamic technologies (disciplinary societies).

Crowds, Classes and Publics

If the cooperation between brains expresses itself first of all in the form of public opinion, that is, as judgements formed and held in common, it then develops as the creation of percepts and concepts that are also formed and held in common (collective perception and collective intelligence), thanks to the technologies of television and the internet. The internet integrates and differentiates the various metamorphoses of public opinion, perception and collective intelligence.

But let us consider for a moment the public; or the publics (for there are several) and the novelty they introduce into action and being together. The public sphere is the form of subjectivation which best expresses the plasticity and functional indifference of the 'whatever' subjectivity (monad). The relation of belonging that individuals and publics have to one another is not a relation of exclusion and identity: though an individual can only belong to one class or crowd at a time, he or she may instead belong, at the same time, to different publics (multi-membership, to use current sociological terminology). Tarde's individual, straddling different possible worlds, is like the artist whom Plato wanted to exclude from his Republic. He is a multiple and mimetic man, but within the constitutive and evolving dynamics of several publics.

These publics express new subjectivities and forms of socialisation which were unknown in disciplinary societies. Indeed, 'the formation of a public supposes a far more advanced mental and social evolution than the formation of a crowd or a class' (Tarde 1989: 38–9).

With the emergence of this variety of publics, society draws even closer to Tarde's privileged metaphor: the brain. In the public, invention and imitation are disseminated in a manner which is 'almost instantaneous, like the propagation of a wave in a perfectly elastic milieu', thanks to technologies that make possible the action at a distance of one mind on another (quasi-photographic reproduction of a cerebral snapshot by the sensitive surface of another brain). With the public 'we rush toward this strange ideal' of sociability where brains 'touch one other at each and every instant through multiple communications', as is the case today with the internet (ibid.: 39).

The division of society into a plurality of publics 'is superimposed more and more obviously and effectively on its religious, economic, aesthetic and political divisions'. It does not replace them. In the 'elastic milieu' of the cooperation between brains and of intercerebral relations, publics delineate fluctuations and bifurcations which reformulate the rigid and univocal segmentations represented by classes and social groups: 'By substituting or superimposing themselves on older groupings, the new – increasingly more extended and massive – groupings which we call publics not only make the reign of fashion follow that of habit, and innovation that of tradition; they also replace the clear and persistent divisions between the multiple varieties of human associations and their interminable conflicts with a complete and variable segmentation (whose limits are blurred) in the process of perpetual renewal and mutual penetration' (ibid.: 70).

Thus, the processes of social segmentation become flexible, or, in Deleuze's terms, deterritorialised. The difficulty of imagining and grasping these new processes of subjectivation after the breakdown of social classes is surely bound, on the one hand, to the difficulty of understanding the laws of constitution and variation of these moving and changing segmentations, which seem devoid of objective bases, on the other, to the Marxist theoretical tradition, which reduces the modalities of association of publics to ideology.

In a science-fiction story which was conceived in 1879, finished in 1884 and appearing for the first time in 1896, Tarde provides us with an effective synthesis of the passage from disciplinary societies to the societies of control: 'the anarchic regime of covetousness is followed by the autocratic government of opinion, which has become omnipotent' (Tarde 2000: 35). The political and economic functions of opinion cannot be brought back to the mechanisms of exploitation and subjection specific to disciplinary societies and the market (the anarchic regime of covetousness).

The control of opinion, of language, of regimes of signs, of the circulation of knowledge, of consumption, and so on, refers to unprecedented techniques of power which will be described, after Tarde, in the work of Bakhtin in the Soviet Russia of the 1920s and in the philosophy of Deleuze and Guattari around 1968.

Bakhtin shows us how the multiplicity of languages, forms of enunciations, and semiotics within the pre-capitalist world (multilingualism) are repressed and subordinated to a language which, by imposing itself as majoritarian, becomes the normative coding of expression (monolinguism) (Lazzarato 2004: Chapter 4). Deleuze and Guattari describe techniques of the constitution of multiplicity qua 'majority' which, by levelling differences, produce a model that serves as a standard, in which one can see the prototype of the construction and measurement of television audiences or of opinion through surveys.

The concept of exploitation, built on the dialectical capital–labour relation, is absolutely inadequate for grasping these techniques for the semiotic control of the expression of multiplicity which accompanied, and often anticipated, the advent of capitalism.

The techniques of subjection in the societies of control did not replace those of the disciplinary societies, but were superimposed upon them, becoming more and more invasive, to the point that today they constitute the indispensable presupposition of capitalistic accumulation.

Both the exploitation and accumulation of capital are simply impossible without the transformation of linguistic multiplicity into the majoritarian model (monolinguism), without the imposition of a monolingual regime of expression, and without the constitution of the semiotic power of capital.

Life and the Living

If the technologies of action at a distance and the machines of expression become the fundamental means for the capture of multiplicity in an open space and if public opinion is the first new institution of multiplicity, which are the new forces that are manifested in these power relations?

It is only after having defined these new forces that we will be able to return to the notion of modulation. To understand all the implications contained in this notion, we must investigate the concepts of life and of the living, because it is life and living beings which are, in the final analysis, the objects of modulation.

Biopolitical techniques aim at life, they are directed towards the living being insofar as it belongs to the human species. They seek to regulate the life affected by disease, unemployment, old age, death: the life to which they refer is the reproduction of a population. The techniques of control are also addressed to life, but in a noticeably different sense. It is another concept of life (and of living being) which must be brought into play to understand the power that these techniques try to modulate.

To do this, we must return to Nietzsche, the true inspiration behind Foucault's theory of power. Like Tarde, Nietzsche too often uses the results of the biology and physiology of his time to criticise the theories of the subject. By starting out from the living body and its physiology, molecular biology allows one to question the autonomy, independence and unity of the self propounded by the philosophers. Nietzsche, like Tarde, discovers in 'molecular' biology, in the multiplicity of infinitesimal beings which constitute bodies (infinitesimal beings which want, feel and think), in their relations and their form of political organisation, a concept of subjectivity that differs from the Kantian 'I' and its modalities of action and suffering.

Again, it is by starting from biology that Nietzsche can say that 'being is living' and that 'there are no other beings'. But what more general definition of the living could be drawn from the studies of molecular biology of the second half of the nineteenth century? Memory (the power of actualisation of the virtual) is the irreducible property that both Nietzsche and Tarde, in different ways, place at the basis of their definition of the living. Tarde and Nietzsche alike find this definition of the living in the scientific works of the time, in particular in Ernst Haeckel's books on evolution.

For the German biologist all the infinitesimal elements (plastitudes) of a body, all the organic monads, have a memory, whereas this property (or aptitude) is lacking in the non-living. Tarde interprets Haeckel's molecular biology in the light of the theory of multiplicity. According to him, Haeckel provides a truly remarkable 'monadological', that is, Leibnizian interpretation of the doctrine of evolution.

This definition of the living as memory is a constant in biology and physiology. The definition of the living in contemporary molecular biology is in no way different from that of Haeckel: 'The essence of the living is a memory, the physical preservation of the past in the present. By reproducing themselves, the forms of life bind the past to the present and record messages for the future' (Margulis and Sagan 2002: 64).

According to Tarde, without memory, without this force (a duration that conserves), without this fertile succession that contracts the before in the after, there would be no sensation, no life, no time, no accumulation and thus no growth. For Bergson, Tarde's first 'disciple', without this duration the world would be forced to start anew at every moment. The world would be a present repeating itself indefinitely, always equal to itself. Matter itself would not be possible without this duration. The creation and realisation of the sensible presuppose the activity of memory and attention, as well as their power of actualisation and repetition.

Any sensation, developing itself over time, requires a force which conserves that which is no more within that which is; a duration which conserves the dead in the alive. Without it, all sensations would be reduced to mere excitation. The forces mobilised by the cooperation between brains and captured by the new institutions (public opinion, etc.) are therefore those of memory and attention. The latter is defined as 'intellectual effort' by Bergson and as 'conatus of the brain' by Tarde.

The philosophy of difference is the first to tackle the new molecular biology and the studies on the brain. Bergson's work concerns the living not only because it directly confronts biology and evolutionary theory, but more precisely because of his research on memory, time and its modalities of action: the virtual and the actual

Memory, according to Bergson, is the co-existence of all the virtual remembrances [*souvenirs*] (the famous reversed cone of *Matter and Memory* is constituted by an infinity of circles which open on to the infinite at the top – the virtual – and are closed towards the bottom – the actual). To remember something does not consist in looking for a remembrance in memory, as though one were rummaging through a drawer. To remember something – like every activity of mind – is to actualise a virtual, and this actualisation is a creation, an individuation and not a simple reproduction. This process is described by Bergson as 'intellectual work', and it involves, as in Tarde, both memory and attention:

> So without attention, no sensation . . . Now what is attention? One can answer that it is an effort that aims at the specification of a nascent sensation. But it should be noted that the effort, in its pure psychological guise and abstracting from the concomitant muscular action, is a desire. (Tarde 1895: 337)

Memory, attention and the relations whereby they are actualised become social and economic forces that must be captured in order to control and exploit the assemblage of difference and repetition. It is by remaining faithful to this intellectual tradition that Deleuze can affirm that in 'a life there are nothing but virtuals' (Deleuze 1995).

We can now return to the concept of modulation. The capture, control and regulation of the action at a distance of one mind on another takes place through the modulation of flows of desires and beliefs and through the forces (memory and attention) that make these flows circulate in the cooperation between brains.

In modulation, as a modality of the exercise of power, it is always a question of bodies, but now it is rather the incorporeal dimension of bodies which is at stake. The societies of control invest spiritual, rather than bodily, memory (contrary to the disciplinary societies). Man qua spirit or mind, who, according to Foucault, was the object of biopower only at the limit, now comes to the foreground.

The society of control exercises its power thanks to the technologies of the action at a distance of image, sound and data which function like machines to modulate, to crystallise electromagnetic waves (Lazzarato 1998) and vibrations (radio, television) or to modulate and crystallise packets of bits (computers and digital networks). These inorganic waves duplicate the waves by which monads act on one another.

We already find indications of this situation at the end of the nineteenth century. Indeed for Tarde, action at a distance, the impression of one mind on another, conserves itself in two ways. First, any impression is conserved, repeated in memory. Second, every expressed impression, 'the entire wave of the soul, so to speak, is prolonged in infinite and indefinitely evolving undulations'. These undulations manifest themselves according to certain regularities and the technological *dispositifs* act by intervening on these regularities.

If memory and attention are living engines functioning on anorganic energy, that is to say, on the virtual, the technologies of action at a distance are artificial engines, artificial memories that assemble themselves with the living engines by interfering with the functioning of memory.

The machines for crystallising or modulating time are *dispositifs* capable of intervening in the event, in the cooperation between brains, through the modulation of the forces engaged therein, thereby becoming preconditions for every process of constitution of whatever subjectivity. Consequently this process comes to resemble a harmonisation of waves, a polyphony (to borrow Bakhtin's expression).

It is thus necessary to distinguish life as memory from life as the set of biological characteristics of the human species (death, birth, disease, etc.). In other words, we must distinguish the 'bio' contained in the category of biopower from the bio contained in memory. In order not to name such different things with the same word, one could define the new relations of power which take memory and its *conatus* (attention) as their object, lacking a better term, as noo-politics.[5] Noo-politics (the ensemble of the techniques of control) is exercised on the brain. It involves above all attention, and is aimed at the control of memory and its virtual power. The modulation of memory would thus be the most important function of noo-politics.

If disciplines moulded bodies by constituting habits mainly in bodily memory, the societies of control modulate brains and constitute habits mainly in spiritual memory.

We thus have the moulding of the body ensured by disciplines (prisons, school, factory, etc.), the management of life organised by biopower (Welfare State, politics of health, etc.), and the modulation of memory and its virtual powers regulated by noo-politics (Herzian, audio-visual and telematic networks, constitution of public opinion, of perception and of collective intelligence). Sociologically we have this sequence: working class (as one of the modalities of confinement), population, publics.

The set of these *dispositifs*, not just the last, constitutes the society of control.

These three different *dispositifs* of power, born in different periods and serving heterogeneous purposes, do not replace one another, but are instead assembled with one another. The United States represents today the most complete model of a society of control integrating the three *dispositifs* of power. The disciplinary *dispositifs* of confinement have made extraordinary strides there, particularly when it comes to prisons. The two million prisoners currently occupying American prisons represent a total percentage of the population that no disciplinary society has ever managed to attain. The biopolitical *dispositifs* for the management of life do not disappear, but, on the contrary, expand and are profoundly transformed: from welfare to workfare, from insurance against social risks (unemployment, retirement, disease) to interventions in the life of individuals forcing them into employment, into servitude to subordinate work. The new *dispositifs* of noo-politics (the first of which nevertheless date from the second half of the nineteenth century) have undergone unprecedented development thanks to informatics and telematics. The difference between them lies in the degree of 'deterritorialisation', as Deleuze would put it. We could say that noo-politics commands and reorganises the other power relations because it operates at the most deterritorialised level (the virtuality of the action between brains).

It is nevertheless true that at a global level we are witnessing a boom in disciplinary institutions. For instance, both the factory and work, as Marx and the economists understand it, are not in retreat but, on the contrary, in full development. The International Labor Organization (ILO) has pointed out that 246 million children between the ages of 5 and 17 years are currently working. Similarly, in western countries, the wage regime is expanding when compared to the period of Fordism. But this does not alter the fact that the paradigm within which these phenomena are inscribed has changed radically. The inability to understand this change on the basis of the paradigm of the work-subject is even more manifest on the political than on the theoretical level.

Industrial work is no longer at the centre of capitalist valorisation, nor is it a model of political and social subjectivation valid for all social forces, nor indeed is it the exclusive force able to produce institutions and forms of politicisation in the societies of control. In western countries, the wage remains the dominant form in which capitalism exploits cooperation and the capacity for invention of whatever subjectivities, but it has exploded into a multiplicity of activities and statuses, expressing subjectivities and expectations which cannot be reduced to the traditional concept of class.

But the problem is even more radical. It is not just a question of saying that industrial work is no longer at the centre of capitalist valorisation. Once we have inventoried all the new forms of activity, once we have affirmed that languages, affects, knowledges and life become – in their assemblage with reproductive work – productive, we still do not understand the dynamic that makes possible this creation and its exploitation: the dynamic of difference and repetition. It is the paradigm of the work-subject which prevents us from seeing this dynamic.

The Labour Movement and Disciplinary Societies

To supplement Foucault's research on disciplinary societies, it would be necessary to carry out studies of the relations that these societies entertained with the institutions of the labour movement. Born and developed at the beginning of the nineteenth century against the logic of disciplines, these institutions became, in the twentieth century, fundamental cogs in the practices of confinement. The twentieth century was the stage for a convergence between capitalism and socialism, in particular in the politics of planning, which represent the apogee of the disciplinary societies and the fulfilment of the logic of reproduction. The unpredictability, uncertainty and possibility of variation presupposed by the assemblage of difference and repetition, together with the monstrous subjectivation this assemblage implies, were strictly codified and neutralised at both the economic and social levels. The 'pre-established harmony' was embodied during the Cold War, without any fundamental difference, in socialist and capitalist planning policies alike.

There is no need to recall that the idea of planning is a socialist and Leninist idea, taken up by Rathenau during the Weimar Republic, which then became the fad for all senior civil servants after the Second World War.

If planning is endowed with specificity compared to the disciplinary societies of the eighteenth and nineteenth centuries, it is in the role and function played within it by work, conceived as both the substance and measure of planning. Work revealed itself to be the most effective means of regulating the entirety of society. In the factories, it disciplines the new working class (the OS, *ouvriers spécialisés*, or unskilled workers) by preventing it from manifesting itself as multiplicity and critique of the wage. Until the 1970s, and on France until the 1980s, the trade-union and political institutions of the labour movement fought against the emergence of the OS, or unskilled operatives, as a new political subject (which no longer corresponded to the working class as understood by Marx) and against their refusal of reproductive work.

In the planned society, the access of women, children and the elderly to social rights (welfare) passes through the worker's wage: even the production and reproduction of the norm of heterosexuality passed through work. The institutions of planning are completely traversed and configured by the idea of work, which assembles together disciplines and biopower, confinement and management of life, thereby realising the contours of society as an 'iron cage', according to Weber's expression. Work also becomes the constitutional power of the new republics born out of the collapse of fascism (the Republic of Italy, for example, is founded on work, as its constitution clearly states).

So does that mean that Foucault was wrong and the Marxists right? Is work then the foundation of all social and power relations? To answer this question, it is necessary to highlight a fundamental difference between planned societies and the disciplinary societies that existed before the First World War. With the advent of planning and Fordism, work is no longer the 'spontaneous' ontological power of constitution of the world which Marx spoke about. In Fordism, the power of work and its regulative capacity are bound to the political logic which instituted it as the substance and measure of society. If work then appears as the ground on which social relations are built, it is no longer because it is that which constitutes the social world, but rather because the social and political compromise between trade unions, owners and the state constituted itself around the idea of work. The geopolitical division of the world rested then on the workerist dynamics which aim at the reproduction, control and neutralisation of any assemblage of difference and repetition by integrating the institutions of the labour movement into the logic of the reproduction of power. Economic reproduction and political reproduction thus coincided through the intermediation of work. We can regard the twentieth century as the stage for the long and irreversible crisis of work and subject insofar as these are seen as the constitutive powers of self and world. If the subject/work paradigm functioned as the system of regulation after the Second World War, it was only because of an entirely political overdetermination.

In the second half of the twentieth century, the apprehension of the process of constitution of the world through the concept of praxis played a conservative or, at best, regulatory role vis-à-vis power relations. If Marx's theory had revolutionary effects in the cycle of struggles which went from the days of 1848 to the Paris Commune, a century later it can be seen to have functioned as a powerful means of integration.

Today, many have forgotten this not-so glorious phase in the history of the labour movement. They glorify Fordism and its certainties *a posteriori*, which amounts to a mystification and neglect of history.

The movements of '68 were not mistaken to regard as their adversaries all the (socialist and capitalist) advocates of the neutralisation of the assemblage of difference and repetition. The (socialist and capitalist) bureaucrats of the planned society were correctly identified as the guards of the iron cage and of the imposition of dualisms. Remaining with the examples developed above, the year 1968 was precisely a point of rupture and flight from the logic of class and the heterosexual norm.

Long after the capitalists and the state abandoned it as the means for disciplining society, the institutions of the labour movement have continued to live within the logic of political compromise in which work constitutes a regulating power. The problem is that the labour movement has nothing to put in the place of praxis. It can't imagine a process of constitution of world and self which is not centred around work.

The only alternative it has been able to imagine is that of employment. The passage from work to employment is another sad chapter in the decline of the labour movement. If work became the centrepiece of the disciplinary societies at the time of their exhaustion (Fordism), employment constitutes one of the principal forms of regulation in the societies of control.

References

Deleuze, G. (1984), *Foucault*, Paris: Minuit.
Deleuze, G. (1990), 'Post-scriptum sur les sociétés de contrôle' in *Pourparlers*, Paris: Minuit.
Deleuze, G. (1995), 'Immanence: une vie', *Philosophie*, 47.
Foucault, M. (2003), *Le Pouvoir psychiatrique*, Paris: Gallimard/Seuil.
Lazzarato, M. (1998), *Videofilosofia*, Roma: Manifestolibri.
Lazzarato, M. (2004), *Les Révolutions du capitalisme*, Paris: Les Empêcheurs de penser en rond /Le Seuil.
Margulis. L. and Sagan, D. (2002), *L'Univers bacterial*, Paris: Seuil.
Tarde, G. (1895), *Essais et mélanges sociologiques*, Lyon: Storck.
Tarde, G. (1989), *L'Opinion et la foule*, Paris: Presses Universitaires de France.
Tarde, G. (1999), *Les Lois sociales*, Paris: Synthélabo.
Tarde, G. (2000), *Fragment d'histoire future*, Paris: Séguier.
Tarde, G. (2003), *Les Transformations du pouvoir*, Paris: Les Empêcheurs de penser en rond/Le Seuil.

Notes

1. **Editorial note:** This chapter appears in M. Lazzarato, (2004), *Les Révolutions du capitalisme*. Translated by Akseli Virtanen and Jussi Vähämäki, revised by Alberto Toscano.
2. One could even say 'differentiation' [*différentiation*] (calculation of a differential) to pursue the implications of the mathematical model of the infinitesimal calculus.
3. The difference in perspective between Foucault and Deleuze regarding the action and efficacy of repression is due to the primacy that Deleuze, unlike Foucault, accords to the assemblages of desire over the assemblages of power.
4. Introduced in 'Post-scriptum sur les sociétés de contrôle', in Deleuze 1990.
5. To understand this neologism, we not only need to know that in Aristotle *noos* (or *noûs*) means the highest part of the soul, the intellect, but also that it is the name of an internet service provider.

Chapter 10

Nomad Citizenship and Global Democracy

Eugene W. Holland

The concept of nomad citizenship developed here derives from the concepts of nomadism and nomadology expounded by Deleuze and Guattari in *A Thousand Plateaus* (Deleuze and Guattari 1987). As I have explained elsewhere, this concept of nomadism should not be understood primarily in reference to nomadic peoples, despite the familiar connotations of the term. Rather, nomadism as Deleuze and Guattari understand it can refer to a wide range of activities, including 'building bridges or cathedrals or rendering judgments or making music or instituting a science, a technology' (ibid.: 366). In the same vein, I will in what follows discuss nomad science, nomad music, nomad games – and eventually nomad management and nomad citizenship. We begin with nomad science, since it is a concept Deleuze and Guattari develop at some length by contrasting it with what they call royal or state science.

Nomad Science

Much could be said about these two 'versions' of science; for our purposes, two points are essential. One is the difference between the principles of 'following' and 'reproducing' that characterise the two kinds of science; the other involves the social consequences that follow from this difference.

Royal science proceeds by extracting invariant ('universal') laws from the variations of matter, in line with the binary opposition of form and matter: matter is essentially variable, but 'obeys' formal laws that are universal. Reproducing the results of a successful experiment is crucial to establishing the veracity and universality of the hypothesised law that the experiment was designed to test. Nomad science, by contrast, proceeds not by extracting a constant but by following the variations or 'singularities' of matter. Its operations are better mapped by the four-fold Hjelmslevian distinction between 'content' and 'expression', each of which involves 'form' and 'substance', rather than the binary opposition of form and matter (Hjelmslev 1961; Deleuze and Guattari 1987: 40–5, 66–7, 108, 142–3).

Let's take, as an illustration, a piece of wood. Royal science will want it milled to established specifications – as a 2 by 4, for instance – so it can be used in building construction whose designs are based on the availability of lumber conforming to certain predictable 'constants' (size, regularity of grain, strength, surface appearance, etc.). Any knots that occur are considered mere imperfections, and may indeed lower the quality rating of the piece of wood as construction lumber, or preclude its use altogether. A sculptor, standing in here for the nomad scientist, will assess the piece of wood very differently. For the sculptor, knots and grain irregularities appear as singularities, features that inhere in the wood-matter as its unique form of content. And in the sculptor's hands, each singularity can become a substance of expression: a knot may become the eye of a fish; a grain pattern, the waves of the sea. Or something else entirely: the content–expression relation here is one of contingency, not necessity (Deleuze and Guattari 1987: 409; Massumi 1992: 10–20).

This illustration may appear to be far from scientific, but there are fields within science – of which we are becoming increasingly aware, although some were already known to the Greeks – where singularities rather than constants abound. Fluid dynamics is perhaps the best known of these fields: it is impossible to predict exactly where an accelerating liquid will swerve, or even to which side of a moving stream an eddy will form; there are no constant laws for these phenomena (Deleuze and Guattari 1987: 361–3). Royal science was in fact constituted in part by the rejection of fluid dynamics in favour of solids; but even for solids, gravitational dynamics are only rigorously predictable between two bodies: the effects of gravity on three or more bodies of roughly equal mass and in close proximity become as unpredictable as a liquid whorl.

Here we are broaching the fields of so-called complexity theory and non-linear mathematics, which lie well beyond the scope of this essay (DeLanda 2002; Bonta and Protevi 2004). A more familiar illustration of nomad science, however, is available in evolutionary biology.[1] Crucially, evolutionary science cannot predict evolution or reproduce it experimentally; what it does instead is *follow* its development. (It is no less a science for this.) To put the point another way, there are no universal laws governing evolution, only patterns of what has happened. Even the original notion of 'survival of the fittest' has given way more recently to the notion of 'survival of the sufficiently fit': not only is random mutation (by definition) not predictable or reproducible, but neither is the interaction of a mutation with its environment. Rewind and rerun evolution 100 times, as the scientific wisdom now has it, and *even if* you *could* reproduce the same mutations, you would get up to 100 different results (Gould 2002). Evolution is thus a matter of what Deleuze and Guattari call 'itineration' rather than 'iteration' or reproduction according to universal law: it traces a path that can be followed, but not predicted (Deleuze and Guattari 1987: 372–4).

Turning to the social consequences of the distinction between royal and nomad science, Deleuze and Guattari insist that 'nomad sciences do not destine science to take on an autonomous power, or even to have an autonomous development' (ibid.: 373) – by which they mean autonomous from other social practices. And this difference involves among other things the relations of sciences to work: 'Nomad science does not have the same relation to work as royal science' (ibid.: 368). Of crucial importance here is the distinction between the technical division of labour and the social division of labour. The technical division of labour arises from the level of complexity of tasks, skills, and knowledges involved in a given process of production; but it does not entail any hierarchy of status or power among specialists participating in the process. The social division of labour, by contrast, although it often overlaps with a technical division of labour, involves distinctions of prestige or power that have nothing intrinsically to do with the skills exercised or level of participation in the process. Most notable is the social division between intellectual and manual labour, which is an essential feature of royal science. According to Deleuze and Guattari royal science requires:

> a dequalification of labor. [And although] [t]he State does not give power (*pouvoir*) to the intellectuals or conceptual innovators . . . it makes them a strictly dependent organ with an autonomy that is only imaginary yet is sufficient to divest of all their power (*puissance*) those whose job it becomes simply to reproduce or implement. (1987: 368, translation modified)

Due to the power of royal science to extract abstract concepts from the concrete operations of productive practices, conception and execution become distinct activities, and each gets assigned to a distinct status group. Francis Bacon's programme for the development of early-modern science illustrates this process perfectly: he charged agents of the Royal Academy with the task of visiting local workshops to extract whatever knowledges were in practice there, and then bringing them back to the academy where they would be elaborated into formal scientific knowledge, only to be eventually reapplied to the production process in the form of technology, thereby liquidating the autonomy of the workers and subjecting them to technico-managerial control (Bacon 2000).

It is significant that this is not a directly or obviously political form of control: it stems instead from a form of the division of labour which, howsoever 'natural' or necessary it has come to seem as the gap between conception and execution has widened with the ever-increasing application of technology, nonetheless operates normatively to subordinate manual to intellectual labour. As Deleuze and Guattari insist:

> if the state always finds it necessary to repress the minor and nomad sciences . . . it does so not because the content of these sciences is inexact or imperfect . . . but because they imply a division of labor opposed to the norms of the State. (Deleuze and Guattari 1987: 368)

To the royal conception of science that sees universal laws as distinct from yet applicable to inert matter corresponds a conception of society as being composed of inert subjects susceptible and indeed bound to the application of universal laws by the state (ibid.: 369). From which Deleuze and Guattari will conclude that 'the way in which a science, or a conception of science, participates in the organization of the social field, and in particular [the way in which it] induces a division of labor [intellectual/manual], is part of that science itself' (ibid.: 368–9). I want to argue the same thing about jazz and classical music: the manner in which each contributes to the organisation of the social field is intrinsic to its heuristic value relative to the other, for comparing the two types of music can reveal a great deal about different forms of social organisation in general. At the same time, we will see that improvisational jazz involves processes of 'itinerary following' rather than 'iterative reproducing,' just as nomad science does.[2]

Nomad Music

Jazz is not the only instance in the field of 'play' – playing music, playing sports, playing games – that can be characterised as nomadic. In *A Thousand Plateaus*, for instance, Deleuze and Guattari expound on the differences between go and chess: the one involves a multiplicity of interchangeable pieces operating in an open or 'smooth' space, the other a hierarchy of distinct pieces operating in a closed and 'striated' space (Deleuze and Guattari 1987: 352–3). As for jazz, two points are crucial in linking it to what Deleuze and Guattari say about nomadism and nomad science. For one thing, improvisational jazz repudiates 'reproducing' in favour of following or indeed creating. Whereas classical symphony orchestras today merely *reproduce* in performance what a composer has already created and written down in the score, jazz bands intentionally depart from what is already known in order to improvise and create something new.[3] Even when following a chord-chart, for example, jazz improvisation is far more itinerative than iterative: solos vary in length; there is not necessarily a set order as to who takes one when; a clever soloist can change keys or tempo unexpectedly, and challenge the others to follow his or her lead; and so on.

And this brings us to the second point: in jazz improvisation, there is no need for a band-leader (even if soloists sometimes serve such a function temporarily, and get the band to follow them in a spontaneous key- or tempo-change), whereas classical symphony orchestras always have a conductor as well as a composer. The classical symphony orchestra requires a *transcendent instance of command* in the figure of the conductor to guarantee coordination, whereas coordination arises more spontaneously and in a manner *immanent* to the group activity in jazz. Classical music entails a social division of labour whereby some merely execute what others (composers and conductors) conceive and command. There's none of that to speak of in improvisational jazz.

The importance of the concept of nomadism for social analytics, in sum, depends on the notion that *the manner in which forms of human activity contribute to the organisation of the social field, and in particular the way in which they induce a certain division of labour or not (social versus technical, intellectual versus manual), constitutes an intrinsic part of that activity itself.* Nomadism, then, designates forms of activity where the modes and principles of social organisation are *immanent* to the activity itself, not imposed by a *transcendent* instance from above; where itinerant following and group creation prevail over the issuing and obeying of commands. It should perhaps be noted that this is a heuristic distinction: no real instance of human activity will appear purely immanent or transcendent. The contrast between jazz bands and symphony orchestras nevertheless offers a useful illustration of nomadism and the key distinction between immanence and transcendence, between what Deleuze and Guattari call the plane of composition and the plane of organisation (Deleuze and Guattari 1987: 154–6, 254–6, 265–72).

Nomad Management

That having been said, it is worth turning to an illustration that appears to belie this distinction, and yet ends up confirming its importance and heuristic value. I am referring to the Orpheus Symphony Orchestra – which prides itself on being 'the world's only conductorless orchestra' (Seifter and Economy 2001). Perhaps equally significant, the business side of the orchestra, the OSO Corporation, now operates entirely without a CEO. How can a symphony orchestra perform without a conductor? How can a business enterprise run without a chief executive officer? Answers are to be found in the management principles developed nearly a hundred years ago by Mary Parker Follett, who is today considered a 'prophet of management' by leading management consultants (Follett 1995 and 1998). Although Orpheus still reproduces pre-composed music from a score, nearly all its other procedures are quite unlike those of a standard symphony orchestra. Most remarkably, the function of conducting has in Follett's terms been 'de-personalised' (Follet 1995: 127–8ff.): instead of being assigned exclusively and permanently to one person – *the* conductor – the conducting function circulates among various members of the orchestra. Whoever is collectively considered to have the best knowledge of and/or feel for a certain piece of music is chosen to conduct it; when the piece of music changes, so does the conductor. Similar Follettian principles apply to the function of artistic director, repertory manager and so on: group deliberation determines who will temporarily fulfil various functions for specific musical choices or periods of time. And remarkably enough, these same principles are being extended from the music to the business side of the Orpheus Symphony Orchestra. The roles of CEO, CFO, marketing director and so on circulate temporarily among the musicians, depending on collective assessment of relative talent and skills in various areas and of the quality of members' actual performance in the different roles. Regardless of the type of music being performed, Orpheus has managed to recast the 'organisation of the social field' of a symphony orchestra along the lines of improvisational jazz.

But de-personalisation is not the only Follettian principle being adopted by leading management theorists such as Peter Drucker (Follett 1995: 1–10; Drucker 1977 and 2001). Central to Follett's conception of management was her critique of what she called 'particularist' individualism: the notion that individuals were discrete atoms and that good management amounted to knowing how to combine them in the most efficient way. Her unit of analysis was instead the group, and the individual was always understood only as a member of a group – indeed, of a multiplicity of groups: 'the individual is not a unit but a centre of forces (both centripetal and centrifugal), and consequently [the group] is not a collection of units but a complex of radiating and converging, crossing and recrossing energies' (Follet 1998: 75). Follett's group, then, amounts to what Deleuze and Guattari call a collective assemblage (Deleuze and Guattari 1987: 80–5). And she was equally careful as they to define what kind of group was involved and the nature of the relation between group(s) and the individual.

The group was to be distinguished most of all from the crowd, from an undifferentiated mass. For what distinguished true group dynamics from a mechanical or organic totality was what she called the *integration* or *interpenetration of difference*. 'Democracy,' she insisted, 'rests on the well-grounded assumption that society is neither a collection of units nor an organism but a network of human relations . . . The essence of society is difference, related difference' (Follet 1998: 7, 33). The power of human groups arises from the articulation of differences, not from the simple aggregation of units, and the articulation of differences cannot occur via the ballot box: it requires a group process that through discussion generates what Follett calls a 'common thought' that 'harmonizes difference through interpenetration' (ibid.: 34).[4] The active, generative nature of group process is key, for 'the essential feature of common thought is not that it is held in common, but that it has been produced in common' (ibid.: 34). Common thought is the outcome of a process whereby differences are not suppressed or superseded but integrated into a whole; and the strength of this whole lies precisely in the preservation and interrelation of difference:

> [The group] needs my difference, not as an absolute, but just so much difference as will relate me. Differences develop within the social process and are united through the social process . . . It is not my uniqueness which makes me of value to the whole but my power of relating. (Follet 1998: 63–4)

The group, functioning as a plane of composition, articulates or integrates difference from the 'bottom–up', whereas the crowd has order imposed on it 'top–down', as a plane of organisation. Crowds, moreover, operate on the principles of imitation or likeness and obedience rather than difference and articulation. Members of an undifferentiated crowd are simply all alike; but even members of a differentiated crowd do not contribute their differences to a group process, but merely imitate roles that have been assigned to them from on high.

From group dynamics emerges a kind of horizontal rather than vertical authority, an authority which Follett insists

> . . . does not come from separating people, from dividing them into two classes, those who command and those who obey . . . [but] from the intermingling of all, of my work fitting into your work and yours into mine, and from the intermingling of forces a power being created which will control those forces. (Follet 1995: 154)

Follett thus posits a crucial distinction between 'power-with' and 'power-over' (Follet 1995: 103–16). Power-with emerges from the articulation of differences each of which contributes positively to a whole that is thereby greater than the merely arithmetic sum of its parts. Power-over, by contrast, operates by constraint and limitation: it is the power to say no or to limit others to the imitation of pre-determined roles, and the power to command obedience. Follett's key distinction has had some influence on recent feminist thought,[5] but needs to be distinguished from the better-known distinction between positive and negative liberty. Negative liberty is simply freedom from constraint, while positive liberty is the freedom to actually do something. Negative liberty and power-over are clearly incompatible: negative liberty is the freedom from control exercised by someone who has power over you. But positive liberty and power-with are not the same. For the 'power-to' do something entailed by positive liberty characterises both planes of composition and planes of organisation, both groups and crowds: a football team or an army battalion certainly has the power-to do something, regardless of its being organised vertically rather than articulated horizontally. The concept of power-with designates more than the mere ability to accomplish something: it highlights the quality of the organisation of the social field entailed by the *form of activity* doing the accomplishing; it designates, in short, the strength of participatory democracy in action.

There is little doubt that Follett's ideas about power-with and the group dynamics of integrating difference first arose from her long commitment to and experience with participatory democracy in the Progressive era neighbourhood organisation movement.[6] But she quickly extended her insights to society at large, conceived of as a group of multiple groups:

> Progress from one point of view is a continuous widening of the area of association . . . [from neighborhoods to] labor organizations, cooperative societies, consumers' leagues, associations of employers and employed, municipal movements . . . the Men's City Club, the Women's City Club; professional societies [which] are multiplying overnight . . . (Follet 1998: 193–4)

The same principle of the articulation and integration of differences would govern the association of groups as did the formation of groups out of individual differences to begin with: 'the same force that forms a group may form a group of groups' (ibid.: 285). Follett thus arrives at a conception of state power and a definition of state sovereignty that are perfectly consistent with what she has seen in the dynamic of neighbourhood and other local group associations: 'The sovereign is not the crowd, it is not millions of unrelated atoms, but men joining together to form a real whole' (ibid.: 283).

> A group is sovereign over itself as far as it is capable of creating one out of several or many. A state is sovereign only as it has the power of creating one in which all are. Sovereignty is the power engendered by a complete interdependence becoming conscious of itself . . . it is the imperative of a true collective will. (Ibid.: 271)

Significantly, however, it was at this point in the development of her thought (and after the debacle of the First World War and the Treaty of Versailles) that Follett turned her attention from social theory to management: coordinating the relatively convergent interests of a neighbourhood group or a business enterprise according to the principles of power-with and articulated difference was one thing; overcoming the antagonism between capital and labour or unifying an entire nation of groups into a single truly collaborative state association according to the same principles would be something altogether different. She did propose 'collective self-control' as a third way between *laissez-faire* capitalism and state socialism, but she turned most of her own attention to refining the principles of management.[7]

Nomad Citizenship

What prevailed in place of Follett's conception of state sovereignty was a more Hegelian view that saw the role of the state not as articulating and enriching the lives and interests of its citizens, but rather as transcending all such private interests and subordinating them to the advancement of the 'objective spirit' of a nation through warfare (Hegel 1996). The view opposed to Follett's would crystallise in the writings of Carl Schmitt, whose *The Concept of the Political* (1996), though written well after Follett's *The New State*, appears to counter her conception of the state practically point by point.[8] Where for Follett the unification of the state – up to and including a world-state – is determined immanently and *internally*, as we have seen, by the growing strength of groups whose differences are articulated to their mutual benefit, for Schmitt the unity of the state is determined purely *externally*, by the relation of enmity between friend and foe. As he insists,

> [Any] political entity presupposes the real existence of an enemy and therefore coexistence with another political entity. As long as a state exists, there will thus always be in the world more than one state. A world state

which embraces the entire globe and all of humanity cannot exist. (Schmitt 1996: 53)

Schmitt recognises, of course, that any social body will contain a number of heterogeneous allegiances in addition to allegiance to the sovereign state: someone can, he acknowledges, be 'a member of a religious institution, nation, labor union, family, sports club, and many other associations' (ibid.: 41). Characteristic of what we can call these 'horizontal' affiliations is that they 'impose on him [sic] a cluster of obligations in such a way that no one of these associations can be said to be decisive and sovereign' (ibid.: 41). But there is according to Schmitt one 'vertical' allegiance that transcends all others, and stands out from them as *the master-allegiance* – and this is, of course, allegiance to the state. And the reason the state commands supreme allegiance from its citizens is that it has a near-monopoly over matters of life and death, and an absolute monopoly on declarations of war between friend and foe:

> The ever-present possibility of a friend-and-enemy grouping suffices to forge a decisive entity which transcends the mere societal-associational groupings. The political entity is something specifically different, and vis-à-vis other associations, decisive. (Schmitt 1996: 45)

Against liberal and pluralist (or Follett's federal) conceptions of the state according to which it appears 'at times . . . as one association among other associations, at times as the product of a federalism of social associations or an umbrella association of a conglomeration of associations' (ibid.: 44), Schmitt's state distinguishes itself absolutely from all other forms of social allegiance because it can declare war. Thereby it legitimates killing in its name and demands the sacrifice of citizens' lives for its own sake: 'By virtue of this power over the physical life of men, the political community transcends all other associations or societies' (ibid.: 47). Political or state citizenship, for Schmitt, thus turns entirely on the distinction between friend and enemy; and it is the role of the state – and only the state – to decide for a social body who its enemies are, and thereby mobilise it for war.

Now if Schmitt's transcendent view of state sovereignty and state citizenship has prevailed over Follett's immanent conception, this is not because Schmitt's view is more cogent than Follett's (it is not), but because his view seems to represent the behaviour of nation-states in recent European history better than hers: the primary function of the modern state has indeed been and continues to be to wage war. It is in this context that the concept of nomad citizenship is so useful, inasmuch as it presents a mode of citizenship *not* limited to politics and the state – indeed, it recommends a mode of citizenship that would ideally *supplant* political citizenship as it is conventionally understood and *replace* it with other modes of citizenship. But before turning to these alternative modes of citizenship, it is important to understand what's wrong with citizenship as defined exclusively or primarily in relation to the state. Why is state sovereignty in decline? Why is allegiance to the state increasingly difficult to sustain, and why are the necessarily desperate measures to sustain it so disastrous? And why should what's left of state citizenship be curtailed, if not eliminated, in favour of other modes of citizenship?

It would be too simple to say only that instead of reconciling and articulating difference into a unified whole, as Follett prescribes, the state has since she wrote usually taken the side of capital against labour and aggravated the gap between them – as true as this may be in a general sense. For there must be limits to the state's ability to command the allegiance of its citizens if it too obviously takes sides against the majority. And to say that the state's primary function is waging war does not mean that such is its *only* function, but rather that waging war increasingly supersedes all others functions, which the state finds increasingly difficult to fulfil. What about public-sector functions other than war, forms of sovereignty other than that based on friend versus foe? Here it must be said that the state today is very hard pressed. Take for example the issue of economic sovereignty: even the United States – and despite its undisputed military hegemony – no longer has sovereignty over commerce; this has been ceded to supra-national organisations and trade agreements (WTO, IMF, GATT, etc.) in the service of transnational capital; no country can any longer take responsibility for protecting the environment or the health (much less the earning-power) of its citizens if these run counter to the strictures of the transnational trade agreements. Or take the state's rapidly declining role in the provision of social services: public education, health care, urban development, public transportation and housing, not to mention the arts – they all get cut back, if not cut out altogether, because of the constant pressure of capital to reduce reproduction costs, either directly, by reducing corporate taxation, or indirectly, by displacing such costs on to citizen/taxpayers who can no longer afford to pay them out of their individual wages. What possible allegiance could citizens owe to a state that does so little for them?

This does not, however, mean that capital can simply do without the state: on the contrary, the function of the state is now that of 'organising conjunctions of decoded flows' in the service of capital accumulation (Deleuze and Guattari 1987: 451). And waging war is in fact a crucial mechanism for guaranteeing the realisation of surplus-value for capital and avoiding its endemic crises of overproduction. Nothing addresses overproduction and keeps the wheels of industry turning like a good war – especially today's high-tech wars in which each guided missile strike or smart bomb explosion means instant millions of dollars in replacement costs. State expenditure on war may seem to contradict the general impoverishment of the public sector outlined above, but the military–industrial complex is predominantly private sector and notoriously capital-intensive, especially compared to the capital non-intensive public sector. Schmitt may be right that war is the state's essential political *raison d'être*, but war's being the very lifeblood of capitalism as the perennial solution to its perennial crises of overproduction must come in a close second.[9]

War, finally, is at the same time the prime means of mobilising popular/ electoral support: it may not yet be the only thing that excites citizens/ voters, but it is certainly what excites them the most, as George Orwell (among others) showed us over fifty years ago. In the absence of other, more positive, internal inducements (for the reasons explained above), the modern democratic state *must* continually reinvent Schmitt's external friend-or-foe dichotomy and constantly mobilise for one damned war after another – Grenada, Panama, the 'war on drugs', Gulf War Sr, Gulf War Jr, and so on – in order to command any allegiance of its citizens at all. In other words, and as Paul Virilio has shown, the modern state only functions via terrorism – that is, by terrorising *its own citizens* (not to mention the external others) into constantly fearing threats to its 'way of life' supposedly coming from some foreign foe or other (Virilio 1975). Terrorising and patriotising state citizens are two sides of the same coin. This is the sense in which Schmitt was right – but only because state terror is the only way left to sustain citizens' master-allegiance to the state.

To all of this, nomad citizenship offers a critical alternative. Its main thrust is to redefine citizenship so that it includes and legitimates a wide range of group-allegiances of the kind Follett emphasised – and especially to deprive the state of its claim to any transcendent master-allegiance. These multiple group allegiances would be, in the sense that Deleuze and Guattari along with Follett describe, *immanent*: their power – their power- with – arises from participatory democracy and the self-coordinating articulation of differences to the mutual benefit of all concerned; they would serve and foster the enrichment of life internally or locally rather than thrive on and foster external threats to it, as the transcendent allegiance of state-citizenship does. Developing multiple allegiances to social groups 'beneath' the level of the state would extend the benefits and responsibilities of citizenship throughout social life, would in effect dissolve the boundaries separating the state and electoral politics from civil society, and would ideally encourage the growth of smaller-scale participatory democracy in numerous venues to accompany – and eventually to supplant – the large-scale representative system we have now. So-called 'entreprises citoyennes' – said to represent approximately 10 per cent of European employment today (Rouillé d'Orfueil 2002) – offer a prime illustration of such socially redistributed citizenship, where the quality of the social relations of production as well as the social impact of the products or services produced count for more than the mere 'bottom line' of profitability.

But nomad citizenship includes as well a global component, in addition to this small-scale, local component – and here Deleuze and Guattari enable us to move decisively beyond Mary Parker Follett's perspective, as prescient and insightful as it was. For nomad citizenship is not just local, it is also a citizenship of planetary scope, quite unlike the citizenships available for small-scale groups like Follett's that meet face-to-face or define themselves – however broadly – as 'friends' or as somehow 'the same'. We might call this the economic or market component of nomad citizenship, in contrast to the political nature of state citizenship. For it depends on the capacity of market exchange to link far-flung groups or individuals together in a social bond that defines them *neither* as *friends nor* as *enemies*, but simply as temporary partners in exchange. In this way, the market is able to capitalise on differences without converting them into military hostilities. For the virtue of market exchange – *provided of course* that it is voluntary and fair – is that it enriches the lives of interested parties by making regional, ethnic, religious, cultural (and many other) differences available to all. That is, of course, a huge proviso: that market exchange become voluntary and fair.[10] But with a world market freed from the transcendent command of capital, we could become nomad citizens whether we chose to leave home or not – for market exchange would do as much (or as little) of the travelling for us as we wished.

Deleuze and Guattari arrived at their assessment of the positive potential of markets and their preference for economics over politics based on a comparison undertaken in the *Anti-Oedipus* (1983) between capitalism and other modes of production. They contrast older modes of social organisation based on qualitative codes and representation with capitalist social organisation, which is based instead on the quantitative calculus of the market. What is distinctive about the market is for one thing that it neatly deconstructs the ur-political dichotomy of friends and enemies: partners in free-market exchange are neither, which gives market relations extraordinary flexibility and world-wide scope. For another thing, the market effectively frees desire from capture in codes, a positive effect of capitalism, which is in Deleuze and Guattari's view even more important today than its extraordinary productivity, which was so admired by Marx and Engels (1998). Money and markets, in essence, operate to free individuals from relations of personal sub-servience and/or political subordination. Ultimately, however, Deleuze and Guattari conclude that capitalism has both an immanent, 'power-with' component – the tremendous deterritorialising force of money and markets – and a transcendent or quasi-transcendent, 'power-over' com-ponent – the forces of reterritorialisation acting in the service of private capital (Deleuze and Guattari 1987; Holland 1999: 59ff.). Economics, or more precisely the abstract calculus of the market, subverts the older power relations of explicit domination, and knits new social ties beneath the level of political authority, subjugation and representation. Yet cap-italism at the same time installs a new form of 'power-over' by yoking the dynamics of market exchange to private capital-accumulation. The transcendent 'power-over' of private capital, in this view, acts as a brake and a limit to the immanent dynamics of the market, which left unfet-tered would generate increasing freedom and material abundance for all.

In a more thoroughly historical set of studies of the emergence of capitalism in early modern Europe, Fernand Braudel arrived at a similar conclusion, which he casts in terms of markets and anti-markets (Braudel 1973). For Braudel, the free-market exchange of commodities continu-ally enriches, diversifies and enlarges human capabilities and sensibilities. Anti-market monopolies and oligopolies, however, because of their size, wealth and/or political clout, can control the market to their own advan-tage, thereby limiting its dynamics according to the dictates of private accumulation – both qualitatively (what gets produced) as well as quan-titatively (how much is available for public consumption). If we agree, in line with the conclusions of Braudel and Deleuze and Guattari, that a truly free market would sponsor new social relations of greater freedom, diversity and material abundance once the 'power-over' of capitalist anti-market forces are eliminated, then we have a conception of the material basis and historical possibility for nomad citizenship: the world market would become a vehicle for the coordination of difference so as to enrich and enhance life rather than to exploit and threaten it.

Under these circumstances, both associational groups – residential, occupational and whatever else – and the world market as a whole would operate on the nomadic model of improvisational jazz: order would emerge immanently 'from below', from the interactions of a multiplic-ity of social agents both within self-organising enterprises and on the world market, rather than being imposed or constrained from above by institutions of power and accumulated wealth. This free market would respond to supply and demand, not to dictates of capital and the anti-market pressures of private accumulation; rather than being devoted to the restrictive valorisation of privately owned capital, social production would be devoted to the continual enhancement of production, consumption and social relations themselves: this is the sense in which the immanent sociality of jazz improvisation can serve as an instructive example for nomadic citizenship.

References

Allen, A. (1998), 'Rethinking Power', *Hypatia*, 13:1.

Bacon, F. (2000), *The Advancement of Learning*, Oxford: Clarendon.

Bailey, D. (1982), *Musical Improvisation: Its Nature and Practice in Music*, Englewood Cliffs, NJ: Prentice-Hall.

Bonta, M. and Protevi, J. (2004), *Deleuze and Geophilosophy: A Guide and Glossary*, Edinburgh: Edinburgh University Press.

Braudel, F. (1973), *Capitalism and Material Life: 1400–1800*, New York: Harper and Row.

DeLanda, M. (2002), *Intensive Science and Virtual Philosophy*, London: Continuum.

Deleuze, G. and Guattari, F. (1983), *Anti-Oedipus: Capitalism and Schizophrenia*, trans. R. Hurley, M. Seem and H. R. Lane, Minneapolis: University of Minnesota Press.

Deleuze, G. and Guattari, F. (1987), *A Thousand Plateaus: Capitalism and Schizophrenia*, trans. B. Massumi, Minneapolis, University of Minnesota Press.

Drucker, P. F. (1977), *People and Performance: The Best of Peter Drucker on Management*, New York: Harper's College Press.

Drucker, P. F. (2001), *The Essential Drucker: Selections from the Management Works of Peter F. Drucker*, New York: HarperCollins.

Follett, M. P. (1995), *Mary Parker Follett – Prophet of Management: A Celebration of Writings from the 1920s*, Boston: Harvard Business School Press.

Follett, M. P. (1998), *The New State: Group Organization the Solution of Popular Government*, Pennsylvania: The Pennsylvania State University Press.

Gould, S. J. (2002), *The Structure of Evolutionary Theory*, Cambridge: Harvard University Press.

Hartsock, N. (1981), 'Political Change: Two Perspectives on Power', in C. Bunch et al. (eds), *Building Feminist Theory: Essays from Quest*, New York and London, Longman.

Hegel, G. W. F. (1996), *Philosophy of Right*, Amherst, New York: Prometheus Books.

Hjelmslev, L. (1961), *Prolegomena to a Theory of Language*, Madison: University of Wisconsin Press.

Holland, E. W. (1999), *Deleuze and Guattari's 'Anti-Oedipus': Introduction to Schizoanalysis*, New York and London: Routledge.

Marx, Karl and Engels, F. (1998), *The Communist Manifesto: A Modern Edition*, ed. Eric Hobsbawm, London and New York: Verso.

Massumi, B. (1992), *A User's Guide to Capitalism and Schizophrenia: Deviations from Deleuze and Guattari*, Cambridge: MIT Press.

Perkins, J. (2004), *Confessions of an Economic Hit Man*, San Francisco: Berrett-Koehler.

Rouillé d'Orfueil, H. (2002), *Economie, le réveil des citoyens*, Paris: La Découverte.

Schmitt, C. (1996), *The Concept of the Political*, Chicago: University of Chicago Press.

Seifter, H. and Economy, P. (2001), *Leadership Ensemble: Lessons in Collaborative Management from the World's Only Conductorless Orchestra*, New York: Times Books/Henry Holt.

Virilio, P. (1975), *Art of the Motor*, trans. J. Rose, Minneapolis: University of Minnesota Press.

Zack, M. H. (2000), 'Jazz Improvisation and Organizing: Once More from the Top', *Organization Science*, 11: 2.

Notes

1. Deleuze and Guattari 1987 reject evolutionism in anthropology (as a form of the myth of linear 'progress') but not the theory of evolution itself, whose contemporary versions are in fact non-linear in important respects (Gould 2002).
2. There are many different kinds of jazz, involving different degrees of improvisation; Zack 2000: 232 provides a chart distinguishing the minimal freedom of 'interpretation' characteristic of classical music from the 'embellishment' and 'variation' characteristic of traditional (Swing) jazz and bebop, respectively, reserving the term 'improvisation' for the maximum freedom characteristic of post-bebop or free jazz, where not just the melody but the complete musical structure is played *with* rather than played *within*.
3. At the moment of emergence of what we today call classical music there was a considerable amount of improvisation, but it was rarely group improvisation of the kind that characterises jazz, see Bailey 1982.
4. This notion of 'common thought' clearly bears strong resemblance to Spinoza's idea of 'common notions' – and indeed much of what Follett says about society has strong Spinozan resonance. She is careful to distinguish her view of the integration of differences into an articulated whole in group dynamics from the Hegelian synthesis of contradictions, Follett 1998: 300; Follet 1995: 115–18.
5. See Follett 1998: xvii–xxii; see also Allen 1998 and Hartsock 1981.
6. See for instance Follett 1998: 'in a neighborhood we have . . . life . . . enlarged and enriched by the friction of ideas which comes from the meeting of people of different opportunities and different tastes and different standards . . . different education, different interests, different standards. Think of the doctor, the man who runs a factory, the organist and choir leader, the grocer, the minister, the watch-maker, the school-teacher, all living within a few blocks of one another' (Follet 1998: 196). On her intellectual evolution from politics to management theory, see Follett 1998: xxxi–lix.
7. See Follett 1998: 162–85, where she addresses alternatives to both *laissez-faire* capitalism and state socialism.
8. See Schmitt 1996. Schmitt was in fact responding explicitly to French syndicalism (Sorel and Duguit) and English pluralism (Cole and Laski); see especially: 39–42.
9. The other modern state function, in addition to waging war, is implanting permanent debt, whether through Keynesian spending for war, or through the export of capital to an underdeveloped world which cannot possibly pay it back (IMF, World Bank); on this latter, see Perkins 2004.
10. The best guarantee of that proviso is what I call 'free-market communism' – a post-capitalist market system based on the elimination of wage-labour (and therefore of capital and exploitation) and its replacement with production cooperatives (Follett's self-organising occupational groups).

Chapter 11

Deleuze, Change, History

Jussi Vähämäki and Akseli Virtanen

Gilles Deleuze is a philosopher of revolution and may even be a revolutionary thinker. Revolution is certainly the milieu of his thinking, where he breaks things open.

Whatever their target, his critiques have nothing to do with understanding, nor with attentive or thoughtful action. Instead, Deleuze misunderstands things and these misunderstandings have rules – that is, they repeat. Repetition sets things in motion, transforming them, and Deleuze's metaphysics is constructed for this virtual context of movement and change.

Here understanding offers only a weak mode of thought because understanding is always bound to its historical contingencies. The concept of change, by contrast, which grounds Deleuze's critique, must be radically distinguished from the concept of history. It is in this difference that the effective revolutionary nature of his work may be found.

Revolution *is* Change

What characterises revolution? In one word: *duration*. And duration is always something that resists, something that endures. Resistance always has a poetic aspect. Duration goes beyond the limits of the linear or spatial conception of time. In this sense revolutions are monuments of collective action, they are *aere perennius*, but without spatial existence. There is no room for them. Revolutions exist only in memory, in time. This means that revolution never 'is' but rather 'goes on'. It is an event in time. This temporal, enduring dimension of revolution is also its metaphysical dimension.

Revolutions may make history, they may produce results, they may have outcomes and consequences. They may also end in disaster. But they never *are* their outcomes or their consequences, their history or their disaster.

They cannot be reduced to their historical conditions because they are manifestations of the subjectivities and desires of people. Already the advocates and adversaries of the French revolution agreed about this. Revolutions change; they are change. And change does not originate in history, it takes place without reasons, it proceeds *in their place*, instead of that which always already is (the *logos*). It is not born of reactions or answers; it has nothing to do with communication. Change is creation without a reason, action without a cause. It is not possible to reduce it to its preconditions, to pre-existing reasons or laws. Revolutions are careless and haphazard (and in this sense there is something anti-Heideggerian and creative in them). They are not born from this or that injustice, they do not proceed from any configuration of being.[1] Indeed, there is always something to come in them, a change, a becoming. That is why we could say that in Deleuze there is an anthropological idea of the human animal: the human being is not a reactive creature that responds to the stimulus that comes from its environment, its ambience. Humans pose problems – they are problems – and through the posing of problems they extend their power. The flexibility of humans, their capacity to live in almost every imaginable environment, to bask in any conceivable ambience, is an active and not a passive faculty. The human being creates its own ambience and its own problems. It is an animal that is able to change its fate.[2]

Revolution is neither past nor future, nor is it only present. The tense of revolution is rather indeterminate duration – a temporality that cannot be measured or divided into parts, meted or rationed out. Henri Bergson taught us that time is indeterminate. It is that which prevents everything from being immediately given, that which prevents beings from being reducible to their manifestations in space or to their positions in the chronological continuum of time. Time slows us down, or, rather, 'time is slowness'. In this sense it must be creative. It must be 'a means of production' and its existence proves that there is indeterminateness in beings: 'time is exactly this indeterminateness' (Bergson 1991: 133). As duration, revolution is characterised by this indeterminate movement and motion and is therefore without a subject. Revolution never takes up a position in space, never takes place; on the contrary, it perpetually encroaches upon the hierarchies of space. It rolls back the boundaries of the territory. It is change.

But what is change made of if not of causes and effects in space of measurable and divisible moments in time? Is what we have already called the metaphysical dimension of Deleuze's thought simply a referential gesture to a mythic or vitalistic power of life? And is this alleged vitalism only a kind of pseudonym for violence (Girard 1978: 84–120)?[3] Let us state this clearly: to introduce a vitalistic explanation implies that there is a transcendental and privatised (or individual) point in Deleuze's thinking. To speak of vitalism in the work of Deleuze leads to the negation of one of the basic concepts of his work: the concept of multiplicity.[4]

Change is Made of Multiplicity

That which endures, that which resists, is not a vague principle of life. Deleuze approaches duration through the *multitudo*, the notion of a multiplicity. But what is multiplicity?

First, multiplicity resists. Multiplicity's resistance finds its expression in repetition, in what is impossible to replace or to represent. There is not a single point in the multitude that is not in movement. It is constantly vibrating and trembling, rushing out in all the possible directions, always escaping. As Deleuze is concerned to point out, multiplicity is not an adjective or an attribute, because it is a noun. Multitudo is not a 'one' constructed out of the 'many'; it is not composed of individuals or of a diversity of parts that are glued together. It does not amount to pluralism. It has nothing to do with tolerance, which is an attitude that makes sense only from within a majority. Multiplicity is minor. It takes every significant or meaningful political discourse and every rational need to the point where it breaks down. That is, thought can move, extend and connect only after the collapse of meaning, only when it has established a distance as far from the society and its needs as possible. Only then can thought effect a disequilibrium. All the muttering and buzzing of language are indicative of its materiality and its movement from major to minor. Machiavelli was right. Change comes from friction and abrasion, from disagreement and conflict. And this conflict is never a conflict about opinion or meaning; it is always material and sensible.

Second, multiplicity is an essential element that cannot be reduced to spatial distinctions. But in it something happens. It is in the concept of multiplicity and its materiality that we may find the central axis of a politics of immanent capitalism that is able to connect the central questions of politics to change. It is the starting point of Deleuzian politics and Deleuze's political philosophy. Multiplicity is an ontological force, a force that stretches every meaning to the point where it loses its way and meaning itself begins to grope in every possible direction, where it starts to unfold. This groping and unfolding is the movement that opens the a-signifying materiality of desire, liberating a desire that is always multiple and without a specific object, a desire that desires to create the world in its own image. We could even say that it is mimetic and that mimesis is just that: the creative human power to create the world as its own image. Mimesis, mimetic desire, a desire innate to the human and absolutely self-contained (autarchic) and independent from any environment, has no need of pre-established order and security. It is constructive and not destructive; to attribute destructivity to desire is to force a transcendent principle inside it or above it. But it can quite simply not be reduced to a unit and it cannot be represented. It is absolutely devoid of any transcendent common denominator (like violence or destructivity or common sense). It consists of countless subjects, boundless amounts of points in absolutely differentiated constellations. It is a multitude of productive singularities, singularities whose productivity cannot be reduced to actual production: it is an absolute power outside the historical and visible world. But if it is outside this must not be understood spatially. Its exteriority is temporal: it is change, the event in time.[5]

Third, multiplicity resists. Multiplicity happens. Multiplicity endures. What, then, is the duration of multiplicity, or multiplicity's resistance as duration where something happens? Above all it concerns living together or 'with-living', which appears in everyday talk as, 'I have to live with it', 'I have been living with these people since . . .', and so on. It is 'co-existence'. It is a kind of being-with that does not coagulate into some discrete fact separate from the multitude of human beings on which its power could be grounded (such as the state). The 'with-living' is not actual in nature; the things we have to live with are not constantly in our minds but lie, rather, in some kind of indeterminate memory.

In *The Trial* Franz Kafka describes how Joseph K. notices that he seems to recruit women helpers, almost to his surprise; first Fräulein Bürstner, then the wife of the usher, and then that little nurse who appears to have some incomprehensible desire for K. These little helpers are as useless and as careless towards us as we are towards life's trivial things and little creatures: cockroaches or paper clips. But they are also indestructible and resistant. They are insistent. They pop up at the most unexpected moments producing all manner of noise, harm and joy. It is useless to convince a paper clip or a cockroach that the present order is essential to their existence. 'With-living' (co-existence), like desire, does not take place in space, through a particular common cause or a meaning that might be communicated. It does not have a particular reason. In multitude, everyone is 'alone together' or 'within oneself with others'. Everyone is there at the same time but is differentiated. That is why multitude does not actualise in particular actions by which what is revolutionary (or productive) and what is not, or who is revolutionary (or productive) and who is not, could be determined. Yet its being as duration is real. It is ideal but not abstract, real but not actual, heterogeneous but continuous. It is divisable only by a change in nature. This is about how Deleuze defines the category of the virtual, which is multitudo's distracted mode of being, the tense-form of revolution, the duration of change.[6]

Fourth, multitudo is creativity without models. It eschews actual acts, common causes or communicative contents. It is bare potentiality for anything: anything may be expected from it. Though it may be a little daring to connect Deleuze's notion of multiplicity to the classical notion of potentiality, which Giorgio Agamben has recently so aptly recovered for the present, it may clarify things a little to say that the mode of being proper to multiplicity is that of potentiality, *dynamis*. It is this fundamental category of philosophical thought which, according to Aristotle, is the mode in which human beings exist insofar as they know and produce: the human being exists as a purely potential being, without work or function, *ergon*, not engaged in actual activity, *energeia* (Aristotle 1990: 1045b–6a).[7] Potentiality as the ontological condition, the species-being of the human animal is always distinct from its correspondent acts, from the mediation of some use or justification, that is, from history. It is always something non-present but yet real, characterised by *adynamia*, impotentiality, the power not to pass into actuality.[8] What characterises potentiality is its dwelling outside of any function, its opposition to actuality (*energeia*), its dwelling outside history. It tends towards surpassing its own time, its own historical situation into which it is never fully translated. Potentiality is in this sense always outside history, withdrawn from the historical events by which it is never fully exhausted, like Achilles who sulks in his tent when the Trojans attack the camp of the Achaeans.

This means that potentiality cannot be completely actualised in a particular task, a single man or in any of the particular communities of men as if it resides somewhere in a multitude of mankind (Agamben 1996; 2004).[9] The potential character of life is always an experience or, better, an experiment of *power*. And there is no power, no movement and no change outside minorities, because it is the minorities that slow us down. Or as Deleuze loved to cite Paul Klee's slogan 'The people are missing.' It means that there is always something to come, something that remains potential and impotent, non-actualised and non-mediated. This something, which resists and endures, is not a transcendental (and spatial) principle like rationality or 'the social'. It does not belong to the sociological tradition, which would restore the logic of representation and substitution. It is always a multiplicity that contains or unfolds all the relations and it is a singularity that expresses or folds those relations.

Multiplicity as Living Labour

Paraphrasing Marx we may call this experimenting power *living labour*. As a power which is not reducible to any specific act or any specific mode of existence or historical age, living labour is multitudo's mode of being, always outside history and the conditions it presents us with. It is an activity that does not materialise into machinery or products but rather retreats from materiality and from turning into actual products.

Turning living labour into products is always also to restrict its potential nature, to bring it to a state of exception, to reduce it to a particular task, to stop its creative rush into history. Or as Marx writes, 'to discover the various uses of things is the work of history' (1887: I, 3). In other words, history is the result of carrying into effect or actualising different ways of using a substance. In this sense capital is a social relation based upon history in itself: the capitalistic society is the first to place in its centre this a-historical potentiality or non-historical core which is without any place or function but without which there would be no *change* (which must thus be distinguished from history).

Giorgio Agamben, for example, struggles with philosophical terminology in trying to explain the nature of our time which is characterised by the entrance of this a-historical dynamic and power of change directly into history: 'anarchic historicity itself . . . must now come to thought as *such*. It indicates, in other words, that now human beings take on possession of their own historical being, that is, their own impropriety' (Agamben 1996: 89).[10]

According to Deleuze, living labour is virtual and real, but not possible and actual. This is exactly how the transformation of the old Factory society (where it was still possible to distinguish between work and leisure, production and reproduction, life and politics) into the today's post-Fordist society (where the factory-office dissolves into society) has been described. We must understand that the foundation of productivity is 'no longer in the capitalistic investment but in the investment of the social brains. Or in other words: the maximal amount of freedom and the breaking of the disciplinary relations becomes the absolute foundation of creating wealth' (Negri 1998: 139–40). Where multiplicity has entered production, relations of cooperation instead combine in terms of the laws of attraction and rejection. Good are those relations which add power, extend and combine, bad are those which take apart and suffocate. This is where Deleuze's thinking forms an antipode to transcendent morals: it is *against* the morality and society of discipline, and *towards* an exposure of its transformation into the societies of control.

We return to our point of departure. Multitudo, 'living labour', which is central to today's immanent form of capitalism, is the virtual context of Deleuze's philosophy for which he constructs metaphysics. But why do we need metaphysics? Because without metaphysics multitudo remains abstract and without meaning. Without metaphysics, the multitude is a character in a B-movie, a feeble use of brains, activity without experimentation. In other words, without metaphysics, or *memory*, multitudo is little more than a reactive series of sequential sensations and therefore cannot create or change actively. Without memory as the force that keeps what is no longer in that which is, without memory as duration, the world would be forced to start over from scratch every instant. Without this fertile succession that contracts before and after all sensations, sensibility would amount to simple excitation.

Memory is time as subject (Deleuze 1986: 115). That is why Deleuze's project may be characterised as the metaphysics of the revolutionary transformation of capitalism at a moment when capitalism is forced to reveal communication as its moral or moralistic (majoritarian) *Grundnorm* to be obeyed without a second thought. The new post-Fordist society or biopolitical economy, which puts people to work with the entirety of their senses and relations, does not need this kind of metaphysics – a metaphysics that, unlike its predecessors, operates not on the level of space and meaning but on that of duration and time, but it cannot get rid of the cockroaches and paper clips. Like Walter Benjamin's famous dwarf, it is they who make the moves.

Exclusion or Controls?

The concept of multitudo, multiplicity, is the way to connect the central questions of the politics of our time to change. Its entrance into history makes the problem of *the one and the many*, which has characterised classical political philosophy, appear trivial or plainly stupid. This is not just a vague term of derision. Stupidity (*bêtise*) is a specific concept in Deleuze's philosophy, denoting a structure that construes thought as a quiz show in characterising communication (Deleuze 1994: Chapter 3). The problem of the one and the many is stupid because in a biopolitical economy the political question is no longer that of organising many different (people) through a common cause in order for each one of them to be able to express themselves in the best way possible without impeding the others. A common denominator or common language is no longer needed as the condition of cooperation. Multitudo is not conditioned by a common cause or by determinate meanings. It finds its community, its unity, in change.

Moreover, if the issue of the multitude is not that of organising the many, the modern problem of *inclusion and exclusion* becomes exceptionally stupid. Multiplicity does not draw a distinction between the included and excluded, it eschews transcendence absolutely:

> When the pack forms a ring around the fire, each man will have neighbors to the right and left, but no one behind him; his back is naked and exposed to the wilderness. We recognize this as a schizo position: being on the periphery, holding on by a hand or a foot. (Canetti quoted in Deleuze and Guattari 1987: 33–4)

The subject is never inside or outside but always on the edge, always 'alone together', always by itself in conjunction with others.

The antagonism between Deleuze's thinking and the theory of inclusion and exclusion is important because both our political thinking and our politics are focused on the themes of equality and equal rights on the one hand and inclusion/exclusion on the other. Current sociological and political philosophy regards exclusion and the enemy/friend relation as its central theme. Niklas Luhmann, Anthony Giddens and Manuel Castells, to take a few examples, have claimed that social exclusion will be the most central problem in late modern societies (Luhmann 1983; Giddens 1998; Castells 1998). They argue that there will be social displacement and expulsion and that dropping out and falling silent are the greatest social dangers to be combated. Now, we are not claiming that there is no exclusion in contemporary society, that is, that societies of sovereignty are a thing of the past. What we are saying is that it is not through the inclusion/exclusion dichotomy that we will be able to understand contemporary capitalism. True, the globalisation process does seem to back up the analysis provided by Luhmann, Giddens, Castells and others. There are shantytowns, favelas and banlieus everywhere the eye can see. Moreover, the idea of the relative independence and differentiation of the different social realms, so cherished by sociological theories, multiplies the opportunities for exclusion since it is very difficult for an individual to live in all possible 'social worlds'. These observations are important but they are not enough to convince us that the problem of exclusion and inclusion is the most important social and political question of today's societies. This is so especially if the problem of exclusion is examined in relation to the endeavour to reach a universalism of equality and equal rights which characterises modern societies and which serves as the conceptual basis of the modern political order (in abstract human life as such and in the subjective rights of that life: the right to stay alive, the right to security, etc.). Of course this universalism does not come across as such. Exclusion may thrive alongside it. But it could also be argued that modern societies not only tolerate social exclusion but in fact have themselves created it. Exclusion seems to function less as a social mechanism than a sociological and political cramp.

Deleuze delivers us from these cramps: each individual, each body and all understanding extends on the same plane and distinguishes us from one another only by the speed of their combinations. This plane of immanence does not need any theological or politological extension, regardless of whether it is the open transcendence of the state (or sovereign) or the hidden transcendence of Truth (or God). Equal rights and inclusion/exclusion do not constitute the central axis of a politics of immanent capitalism. It does not imply some kind of logic of subsumption nor the idea of a basic relation to which every other relation is reducible.

Exclusion refers always to something negative: to shutting out, to debarring and omitting, to building fences, setting up restrictions and enforcing prohibitions; that is, it is bent on getting something out of the system. But modern societies have aimed, rather, at subsuming and embracing the other, normalising the abnormal and the deviant, constantly redefining and extending its limits. Michel Foucault, in particular, has emphasised that the forms of exclusion are replaced with modern techniques of power that are based on normalising and controlling rather than on spatial confinement and exclusion. As Deleuze noted,

> Foucault is often taken as the theorist of disciplinary society and of their principal technology, confinement (not just in hospitals and prisons, but in schools, factories, and barracks). But he was actually one of the first to say that we're moving away from disciplinary societies, we've already left them behind. We're moving toward control societies that no longer operate by confining people but through continuous control and instant communication. (Deleuze 1990: 230–1)

In the new control societies the boundaries between the inside and the outside have blurred and the various closed institutions, ranging from schools to mental hospitals, from armies to factories, have had to open their gates for continuous education, out-patients, new conceptions of security and new forms of production. The border between inside and outside is working inside this configuration and supervises the moments of indecision and friction. The factory needs to let demand and the consumer directly into the production process, but it has to be the right demand. Learning becomes learning about learning, but there is good and bad knowledge. Prison changes into a system of consequences and hospitals turn into open sites that care for out-patients. The distinction between the interior and the exterior, the institution and its outside is growing dim. Social space has lost its power of confinement. At the same time, the techniques of organisation and control have evolved from uses wedded to particular spaces (schools, factories, hospitals and prisons), where some people spend a great deal of time. Society has become a continuous space occupied by people during the entire span of their lives. According to Deleuze, the changed conception of money perhaps best expresses the difference between these two kinds of societies. Whereas discipline was always related to moulded currencies having gold as a numerical standard, control is based on floating exchange rates, modulations, organisations of the movement of currencies (Deleuze 1990: 230–1).[11] In short, it tries to follow or imitate movements and exchanges as such, paying no attention to their specific contents.

Nor can exclusion be interlaced with exploitation or repression. On the contrary, the exploited is never excluded but is rather a vital component in the functioning of a system. Indeed, it is difficult to understand the idea of exclusion as essential to the functioning of today's societies if it is understood as negative segregation and indifference. Yet, insofar as we are concerned with exploitation and repression, the theory of exclusion and its terminology is inadequate to the task of conceptualising that which only appears as exclusion or inclusion but is in fact exploitation or repression.

The starting point of a renewed theory of exclusion can only be the collapse of closed institutions and the consequent termination of the reproduction of social order on the one hand and individual existence on the other. That is, we must begin with the crisis of the arrangements of mediation such as state, money, language and public space, which characterises modern societies. It is this transformation that gives birth also to the new forms of control, which no longer operate in terms of exclusion and inclusion and at the level of particular institutions typical to them but rather penetrate into the entire process of life. These controls no longer function *indirectly* (by mediation) by positioning and organising people to certain space or to a particular community (a factory worker, a soldier, a pupil). This indirect and mediated control, which aims at subjugating a mass of people into a homogeneous people by reference to a common cause, is replaced by *direct control* (without mediation), which centres on lived time and organises behaviour through the total mobilisation of all the imaginable techniques of repression and subjugation and their concentration in a single moment of time. Direct

control replaces nation-states as forms of organisation with a new formation that Michael Hardt and Antonio Negri have called 'empire'. The
controls in societies of control are always plural and this is why they
seem to offer different options, moments of choice in which the butcher's
knife feels like a form of salvation. This is the background of the concept
of 'mixed constitution' (Hardt and Negri 2000: 304–24).

Deleuze analysed the crisis of closed spaces and meaningful action in
his final works. His central concern here is how language and communication is permeated by capital and hence the necessity of creating
escapes from these new controls. The essential issue of revolution is not
that of preventing exclusion, nor that of getting inside the lines of communication, of infiltrating the public sphere or the common world. It is
rather a matter of taking leave of communication, of fleeing from it. It
is necessary to play along, to be involved and to be seen. That is why
exclusion and inclusion do not constitute the central axis of the politics
of immanent capitalism for Deleuze. Instead, he repeatedly emphasises
that 'the current problem of revolution, the revolution without bureaucracy, will be those new social relations where active minorities, singularities enter into a nomadic space without property and enclosure'
(Deleuze 1969: 18–19).

In other words, multitudo's entrance into production indicates the centrality of direct social relations in the public sphere, the realm of common
language. We enter into these without the mediation of property, quality
and information (or products):

> Capitalism in its present form is no longer directed toward production
> which is often transferred to the remote parts of the Third World . . . It is
> directed towards meta-production. It no longer buys raw materials and no
> longer sells finished products: it buys finished products or assembles them
> from parts. What it seeks to sell is services, and what it seeks to buy is shares.
> (Deleuze 1990: 231)

The capitalistic techniques of control and organisation no longer function on the level of the polarity between direct unconditional participation and indirect mediated participation. According to Deleuze, the new
forms of organisation and control are exposed not only to the disap-
pearance of distinctions and borders but also to the explosion of the ghet-
toes and shantytowns. They cannot operate on the level of local space
but must occupy a global territory and its temporal rather than spatial
processes. This change is important because it concerns our conception
of power, but above all because it restructures our entire political system
and its organisation.

By opposing a traditional disciplinary conception of power and the concept of control, it is possible to say that power operates on particular actions and subjects in space. Its target is the physical or biological human being. Power seeks its justification from particular institutions and their functions (the factory produces, the hospital takes care of illness, research is done in the university, the army wages war). Control, instead, operates on the bare conditions of action, on the possibilities of life in general (both corporeal and incorporeal). Unlike the modern logic of power, which always needs an institutional context and a normal state to justify itself, control avoids committing itself to any particular institution and its particular task. It seeks legitimacy from public opinion and ethical right instead. As a consequence, and as proven by the permanently temporary war on terrorism, morals and public opinion replace formal law and its institutions, the cornerstones of modern democratic societies, as the basis of legitimacy.

Control, in other words, is power that permeates society by withdrawing from the institutions. To say that it withdraws from the institutions is to say that it does not have any particular place of operation or a restricted external reason to refer to, no fixed point of reference or legitimacy like formal law or the particular task of an institution. It has no specifiable boundary. In other words, it is arbitrary.[12] It is uninhibited by fixed reason and judgement; it is without restraint: it is power without *logos*, arbitrary power or pure power, power without ends. This is how the concept of control opens the nexus between the floating currency (or the floating signifier) and the generic human capacities (intellect, perception, linguistic–relational abilities) as means of production. That is, it marks the era when faith in the sign (or in any external reason) is lost and the production of wealth in modalities can no longer be thought or understood by the concepts of modern economy. This new formless form of power as a non-state, non-institutional form of intervention, is the logical form of power within an economy whose foundation has collapsed. We could say that the distinction between power in a traditional sense and control is this: whereas power operates within the juridical order in a normal state, control operates in a permanent state of exception or a state of anomy without institutional legitimation and without determined and recognisable tasks or limits. This is how it spreads into every aspect of life.

Change, History, Communication

What is change? Change is not history, change is not communication. It is an event in time which may produce outcomes or effects in the state of things but which are not reducible to their outcomes or effects. Revolutions change, and change is always inseparable from the 'dead time' where nothing takes place. Change is not born in space but in time. It destroys spatial succession, the self-evidence of common sense that is required by habit, routine and communication. Change is always different from history; it is the dead moment in the series of historical successions. It is something that cannot be reached by way of historical facts, just as the arrow in Zeno's paradox is motionless at every point of its trajectory and seems to annul the reality of motion and change for all those who, in believing in communication and the power of meaningful language, become the laughing stock of the sophist.

Talking with Félix Guattari about their book *What is Philosophy?*, Deleuze distinguished between history and change:

> We talk a lot about history. The only thing is that change differs from history. Between these two there are all kinds of similarities and responses: change is born from history and returns there, but it is not history. And change is not the opposite of history, the eternal. History studies certain functions along with the event and becomes effective; but the event, insofar as it surpasses its own effects, is a change in the substance of a concept, and change is the matter of philosophy. (Deleuze and Guattari 1991: 109–10)

Revolutionary change (the event) is therefore something which surpasses its own effects, its own immediate causes. It unravels beyond its neighbourhoods, over the limits of its space as a meaningless and effective rupture in the sequence of beings. Philosophy must reach out for change; it must grant the event a metaphysics. This is why a philosopher must give in, must turn to these forces in his or her intuition. Heliotropism is characteristic of creative thinking: it seeks to combine with forces which add and extend its own force.[13]

Elsewhere, Deleuze specifies the difference between change and history with a slightly different emphasis:

> It is true that I have become more and more sensitive to the possible difference between change and history. It was Nietzsche who said that nothing important could have been accomplished without a 'non-historical core'. This is not to oppose eternal and historical, or contemplation and action: Nietzsche is talking about the way things happen, about events themselves or about change. What history grasps in an event is the way it is actualized in particular circumstances, but as change the event is beyond the scope of history. History is not experimental; it is just a set of more or less negative preconditions which make it possible to experiment with something beyond history. (Deleuze 1990: 230–1)

Thinking is always experimenting or experiencing. And as such it is the opposite of interpretation. Interpretation expresses the fact that transcendence has already come about and has arrested movement. Interpretation is a reactive and passive experimentation. It is always carried out with reference to something that is supposed missing, by bringing an empty space to continuity. But unity that is organised around the presence or absence of a certain thing is precisely what is missing from multitudo, just as what is missing from change (revolution and eventualisation) is the subject. To impose a unity on multitudo means to transform it into a homogeneous mass or people, just as coercing a subject to change means to freeze it or to stuff it into the confines of history. The reference to Nietzsche here is not accidental:

> [F]or Nietzsche it is obvious that society cannot be the last instance. The last instance is creativity, it is art; or rather art expresses the impossibility or absence of the last instance. From the beginning of his work Nietzsche claims that there are 'little higher' goals than those of the society or the state. His entire work may be gathered around a dimension which is not historical, also not history understood dialectically, and neither is this dimension that of the eternal. This dimension which is at the same time in time and works against time he calls untimely. (Deleuze 1967: 40–1)

The untimely never returns to the political-historical even if it may occasionally dovetail with it.

In politics there are creators, creative movements that stop the sequence of historical happenings that bring 'dead time' into history and politics. These are the untimely masters, the born organisers that surpass their own time, destroy and revolt in order to change and create and not to maintain the status quo like those who are submissive to an other or to a state.

> They come like fate, without cause, reason, consideration, or pretext. They are present as lightning is present, too fearsome, too sudden, too convincing, too 'different' even to become hated. Their work is the instinctive creation of forms, the imposition of forms. They are the most involuntary and unconscious artists in existence. Where they appear something new is soon present, a living power structure, something in which the parts and functions are demarcated and coordinated, in which there is, in general, no place for anything which does not first derive its 'meaning' from its relationship to the totality. (Nietzsche 1887: II, §17)

History – the 'already happened', the *fait accompli* which cannot be affected and is outside the human being, the 'objective foundation' which modern political philosophy has in its different forms taken as its starting point – belongs for Deleuze to the negative. It is absent and missing: 'unity is exactly what is missing from multiplicity, just as the subject is what is missing from events ("rains")' (Deleuze 1990: 194). It is present only as absence or lack. This accords with the Hegelian–Kojevean and psychoanalytic definition: desire is the presence of absence. What does this negative, absent precondition accomplish? Above all it constrains freedom, makes demands, establishes conditions and defines boundaries. It does not reach out to change but paralyses action and participation, prevents production and passes judgement. The history of philosophy is stupid: it is like a TV quiz-show in which something already thought or already done by somebody else, ready made and ready lived, paralyses all activity. It is a question of solving and answering problems set by somebody else in an anticipated and welcomed way, which gives the student-competitor a strange pleasure in submission.

History establishes prerequisites or conditions for action; it arranges common sense as the condition for communication or rules of democratic conversation for a statement. History positions: in its continuum everyone has his or her own place already (it merely needs to be found). In history, movement, change and creativity are only illusions. In history, time itself is an illusion. For Deleuze the question is no longer that of leaving from somewhere or of arriving somewhere, of starting or of finishing, but of what happens 'in between' (Deleuze 1990: 165). We are always in duration, in the interstice, undergoing change and that is why we must start with what is between. This is not just 'something said' nor does it mean that groundlessness or negativity here enters Deleuze's thinking. Rather it is a principle of practical philosophy. Starting from the middle means starting from the experience and moving on from there in two directions: to immediate sensation (the present) and to memory (the past). Between these two there is no qualitative difference as the present is just a contracted moment of the past. The human body and its sensations live in the actual moment and they are exposed to the effects of time. Memory instead preserves and extends time, adds opportunities for action and is able to create other possibilities in the development of real and seemingly necessary circumstances. The replacement of memory by history, by facts that have already happened, means the materialisation of memory, the expelling of indeterminate time and duration from memory and its replacement with mere sequential spatial sensations. It destroys time and by the destruction of time the possibility of creativity and revolution also disappears. History compels us to consider the facts. It compels us to respond, to react and take responsibility, to prefabricate words and deeds suitable for the continuum of circumstances or communication.[14] It casts out change and no event is possible where there is no time.

[P]hilosophy is by nature creative or even revolutionary, because it is always creating concepts. The only condition is that they have a necessity, as well as unfamiliarity, and they have both to the extent that they are a response to real problems. Concepts are what stop thought being a mere opinion, a view, an exchange of views, gossip. Any concept is bound to be a paradox. (Deleuze 1990: 197)

Concepts, paradoxically, refer always to something outside history and beyond communication. The concept has nothing to do with a pre-set task or correct solution. The concept opens a break towards movement, time and change. That is why writing is not an end in itself for Deleuze but something which oversteps the mere repetition or copying of the already said. It organises maps and extends itself into its environment because its task is to free life from the site of its imprisonment. Writing must make life more than a mere personal fact or brand. Indeed, Deleuze says that he writes 'because of a coming people, people who do not yet have a language' (Deleuze 1969: 18–19). Philosophy does not bring this people into existence but it gives them a voice, makes them mutter or hum like a swarm of bees or, as in Gerard Straub's films where the voice arises but what is said hides itself in the ground (Deleuze 1989). Creation is not communication, but resistance. Yet Deleuze saw quite clearly that resistance, too, had become part of the communication quiz-show where different viewpoints and exciting openings are explicitly sought. Resistance cannot rely on 'saying it differently', on the communication of radical opinions, because capital has permeated language itself – and not by accident but substantially. That is why resistance must surpass the horizon of communication and history itself. It may yet be necessary to create 'vacuoles of non-communication', circuit breakers or switches which help us elude controls (Deleuze 1990: 238). We must find the 'dead time' by which to make a break with stasis, and push for change. Only this 'dead time' may constitute an event. That is why concepts may only be born of paradox, from the failure of communication.

Change and the Other

Change is something that oversteps its own time. But it is also something that exceeds the category of being. It is precisely in this sense that it, as a philosophy, exceeds the pre-established boundaries. As Deleuze says, in all of his books he has been seeking the nature of event because it is the only philosophical concept that is capable of replacing the verb 'to be' (Deleuze 1990: 187). Event is change. It is not meditation alongside beings. It has no beginning or end. It is without a cause and a subject.

The people and the revolution are absolutes before which individuals lose their meaning, as is shown in the storms of the French revolution. In April of 1794, the day after the arrest of Georges Jacques Danton, Robespierre spoke of his guilt, and the guilt of Camille Desmoulins. His accusation returned again and again to the core of their deceit: they imagined themselves as superior to other people. According to Robespierre, Danton and his kind sacrificed the fatherland on the altar of their greed, their personal relationships and, perhaps, their cowardice and shame. They were afraid. And fear is the testimony of guilt: those who are afraid, are afraid of losing themselves. This means that they have placed themselves above others and imagine themselves to transcend relations that make them. Here, too, revolution is closely tied to 'living labour'. Revolution is a mass phenomenon in which no one can be above or superior to another. It is missing a subject. The one who does and what is done, the active and the passive, cannot be distinguished at the level of multiplicity. If revolution is duration, duration goes on always in the middle. It does not run from somewhere to end somewhere else. It does not have any particular content, cause or task; it can't be divided, partitioned or represented. Division and partition mean arresting duration and change, making it chronological ('if you act now you may qualify for . . .', 'follow our step-by-step method and obtain . . .'). It ties change down to a being or meaning, to an attribute or property. This bondage prevents the forces of change from free combination and organisation: it weakens them.

But what does it mean, then, to say that for Deleuze the free combination of forces, with-being without the system of mediation and representation, is always the most essential?

Revolution turns into reaction by carrying action out through 'the other', by compelling us to respond and to take responsibility. This ties time down or divides it through space. In short, change is destroyed by locating an actor, a subject. When subjects are exposed, when they come forward in a space, they may be used and easily destroyed. Movement or change does not originate in 'the other', in some real fact outside, or in distinguishing between the included and excluded. That is why revolution cannot begin with listening to others or responding to the demands of the age. Revolutions do not spring from a wrongdoing or injustice we have seen and experienced; we don't turn into revolutionaries because we want to set this or that evil right or want to solve some kind of political–social crossword puzzle. This is precisely how the preconditional 'facts' and communicative requirements work on us. We become revolutionary not through concentration but through failing of concentration, through absent-mindedness (or through distraction to use Walter Benjamin's word) that breaks free of limits and conditions.

In the end, what is it that weakens our power to act? It is often said that one must not waste nor divide one's powers. They must be focused. Action must be concentrated upon something and the exertion of thought must be directed at something. Following Deleuze, however, it is easy to see that such constraints weaken us more than they strengthen us. When we run into something amiss, something wrong or out of place, our powers try to locate and pinpoint the difficulty. They seek to place the trace that it left in us. A portion of our powers needs to keep an eye on the effect that this ill-fitting thing had. We try to objectify the effect by creating a spatial trace, a thing that is distinct from us. We now have our power only through 'the other'. The feeling of sorrow and disappointment originates in our inability to use our powers. As feelings, disappointment and sorrow express submission and powerlessness. It is essential to understand that they originate in an investment of power in some thing or being. That is why our sorrow and powerlessness derive from materialising our capacity and power, from finding a 'cause'.

Following Spinoza, Deleuze (1991) understands joy as the opposite of sorrow. If sorrow is the reduction of our activity and capacity and originates from withholding powers, from eyeballing the 'cause', then joy is always the multiplication of our capacity and an extension of our powers by addition. Joy does not focus or contract powers but expands them. There is no investment in joy; it does not proceed through 'the other'. We are joyful directly, and even in being joyous about the existence of somebody, we enjoy that he or she is. Joy does not reduce or weaken our power. When we meet something that is right for us, we link to it, combine with it and devour it. What we were before fuses with what we encountered and becomes part of a greater and more extensive person. Our powers multiply and increase without any kind of investment, withholding or limitation. They are set in motion and are no longer tied down or invested in a certain point or an unmoving image.

Because Deleuze makes no distinction between the inside and outside, between the excluded and included, the difference between the increase of powers and their reduction and contraction, the difference between joy and sorrow, is not a leap, a transition or a difference in their nature. This is of vital importance for understanding the relevance of Deleuze's thinking and the political relevance of his metaphysics today. The detachment from 'the other' and implicitly from the entire problem of ethics – and thus from the idea that the ethics of 'the other' is a question of the political struggle today – is one of the most important contributions

Deleuze's thinking makes for the analysis of today's society. Insofar as immanent capitalism, the society of 'living labour', no longer operates on the level of contents, particular tasks and communicative meanings, it can't apprehend the creativity, change and time it needs by positioning it and tying it down to a space. It must develop new methods of organisation and control. These should be able to commodify and organise *whatever activity* regardless of its means or its products (activity without content). This means that the new controls cannot function by only organising a divided part of people's time, like working hours, class schedules, homework assignments and leisure activities. The crisis of the old Fordist factory-office, the crisis of the school and university are all crises of separate spaces, closed spaces and their inability to organise and turn immaterial action into products.

The new systems of control need to subordinate and govern all of lived time and not just a part of it. If the old forms of control, which were based on spatial organisation, made life liable and reactive or ethical only in school, at work, in the army and in other such institutions, they must now be used to turn all of life into ethical (moral) life.

Communication becomes a sort of invisible machine that is an indispensable investment, just as the machines in the factory halls were for industrial capitalism, but this machine no longer needs the boundaries of the factory's physical space. Therefore, the crises of the closed spaces, and the organisational forms characteristic to them – the hierarchical structures of command, spatial organisation and external coordination typical to closed spaces – have turned out to be problematic in the face of communicative cooperation. The ability to communicate and relate to the presence of others, which is now essential to the production of value, is not created and controlled simply in the working time of the factory-office. The practices of control and organisation are instead converted into the production of a general interior, a 'second nature' as Aristotle calls it, that conditions ways of behaviour and their associated mentalities, habits and conventions of mind: from the supervision of particular tasks that took place in the space of work by means of wages and direct control, to the management of life demanded by the financier, for whom what is important is not what is done but that something is done in general. Doing, talking and knowing in general become important. Why? Because production can no longer be pre-planned or organised except at the level of general capabilities or general conditions to respond to every possible situation, to any change of demand, customer preference or public opinion. The requirements of both production and work go from being specific products, knowledge, tasks or skills to being capacities of a general kind, or language, communication, reasoning, perception, memory, learning and the ability to relate to the presence of others. These general conditions now begin to organise, form and control all action, talk and knowledge. The organisation of production is only possible through the management of these general capacities or general conditions of human action and communication, which may be best described as the *organisation of organisation*, that is, organising the general conditions of organising. General conditions and the attempts to organise them in organisational practices form the basis of the new methods of control that are used to transform cooperation between minds into predisposed productive services.

We are always trying to save time, which causes us always to put things off. Not the least of these things is the revolution. We would like to participate, but we just don't have time. Some other time, perhaps, but not now. But according to Deleuze, our powers increase and extend outwards from a complicity and participation which is fundamentally antithetical to command. As long as our powers are invested, positioned or materialised, as long as they may be purchased and sold, conquered or seized, our ability to act is reduced. Power weakens us. That is the simple reason why today's political struggle cannot operate at the level of Power. The task of revolution is not to weaken us; it is not to effect, again and again, the division of inside and outside. It is the task of revolution to break with it. Revolution grows only out of insurgency without cause, from the free movement and combination of forces in time. Anything may be expected of it. Deleuze's grandeur, his revolutionariness, lies in the formulation of this philosophy of insurgency, which frees philosophy from history and communication by breaking open an avenue of change. It offers a basis for developing a new metaphysics which is able to give time and memory to the society of living labour – *our* society. This metaphysics helps us to break free from the command and subjugation that bears down upon our lives directly and takes all our time. It helps us to save time.

References

Agamben, G. (1996), *Mezzi sensa fine*, Torino: Bollati Boringhieri.
Agamben, G. (2000), *Il tempo che resta*, Torino: Bollati Boringhieri.
Agamben, G. (2004), 'L'Opera dell'uomo', *Forme di Vita. La natura umana* 1: 117–23.
Aristotle (1990), *Metafysiikka*, trans. T. Jatakari, K. Näätsaari, and P. Pohjanlehto, Helsinki: Gaudeamus.
Bergson, H. (1991), *Oeuvres*, Paris: Presses Universitaires de France.
Castells, M. (1998), 'The Informational City is a Dual City: Can it be Reversed?', in D. A. Schön, B. Sanyal and W. J. Mitchell (eds), *High Technology and Low-Income*

Communities: Prospects for the Positive Use of Advanced Information Technology, Cambridge: MIT Press.

Deleuze, G. (1966), *Le Bergsonisme*, Paris: Presses Universitaires de France.

Deleuze, G. (1967), 'L'éclat de rire de Nietzsche', *Le Nouvel Observateur*.

Deleuze, G. (1969), 'Entretien avec Jeanette Colombel', *La Quinzaine littéraire*, 68.

Deleuze, G. (1972), 'A quoi reconnait-on le structuralisme?', in François Châtelet (ed.), *Histoire de la philosophie*, VII, Paris: Hachette.

Deleuze, G. (1973), 'Lettre à Michel Cressole', *La Quinzaine littéraire*, 161.

Deleuze, G. (1986), *Foucault*, Paris: Les Éditions de Minuit.

Deleuze, G. (1989), 'Océaniques', in *Qu'est-ce que l'acte de creation?*, FR3: 18 May.

Deleuze, G. (1990), *Pourparlers, 1972–1990*, Paris: Les Éditions de Minuit.

Deleuze, G. (1991), *Spinoza: Filosofia pratica*, Milano: Guerini e Associati.

Deleuze, G. (1994), *Difference and Repetition*, trans. P. Patton, London: The Athlone Press.

Deleuze, G. and Guattari, F. (1987), *A Thousand Plateaus: Capitalism and Schizophrenia*, trans. B. Massumi, Minneapoli: University of Minesota Press.

Deleuze, G. and Guattari, F. (1991), 'Nous avons inventé la ritornelle', *Le Nouvel Observateur*.

Giddens, A. (1998), *The Third Way*, Cambridge: Polity Press.

Girard, R. (1978), *To Double Business Bound: Essays on Literature, Mimesis and Anthropology*, Baltimore: Johns Hopkins University Press.

Hardt, M. and Negri, A. (2000), *Empire*, London: Harvard University Press.

Lazzarato, M. (2004), *Les Révolutions du capitalisme*, Paris: Empêcheurs de penser en rond/Le Seuil.

Luhmann, N. (1983), *Struttura della società e semantica*, Roma-Bari: Laterza.

Marx, K. (1887), *Capital, Vol. I*, trans. S. Moore and E. Aveling, Moscow: Progress Publishers.

Negri, A. (1998), *Exil*, Paris: Éditions mille et une nuits.

Negri, A. (2002), 'Pour une definition ontologique de la multitude', *Multitudes*, 9.

Negri, A. (2003), *Il ritorno*, Milano: Rizzoli.

Nietzsche, F. (1887), *Zur Genealogie der Moral*, Leipzig: Verlag von C. G. Naumann.

Notes

1. Giorgio Agamben (2000) for example points out in his *Il tempo che resta* that Marx's idea of revolution has nothing to do with any particular injustice, but justness as such.
2. This idea is one of the keys to reading Deleuze's book on Bergson (1966).
3. This is a suggestion that we find from R. Girard, 'Delirium as System' (1978: 84–120). Even if we are sympathetic to Girard's theory of mimetic desire and violence, his interpretation of Deleuze and Guattari lacks that quality and acuteness so convincing in his other works. For example, it is not so difficult to see that in *Difference and Repetition* Deleuze is dealing with mimetic problems, and that his ideas on intuition try to analyse problems of imitation.
4. See Deleuze's synthetic preface in Antonio Negri 1998.
5. Deleuze calls it also *dehors temporal*, the 'temporal outside', outside as a vital, recurring element, vital not organically but temporally. Also Antonio Negri summarises some characteristic of multiplicity well in accordance with Deleuze's conception, see e.g. *Il ritorno* (2003: 139–40) and 'Pour une definition ontologique de la multitude' (2002: 36–48).
6. Even if the term is not used there, one of Deleuze's shortest and most precise definitions of multiplicity is found in Deleuze 1972.

7. Aristotle derives *energeia* from *ergon* (function, task, work). *En-ergeia* is the state of being in work, functioning (Aristotle 1990: 1050a). Aristotle here ties in also the related notion of *telos* (end, completion, purpose). Because *ergon* is the completed, *energeia* is related to *entelecheia* (being in the state of completion): *energeia* is the functioning of a *dynamis* (potentiality, capacity), its fulfilment and actualisation, normally accompanied with pleasure. From this follows that potentiality is contrary to pleasure, that which is never enacted, which never achieves its end. If pleasure according to Aristotle's definition never takes place in time, potentiality is then essentially *duration*.
8. The essence of potentiality is the relation it has with its own privation, *steresis*, its non-being. See Agamben 1986 for a discussion of potentiality with exceptional clarity.
9. Agamben insists this both in the first chapter of *Mezzi sensa fine* (1996: 18), and in his recent article 'L'Opera dell uomo' (2004: 1, 117–123).
10. Unless otherwise indicated, all translations are ours.
11. According to Deleuze, Foucault's conception of pastoral power belongs to the disciplinary formation. See also Maurizio Lazzarato 2004.
12. 'International legality' (Kuwait 1991), 'humanity' and 'human rights' (Somalia 1993; Bosnia 1995; Kosovo 1999), 'enduring freedom' (Afganistan 2001), 'fight against terrorism' (Iraq 2003).
13. We return to this at the end of the article when dealing with the role of 'the other' in Deleuze's thinking, especially in regard the role of 'the other' and ethics in restraining and weakening forces.
14. Indeed, Deleuze is strongly against studying the history of philosophy because it congeals any chance of change and makes philosophy a quiz-show for nice boys and girls under the supervision of the teacher-host. Deleuze opposes philosophy as communication because the consensus required by communication or the presumed 'democratic rules of discussion' are not at all enough for creating concepts. Of Deleuze's relation to the history of philosophy see e.g. Deleuze 1973: 17, of communication see Deleuze and Guattari 1991: 109.

Part V
Social Constitution and Ontology

Chapter 12

Society with/out Organs

Niels Albertsen and Bülent Diken

The aim of this chapter is threefold. First we wish to explicate our understanding of the Deleuzian understanding of 'the social'. Then we employ our explication in an experimental mapping of the field of social theories by means of a diagram based on two orthogonal axes: a vertical continuum between order and chaos and a horizontal continuum between purity and heterogeneity. The result of this mapping is a mobile perspective on 'the social' and on social theories showing a dynamic field of 'forces' that strive to push social theories across their pre-established boundaries and to pull them back. Finally we turn to our third aim, which is to reflect on the following question: what happens to critique, when the mobile nomadism of Deleuzian critique seems to be captured by the control society of contemporary capitalism?

We hope that the chapter as a whole will convince the reader of the powers of a Deleuzian approach to transcend the limitations of the various visions of 'the social' provided by social theories as well as to plug these visions into each other.

The 'Society without Organs', Molar and Molecular Segmentation and Lines of Flight

The body without organs (BwO) is 'what remains when you take everything away' (Deleuze and Guattari 1987: 150) from organised, articulated, stratified, functionally integrated bodies with differentiated organs. The BwO is 'nonstratified, unformed, intense matter, the matrix of intensity, intensity = 0' (ibid.: 150). In case of 'the empty BwO' we have pure chaos, 'a chaos so perfect, so pure, so complete that in it all differences, all articulations are effaced . . . the zero degree of difference' (Callinicos 1982: 94). Filled with intensities the BwO becomes the 'full BwO', a plane of consistency without which no social, mental or physical order would exist.

There is also a 'cancerous' BwO, which pertains to the proliferation of strata. Thus too violent destratification ('empty BwO') on the one hand and too much stratification ('cancerous BwO') on the other should be distinguished from the 'full BwO' as the plane of consistency or immanence (Deleuze and Guattari 1987: 153, 162, 163).

Here we approach the Deleuzian distinction between transcendence and immanence; the vertical and the horizontal. The crucial question is whether thinking and action are oriented towards a vertical plane, where all 'organization . . . comes from above' (Deleuze 1988b: 128) or whether '[w]e head for the horizon, on the plane of immanence' (Deleuze and Guattari 1994: 41). The vertical plane, pertaining to all forms of stratification, is a 'plane of transcendence', since there is always a hidden steering at work, a creator God, an evolution in the supposed depths of nature, or a society's organisation of power (Deleuze 1988b: 128) – 'the strata constitute the Judgement of God' (Deleuze and Guattari 1987: 502). But if we, on the other hand, 'head for the horizon', there will be nothing beyond, no 'additional dimension', and everything will be a common 'plane of immanence' (Deleuze 1988b: 128, 124).

Just as the plane of consistency or immanence pertains to the full BwO, and the plane of transcendence or organisation to the cancerous BwO, there is also a plane pertaining to the empty BwO: 'a pure plane of abolition or death', a plane of suicidal or complete destratification, of 'regression to the undifferentiated' (Deleuze and Guattari 1987: 270).

We can conceive of the society's BwO as a sort of 'Society without Organs'. Here the notion of the BwO serves to model 'the social' as a disorganised, 'anorganic body . . . not defined by its constitutive organisation, but by its states' (Lingis 1994: 289–90). As such 'the social' in the Deleuzian sense strongly contrasts to the way in which classical social theory conceives of 'society' as a body, as an organism, with organs, defined by fixed and complementary functions. The social space as a body without organs breaks with the representation of the social, which reduces the 'social body' to its 'organs'. The 'Society without Organs' can be thought of as the undivided, in(di)visible society conceived as a complex surface of relations, connections and interactions, including those which are usually dismissed as anomalies or ambivalences in conventional representations of society.

Further, the BwO is not a state that precedes social organisation but one produced or imagined from within the social. Social theory traditionally imagines the social as something that emerged from an undifferentiated mass (e.g. Hobbes' 'state of nature' or Lévi-Strauss' 'zero-institution'), but according to Deleuze and Guattari the social systems of difference do not differentiate a pre-given chaos. The BwO of 'society' is not 'the expression of a "de-differentiated" . . . organism stuck back together that would surmount its own parts'. The BwO is not the origin of the social but its limit, its delirium, its 'tangent of deterritorialization, the ultimate residue' (Deleuze and Guattari 1983: 327–8, 281).

As the residue of 'the social' the BwO has two virtual poles: paranoia, that is, molar stratification or organisation on the one hand, and schizophrenia, that is, molecular destratification and deterritorialisation on the other (Deleuze and Guattari 1983: 281–5). Molar stratification, or systematic aggregations of disciplined functions, involves the creation of a plane of transcendence of 'society', and, opposed to this plane, there is a plane of immanence, resulting from schizophrenic movements of deterritorialisations and connections ('and' . . . 'and' . . . 'and then'). These are also two states of 'the social' defining the direction of social change. Relentlessly oscillating between these two virtual destinations, 'the social' is actualised as a dissipative assemblage, facing strata (and the cancerous BwO) on the one hand and the plane of consistency (and the full BwO) on the other.

To understand how 'the social' is constantly territorialised and deterritorialised by molar and molecular movements, it is necessary to dwell on the concept of segmentation that characterises every kind of stratification.

> We are segmented from all around and in every direction . . . Segmentarity is inherent to all the strata composing us. Dwelling, getting around, working, playing: life is spatially and socially segmented. The house is segmented according to its rooms' assigned purposes; streets, according to the order of the city; the factory, according to the nature of the work and operations performed in it. We are segmented in a *binary* fashion, following the great major dualist oppositions: social classes, but also men–women, adults–children, and so on. We are segmented in a *circular* fashion, in ever larger circles, ever wider disks and coronas, like Joyce's 'letter': my affairs, my neighborhood's affairs, my city's, my country's, the world's. . . . We are segmented in a *linear* fashion, along a straight line or a number of straight lines, of which each segment represents an episode or 'proceeding': as soon as we finish one proceeding we begin another, forever procuring and procedured, in the family, in school, in the army, on the job . . . Sometimes the various segments belong to different individuals or groups, and sometimes the same individual or group passes from one segment to another. (Deleuze and Guattari 1987: 208–9)

Here Deleuze and Guattari describe *molar* or 'rigid' segmentation with its three forms: binary segmentation, controlled by direct binarisation; circular segmentation, which tends to become concentric and root its focal points in a single centre that is in permanent movement but remains invariant through its movements; and finally linear segmentarity, which nourishes overcodings that constitute a homogeneous space and distils determinate forms, substances and relations (ibid.: 212). Rigid segmentarity functions according to the dichotomic principle of arborescence, like a tree, 'an axis of rotation guaranteeing concentricity; it is the structure or network gridding the possible' (ibid.: 212).

The rhizome, on the other hand, is a metaphor of *molecular* segmentarity. The rhizome is a non-hierarchical, horizontal stem that develops underground, operates by variation, expansion, conquest, offshoots, and as such it is 'absolutely different from roots and radicles' (ibid.: 7). The rhizome is an acentred system in which 'communication runs from any neighbor to any other, the stems or channels do not preexist, and all individuals are interchangeable, defined only by their *state* at a given moment' (ibid.: 17). Which kinds of social relations are rhizomic in character? Deleuze and Guattari mention mass-phenomena like packs, bands and even high-society groupings as examples of rhizomic, 'fuzzy' social aggregates, which consist of multiplicities in continuous metamorphoses, and which are characterised not by centralisation but by diffusion of power (ibid.: 249, 358). One should distinguish, then, between masses or flows, with their molecular segmentarity (based on mutations, quanta of deterritorialisation, connections and accelerations) on the one hand, and classes or solids, with their rigid segmentarity (binary organisation, resonance, accumulation, overcoding), on the other. '*Mass* and *class* do not have the same contours or the same dynamic, even though the same group can be assigned both signs' (ibid.: 221).

Thus, against the Durkheimian sociology with its focus on 'great collective representations, which are generally binary, resonant, and overcoded', Deleuze and Guattari side with Tarde's microsociology, arguing that what needs explanation is precisely what is presupposed in Durkheim's sociology, that is, 'the similarity of millions of people' (ibid.: 218). Tarde's focus was on detail: first, on imitation (proliferation of flows); second, on oppositions (binarisation of flows); and third, on inventions (connection of flows) (ibid.: 218). What we have here is, in other words, a 'society' of flows, a mobile society. The difference between 'macro' and 'micro' is not one of scale, but one of quality. The difference is not between 'society' (macro) and the individual (micro) but between the molar and the molecular, both traversing 'the social' and the individual at the same time.

To elaborate more on this difference, Deleuze and Guattari draw on Michel Serres' work on the history of sciences and speak of two different sciences, the (molar) state science and the (minor) nomad science. Whereas the first is a theory of solids, treating flows (fluids) as a special case, the second is characterised by a hydraulic model, which has roots in ancient atomism, and which treats flows and fluids as the reality, as consistency. Whereas the first is a science of the stable, the unchanging, the identical, the second model is of becoming and heterogeneity. Whereas the first, positing a closed grid space for solid things, can portray movement only in the form of a linear, or 'laminar', flow, the second depicts movement as a vortical inclination forming spirals and vortices in a smooth space. Whereas the first model is theorematic, focused on differences between a genus or a stable essence and its species, the second considers every figure from the viewpoint of affections that come to pass through them and accidents that determine them, so that every figure under consideration designates an event. In short, then, there is a state science that strives to limit movements to laminar flows, and a nomad science that is interested in movements that surpass all limitations imposed on them (ibid.: 361–2). 'History is always written from the sedentary point of view and in the name of a unitary State apparatus, at least a possible one, even when the topic is nomads. What is lacking is a Nomadology' (ibid.: 23).

'The social' as a smooth, nomadic space of contact and connection in contrast to the visual, striated (Euclidian) space, is composed of quantum flows, which involve 'something tending to elude or escape the codes; quanta are precisely signs or degrees of deterritorialization in the decoded flow' (ibid.: 219). Whereas laminar flows are defined by a linear, regulated movement from one point or position to another, quantum flows are defined by their speed, that is, their deviation. Therefore it is necessary to distinguish speed and movement:

> a movement may be very fast, but that does not give it a speed; a speed may be very slow, or even immobile, yet it is still speed. Movement is extensive; speed is intensive. Movement designates the relative character of a body considered as 'one', and which goes from point to point; *speed, on the contrary, constitutes the absolute character of a body whose irreducible parts (atoms) occupy or fill a smooth space in the manner of a vortex*, with the possibility of springing up at any point. (Ibid.: 381)

There are three forms of flows, or synonymously, lines passing across 'the social'. First, molar lines forming a rigid segmentarity, which are forming a striated contour, an arborescent system. Second, there are molecular lines, of the rhizome type passing between points – the rhizome is an *intermezzo* – and forming a smooth space, in which movement does not designate a localisable relation going from one point to the other and back again, but 'a transversal movement that sweeps one *and* the other away, a stream without beginning or end': 'and . . . and . . . and . . .' (ibid.: 25). And third, there are 'lines of flight'. Before considering this type of lines, we shall take a closer look at the molar and molecular lines.

Every society, even the fascist one, has both molar and molecular components/lines at the same time. Indeed, 'what makes fascism dangerous is its molecular or micropolitical power, for it is a mass movement', a proliferation of molecular interactions before it begins to resonate together in a totalitarian state (ibid.: 214–15). It is, therefore, 'too easy to be antifascist on the molar level, and not even see the fascist inside you' (ibid.: 215). In other words, a simple opposition between rigid and molecular lines is misleading for they always overlap and get entangled. Power is on both molar/arborescent and molecular/rhizomatic lines, simultaneously. What matters is to see the rhizome in the tree and the tree in the rhizome.

Everything and everyone seeks a territory, carries out deterritorialisations, and reterritorialises on 'almost anything – memory, fetish, or dream' (Deleuze and Guattari 1994: 68). In terms of psychosocial figures, the immigrant, or 'the stranger', who moves from one setting to (re)territorialise on another (like laminar flows), symbolises *relative* deterritorialisation, whereas the nomad, constantly on the move (like quantum flows), symbolises *absolute* deterritorialisation (Deleuze and Guattari 1987: 380–1). But it is important to note that the nomad is primarily defined not by being itinerant (even though this might be case) but by occupying a smooth space and by speed, which, as mentioned, does not necessitate extensive movement as such but rather intensity and a deviation from the force of gravity, or from the plane of transcendence (see ibid.: 410). For that matter, if asked precisely who the nomad is, Deleuze and Guattari would probably answer that they have never seen a nomad, just as Deleuze says his favourite sentence in *Anti-Oedipus* is 'No, we've never seen a schizophrenic' (Deleuze 1995: 12). For the nomad is everywhere. It is therefore important not to reify the concept of deterritorialisation as if it pertains to certain phenomena. In other words, deterritorialisation is not simply an 'absolute, self-positing concept because it deterritorializes itself in the moment it is created' (Goodchild 1996: 58), as happens in Deleuze and Guattari's considerations on the nomad.

Let us now turn to the third kind of line passing across 'the social', the line of flight. Contrary to the molecular lines that only designate relative deterritorialisation and reterritorialisation by the strata, the lines of flight break free as absolute deterritorialisation. This is most crucial for 'the social' because it is defined much more by what escapes it than by its zones of power (cf. Deleuze and Guattari 1987: 217). Every society has zones of power (the state, homogeneity), zones of indiscernibility (the molecular fabric of the society), and zones of impotence (that is, lines of flight). Every social phenomenon confronts escapes and breakaways and thus inversions. 'Linearization and segmentation are where flows run dry, but also their point of departure for a new creation . . . something always escapes' (ibid.: 217). Every creative potential, and every profound movement in society, originates in escape, it does not spring from antagonisms or contradictions between rigid segments (ibid.: 220). Even though social movements are unavoidably 'represented' as a contradiction between molar segments, it is the lines of flight, leaking between segments, escaping organisation and centralisation, that explain what is happening. Therefore, in a sense, the originary social relation is marked not by oppositions as in traditional Marxian analysis or in the schmittian friend/enemy opposition, but by the paradoxical relation of the line of flight (deterritorialisation) to a given social situation (territorialisation).

Deterritorialisation, always seeking connection with something else, means becoming as opposed to being, that is, being part of the three main strata: organism, language and subjectification. Against organism deterritorialisation means becoming a body without organs (Deleuze and Guattari 1987: 149–68); against language deterritorialisation means becoming 'a foreigner, but in one's own tongue' (ibid.: 98); and against subjectification (as human, male, white and so on) deterritorialisation means becoming-animal, woman, black, molecular and so on. Becoming involves 'the transversal relations that ensure that any effects produced in some particular way . . . can always be produced by other means' (Deleuze 1995: 11). Becoming-animal, therefore, is 'not a question of . . . seeing yourself as some dumb animal, but unraveling your body's human organization, exploring this or that zone of intensity' (ibid.: 11). Becoming breaks up hierarchical organisation and is, as such, synonymous with the 'war machine'. The war machine is a free assemblage oriented along a deterritorialising line of flight. Consisting of flows (speed), operating in a smooth space, and untying the social bond (codes) into a multiplicity, the war machine is that which cannot be contained in the striated, rigidly segmented social space. 'War' here must be understood as a mechanism against rigid and overcoded social organisation. A war machine as an assemblage has as its object not war – war is only the supplement of the war machine – but the constitution of a creative line of flight, a smooth space. War is simply 'a social state that wards off the state' (Deleuze and Guattari 1987: 417).

Lines of flight are neither good nor bad in themselves; they are open-ended processes. A line of flight can continue folding and making new connections. When this is the case, it can be said to be rhizomatic, an intermezzo or inter-being. There are, however, three dangers. The first is that a line of flight can become re-stratified: in the fear of complete destratification, rigid segmentation and segregation may seem attractive. Whenever an organisation, institution, interpretation, a black hole and so on stop a line of flight, a 'reterritorialisation' takes place. In this case the 'mass' is metamorphosed into strata, for example a 'class'. The second danger, which is less obvious but more interesting is 'clarity'. Clarity arises when one attains a perception of the molecular texture of 'the social', when the holes in it are revealed. What used to be compact and whole seems now to be leaking, a texture that enables indistinctions, overlappings, migrations, hybridisations, a transgressive delirium.

> Instead of the great paranoid fear, we are trapped in a thousand little mono-manias, self-evident truths, and clarities that gush from every black hole and no longer form a system, but are only rumble and buzz, blinding lights giving any and everybody the mission of self-appointed judge, dispenser of the justice, policeman, neighborhood SS man. (Deleuze and Guattari 1987: 228)

The 'mass' does not only reproduce the dangers of the rigid in a miniature scale; it becomes microfascism. The third danger: a line of flight can lose its creative potentials and become a line of death. Fascism is the result of an intense line of flight that desires its own repression and 'death through the death of others' (ibid.: 230). The point at which escape becomes a line of death is the point at which war (destruction) becomes the main object of the war machine rather than its supplement. This is another reason why it is 'necessary to retain a minimum of strata . . .' (ibid.: 270). Again, the danger is the creation of a rigid plane of transcendence on the one hand, and a complete destratification, resulting in erasure of all consistencies, on the other. In both cases the immanence of 'the social' is destroyed.

Becoming Deleuzian in Social Theory: a Diagrammatic Experiment

Against this background, 'the social' can be described as a dissipative assemblage. To illuminate this assemblage, we experiment with a diagram (Figure 12.1) that starts from an understanding of 'the social' as hybrids of human and non-human elements. The two poles of nature and society, which modernity has sought to purify, do not pre-exist as 'pure' entities. They rather involve, to use the phrasing of Bruno Latour, the heterogeneous proliferation of hybrids (Latour 1993: 51). This idea serves as the

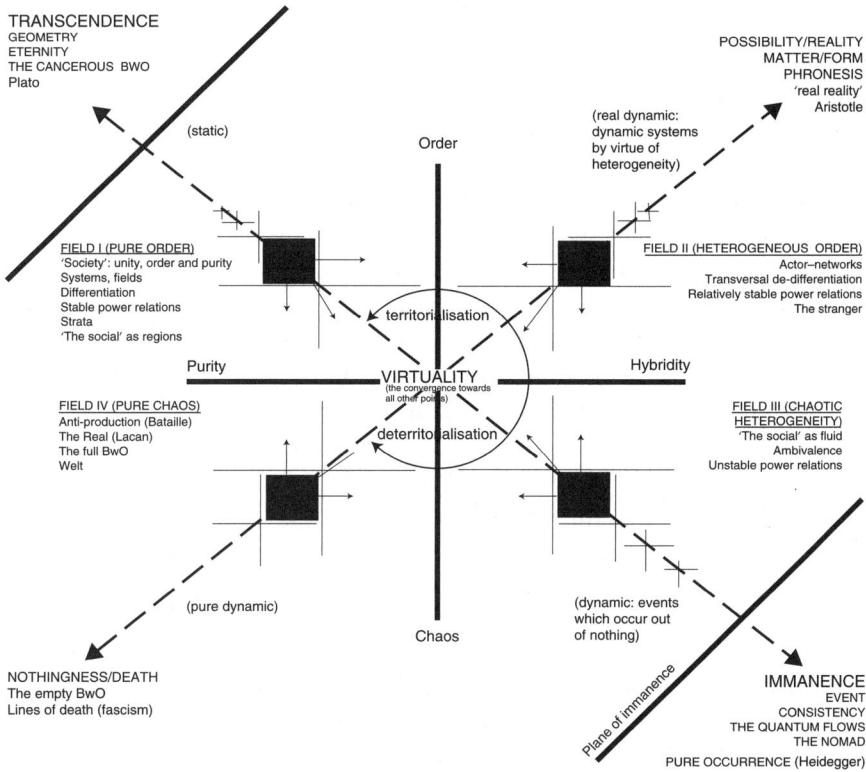

Figure 12.1 The social in a dynamic diagram

horizontal axis of our diagram, where the relationship between purity and heterogeneity is that of a continuum, a process of hybridisation or purification. The same logic applies to the second axis, that of order and chaos: the relationship between them is not given in advance but must be thought of as stabilisation or destabilisation processes. 'Chaos' is what disorganises any consistency in infinity and concomitantly order is 'systematic consistency' (Deleuze and Guattari 1994: 42). The 'area' between order and chaos can, again, be characterised as a continuum, as including what has attained a 'certain consistency without losing the diversity of different motions' (ibid.: 42). This relational thinking allows for a differentiation between order and purity on the one hand, and between heterogeneity and chaos on the other: order is not identical to purity just as heterogeneity is not identical to chaos. Consequently, we can refer to four 'ideal-typical' vanishing points or lines: pure order, ordered or organised heterogeneity chaotic heterogeneity and pure chaos.

In regard to the stratification and segmentation of 'the social' Deleuze and Guattari's perspective borders on the theories of modernity which emphasise the ordered and stable aspects of a differentiated sociality in the form of fields (e.g. Pierre Bourdieu 1996) or autopoietic systems (e.g. Niklas Luhmann 2000). However, in contrast to systems and fields, the Deleuzian understanding of the social incorporates hybridity and ambivalence into the theory itself. Ambivalence or paradox does not pertain to a system only to be temporalised and spatialised, that is, to be ordered (Luhmann). Nor do they become stable and routinised 'practices' (Bourdieu). Having an eye for the heterogeneous and the inconsistent, the Deleuzian approach can move beyond differentiation and depict 'the social' in terms of de-differentiation as well.

Dealing with different forms of social heterogeneity which are excluded from but constitutive of sociality, Deleuze and Guattari's theory parallels other contributions to this theme as found in Zygmunt Bauman's concept of ambivalence with spontaneous and unregulated ethics as the excluded ground of sociality (Bauman 1993), Slavoj Žižek's version of Lacanian social theory that incorporates radical negativity and the processes of sublimation into social analysis (Žižek 1989), and Laurent Thévenot's pragmatic sociology with its central emphasis on heterogeneous moral modes of engagement through regimes of action including both humans and things (Thévenot 2001). The central point is that the coherence of 'the social', the classical problem of social order, cannot be understood without 'polluting' the purified concepts of the social with heterogeneity. The social is not sui generis. Social facts are not explained by pure social causes, as Durkheim would have it.

In terms of de-differentiation (Field II of our diagram), the Deleuzian understanding of 'the social' has most visibly inspired the actor–network theory, which focuses on relatively stable but heterogeneous orderings with an emphasis on objects as actors (actants) and the social as a hybrid network. According to Latour actor–network theory could just as well be called 'actant-rhizome ontology' (Latour 1999: 19). Deleuze and Guattari, however, contrast the rhizomatic networks to the stable structures: the rhizome exists only in the state of metamorphoses and constant hybridisation (cf. Deleuze and Guattari 1987: 21). Their model is 'one of becoming and heterogeneity' (ibid.: 361). From a Deleuzian perspective, actor–network theory would therefore seem to be too focused on ordering mechanisms and their functioning, that is, on 'heterogeneous orders'. Interestingly in this respect, mainstream social theory understands the 'flows' around which the 'network society' is constructed, merely as 'purposeful, repetitive, programmable sequences of exchange and interaction between physically disjointed positions held by social actors in the economic, political, and symbolic structures of society' (Castells 1996: 412), that is as laminar flows in the sense of Deleuze and Guattari. In contrast, they emphasise the difference between the laminar flows (ordered movements between stable points or positions) and the quantum flows (disordered and deterritorialising lines of deviation). Thus their concept of 'flow', in the sense of deviation and becoming, takes us to Field III of the diagram.

So far our Deleuzian topology of 'the social' can be summed up in the idea that 'the social' does not exist as a single spatial type. Rather, as Annemarie Mol and John Law have argued, 'the social' performs more than one kind of space:

> First, there are regions in which objects are clustered together and boundaries are drawn around each cluster. Second, there are networks in which distance is a function of the relations between the elements and difference a matter of relational variety. These are the two topologies with which the social theory is familiar. The first is old and secure, while the second, being newer, is still proud of its ability to cross boundaries. However, there are other kinds of space too . . . [where] neither boundaries nor relations mark the difference between one place and another. Instead, sometimes boundaries come and go, allow leakage or disappear altogether, while relations transform themselves without fracture. Sometimes, then, social space behaves like a fluid. (Mol and Law 1994: 641)

If 'the social' is understood as consisting of 'regions' (e.g. systems or fields), then the focus is on the strata and differentiation. Understood as 'networks', 'the social' has been articulated by Deleuze-inspired theories such as the actor–network theory. In Field III, however, 'the social' is neither solid nor stable, not even relatively, but disordered and hybrid. 'It is all contingent' because it is fluid (ibid.: 663). Hence Deleuze and Guattari employ the distinction between the solid and the fluid to refer to the above-mentioned distinction between (molar) state science and the (minor) nomad science. Whereas the first is a theory of solids, treating flows (fluids) as a special case, the second is characterised by a hydraulic model which treats flows and fluids as the reality, as consistency.

The fourth field in the diagram, on which mainstream social theory is completely blind or silent, can relate the social to the body without organs, understood as 'pure chaos'. 'The social', then, is constituted by differentiated strata as well as networks, flows and the BwO. What is important here is of course to understand how they relate to each other as well as how they differ from each other. If the basic movement made possible (i.e. visible) by the Deleuzian approach pertains to the two poles of (re)territorialisation and deterritorialisation, territorialisation is the stabilising movement from Field IV to III, II, and I. Inversely, the desta-bilising movements the other way around signify deterritorialisation as the limit to the clean-cut distinctions between territories and the creation of 'zones of indistinction' characteristic of modernity (Agamben 1998). The Deleuzian perspective on 'the social' thus is a mobile perspective, and the different mobilities introducing (dis)continuity into 'the social' generate different types of relations. First, there can be *mutually supportive* relations among the strata, networks, flows and the BwO where each plays the role of the 'parasite' (Serres 1982) in its relation to the others in that they derive meaning from each other. Second, there may emerge *conflictual* relations where they seek to stratify, dominate or codify one another. For Deleuze and Guattari, the strata clearly endeav-ours to 'capture' the flows. Third, one can find *parallel* relations, since the strata, networks, flows and the BwO all constitute themselves as a series heterogeneously organised by difference.

> Each series tells a story: not different points of view on the same story, like the different points of view on the town we find in Leibniz, but completely distinct stories which unfold simultaneously . . . Each series explicates or develops itself, but in its difference from the other series which it implicates and which implicate it. (Deleuze 1994: 123–4)

This opens up the social world to virtual possibilities. Virtuality, defined as the state of being 'real without being actual' (Deleuze and Guattari 1987: 94), refers to possibilities in relation to which 'the social' can perform or position itself. Actual social positions are not the same as the virtual domain of possibilities around them. This huge, non-actualised domain that consists of possibilities constitutes a central feature of the Deleuzian perspective on the 'social'. The social world is also virtual; it consists of possibilities of movement, of change of position, of transi-tions. Movements along lines of flight and virtuality are thus closely related to each other.

In this experiment we have reconstructed Deleuze's mobile ontology of 'the social' from a certain viewpoint, building upon the idea that the dimensions of order–chaos and purity–heterogeneity are significant tools of 'world-viewing'. This may seem a limitation to our diagram, and it is, but within these limits the diagram can claim a generalisable validity insofar as the diagram can contain itself within itself, 're-enter' itself (Brown 1969), repeat itself within its different fields. The dimensions of order and chaos, purity and hybridity can be found not only among the fields, but also within the fields. Is this not also the whole point of looking for the rhizome in the tree and, inversely, the tree in the rhizome? This point takes us to the twofold argument that, first, every single field contains 'forces' that push in the direction of the other fields, and second, every field also pulls itself towards the 'purity' of itself.

Let us exemplify the first point by applying our Deleuzian approach to Luhmann's system theory. The question here is: does Luhmann's theory of differentiated autopoietic systems have some lines of flight pushing it in other directions? Let us, in this context, recall Luhmann's concept of 'the world' (Welt) and its relationship to art. According to Luhmann the basic operation of the art system, with regard to both the making and the reception of art, is observation (Luhmann 1993: 224). Observation means the operation of making a distinction and marking one side of the distinction as distinct from the other. Thus 'an inner and an outer side' of the distinction emerge, both of which, taken together make up a 'form'. The creation of artworks operates with such forms. An originary distinction triggers a process in which connections of form are reworked by crossing the boundaries of the preceding forms (Luhmann 1990: 10, 14). The perception of the artwork similarly consists of deciphering the 'work's structure of distinctions' (Luhmann 2000: 39).

In the making of distinctions the unity of the distinction remains an unobservable 'blind spot'. 'Welt' is Luhmann's concept for this unobservable unity. The blind spot may be observed by another distinction, but then the unobservable unity of this distinction becomes the blind spot. As the unity of the 'unmarked state' prior to observation, the world never appears in observation (Luhmann 1990: 15). It rather goes along with all observations as their blind spot, remaining 'transcendentally presupposed' (ibid.: 20). But, as a reworking of connections of forms, the artwork makes the unobservable unity of one form observable by other forms, which have their own unobservable side. In this sense the artwork makes the invisible visible while the 'invisible is preserved' (ibid.: 14, 20).

For any observer (observing system) Welt is always differentiated into system and environment (Umwelt), the unity of this differentiation being unobservable. The artwork seems to come close to a deconstruction of this differentiation. In the artwork it is as if observation endeavours to observe itself and its own blind spot, while being at the same time unable to do this. The artwork thus pushes the system/environment distinction and the difference between the observation and its blind spot from the purified order of Field I towards the pure chaos of Field IV. Needless to say, Welt is similar to the Deleuzian BwO: both imply an unobservable, undifferentiated, pure chaos. The beginning of everything takes place in Field IV, in the Welt of the unmarked state, which in 'older cosmology', according to Luhmann, precisely was called 'chaos' (Luhmann 2000: 41).

Regarding the second point, the pull towards the purity of the field, we have only some preliminary remarks to make. Taken to the extreme, the forces pertaining to the vector of order and purity (Field I) reveal themselves as a search for the 'pure rule', as in for instance geometry, symbolising total disembodiment and abstraction. The divine power of geometry has from the time when the Egyptian agriculturalists measured the farmlands been a fascinating philosophical issue. Geometry was the mediator that informed Plato of a real, immovable, stable world of pure ideas behind the apparent worlds of movement and change. Later, Spinoza in the *Ethics* would use the inevitability that the sum of the angles in a triangle is 180 (1994: I, 17) as a didactic device for rendering visible the view *sub specie aeternitatis*, the view from eternity. Furthermore, Spinoza was an inspiration to Nietzsche, the early Wittgenstein (Tilghman 1991), Deleuze and Bourdieu (1996; 1999), a fact which seems to indicate that further investigations into 'subterranean' movements between the fields (especially Fields I and IV) may show surprising connections between thinkers one normally would not associate with each other (cf. Albertsen 1995; Albertsen and Diken 2004).

The line of flight characterising the BwO (Field IV) might be nothingness and/or death. It is a line of flight out of all systems. At this point the body without organs becomes an 'empty' BwO, which, in contrast to the full BwO, signals an absence of every kind of determination and strata. The BwO that becomes a line of death can be exemplified by microfascism. In Field II, the line of flight may be the Aristotelian phronesis of the Golden Mean of order and heterogeneity, and ontologically of matter as potential for form. In Field III, the line of flight goes towards the 'event', Heideggerian pure occurrence, accidence, or pure contingency. Events that come out of nothing and merely 'appear'.

Finally, the whole scheme need not be a map-like, flat one, but rather a cylinder folded in such a way that the transcendence of pure order and the immanence of the event meet. Is the pure event that comes out of nothing less pure than the geometrical triangle, and, as coming out of nothing, less ordered in itself? The answer seems to be no. In this sense, too, the scheme re-enters itself.

Control and Critique, Mobility and Deviation

So far 'the social' on the one hand appears as an assemblage of bodies, matter and discourses, quite similar to Foucault's *dispositifs* of power/knowledge (Deleuze and Guattari 1987: 531; Patton 2000: 44). Power is the 'stratified dimension of the assemblage' (Deleuze and Guattari 1987:

531). On the other hand, 'the social' is also determined by mobility. Social assemblages are as much assemblages of movement as of power; indeed, the 'social' is primarily defined by movement and not by its stratified zones of power (ibid.: 531, 217). Indeed, mobility is the most significant dimension to the social field as shown by our diagram. Hence 'what is lacking is Nomadology'. But what happens to the idea of nomadism if power itself goes nomadic as in today's network society? What happens if the lines of flight are accommodated by the apparatuses of capture (ibid.: 424–73) of contemporary power? What if contemporary power thrives well in the forms of justification and critique based on the notion of creativity? Is it still possible and feasible to say 'More perversion!' (Deleuze and Guattari 1983: 321), when perversion has already become a big business?

As Boltanski and Chiapello (1999) argue, the 'new spirit of capitalism' integrates a new regime of justification and critique, which they call the 'project regime'. This new regime is adjusted to network mobility and gives worth to connectionism, always being on the move towards a new project, new ideas, living a life of simultaneous and successive projects. In this connectionist, reticular world, in which a pre-established habitus is rejected, one 'should be physically and intellectually mobile' and be able to respond to the call of 'a moving world'. The 'grand person is mobile. Nothing must disturb his displacements.' He must be 'a nomad' as Boltanski and Chiapello say, referring to Deleuze (ibid.: 168, 183). According to Richard Sennett, thus also the paradigmatic networker Bill Gates seems to be

> free of the obsession to hold on to things. His products are furious in coming forth and as rapid in disappearing, whereas Rockefeller wanted to own oilrigs, buildings, machinery, or railroads for the long term. Lack of long-term attachment seems to mark Gates' attitude toward work: he spoke about positioning oneself in a network of possibilities rather than paralysing oneself in a particular job . . . he has the ability to let go. (Sennett 1998: 62)

One can argue that the grammatician of the project regime is precisely Deleuze and Guattari's 'prince of philosophers', the philosopher of immanence *par excellence*, Spinoza (Deleuze and Guattari 1994: 48, 60). The project regime, just as Spinoza's ontology of immanence and his idea of absolute democracy, valorises activity against passivity, multiplicity against homogeneity, creative change against fixation on rules, freedom and tolerance and everybody's right to self-valorisation in networks. In this sense the new spirit of capitalism paradoxically elevates the philosopher of immanence to its grammatician of transcendent justification.

Spinoza's philosophy serves here as the common principle of equivalence to which one can refer to find out whether a position is advantageous or disadvantageous in relation to networks (cf. Albertsen 2005). Similarly, Augusto Illuminati has reasonably argued that it was Deleuze who first gave this 'post-Fordist twist' to Spinoza (Illuminati 2003: 320).

Deleuze himself emphasised that today's control societies are taking over disciplinary societies: factories are replaced by businesses, schools by continuous education, exams by continuous assessment: 'in control societies you never finish anything – business, training, and military service being coexisting metastable states of a single modulation' (Deleuze 1995: 179). Capitalism is no longer characterised by panoptic, place-bounded discipline forcing people to overtake given subject positions, but by a permanent movement, in which the subject is always in a state of becoming. The symptom of control society is the collapse of the institutional walls, but this does not imply that discipline ends with the deterritorialisation of institutions. Rather, discipline, now freer than ever from territorial constraints, has become more immanent to the social field (Hardt and Negri 2000). In control society subjectivity is 'produced simultaneously by numerous institutions in different combinations and doses'; hence social space tends to lose its delimitation: a person 'is factory worker outside the factory, student outside the school, inmate outside prison, insane outside the asylum – all at the same time. It belongs to no identity and all of them – outside the institutions but even more intensely ruled by their disciplinary logics' (ibid.: 331–2).

Mobility once served as a tool to criticise what was seen as static. In this, concepts such as nomad, rhizome, hybridisation, desire, displacement signify resistance to or escape from power. They all drew attention to what is mobile, and from this point of view discipline was an 'anti-nomadic technique' (Foucault 1991: 218). But contemporary society now operates according to the logic of nomadism. Ours is a 'nomad capitalism' (Williams 1989: 124) that justifies itself with reference to aesthetic inspiration: 'Be Inspired', as a Siemens ad reads. Meanwhile, capitalists themselves boast in new ways – 'I am such a nomad, I am such a tramp' (A. Roddick, the owner of the Body Shop, quoted in Kaplan 1995: 54) – and a new capitalist discourse based on metaphors of mobility promotes the flexible organisational forms that can 'go with the flow' (Thrift 1997: 39). In a nutshell, perhaps today 'we are witnessing the revenge of nomadism over the principle of territoriality and settlement' (Bauman 2000: 13). What once was the exception has become the rule. Deleuze and Guattari had complained that 'history is always written from the sedentary point of view' (1987: 23). But we are today 'condemned to nomadism, at the very moment that we think we can make displacement the most effective means of subversion' (Virilio and Lotringer 1997: 74).

This development confirms that critique is not a peripheral activity; rather, it contributes to capitalist innovations. They assimilate critique. Capitalism received mainly two forms of critique until the 1970s: the social critique from the Marxist camp (exploitation) and the aesthetic critique from the French philosophy (nomadism). However, since the 1970s, capitalism has found new forms of legitimation in the latter form of critique, which resulted in a 'transfer of competencies from leftist radicalism toward management' (Boltanski and Chiapello, quoted in Guilhot 2000: 360). The artistic critique of the 1960s and 1970s today supply businesses with a rhetoric of creative productivity, making aesthetics an element of social cohesion (cf. Holmes 2004). The aesthetic critique has, in other words, dissolved into a post-Fordist normative regime of justification, the notion of creativity is re-coded in terms of flexibility, and difference is commercialised. Even the philosophical concept has been affected:

> [The] most shameful moment came when computer science, marketing, design, and advertising, all the disciplines of communication, seized hold of the word *concept* itself . . . Philosophy has not remained unaffected by the general movement that replaced Critique with sales promotion . . . Certainly, it is painful to learn that *Concept* indicates a society of information services and engineering. (Deleuze and Guattari 1994: 10–11)

Capitalism, then, accommodates creativity and critique. Critique as such is indeed constitutive of capital, which is why Hardt and Negri (2000) argue that the 'multitude' is the fundamental creative force that keeps power and capital afloat. It is, in other words, the multitude that sets capital in motion, not the other way around; the 'final word on power is that *resistance comes first*' (Deleuze 1988a: 89).

So, where does this leave us? If control society accommodates nomadism, how can its mobility be criticised on the basis of mobility? How to ground a mobile critique of control society?

Regarding this tension, there may still be a Deleuzian line of flight. We have already met this line above: *speed as deviation*. It is by deviation and not necessarily by movement that the nomad creates an*othe*r space. It is no surprise, therefore, that Deleuze, who is often criticised for 'romanticising' mobility, is not so keen on travelling. 'You shouldn't move around too much, or you'll stifle becomings,' he writes, adding with reference to Toynbee: 'the nomads are those who don't move on, they become nomads because they refuse to disappear' (Deleuze 1995: 138). Control society proves that neither mobility nor immobility are liberatory in themselves;

they radically change meaning depending on the context. Subversion or liberation therefore must be related to taking control of the production of mobility and stasis (Hardt and Negri 2000: 156). Because, as Deleuze and Guattari say, '. . . everything is a production' (1983: 4).

References

Agamben, G. (1998), *Homo Sacer: Sovereign Power and Bare Life*, Standford: Standford University Press.
Albertsen, N. (1995). 'Kunstværket, en sansningsblok under evighedens synsvinkel: Spinoza, Wittgenstein, Deleuze', in N. Lehmann and C. Madsen (eds), *Deleuze og det æstetiske*, Aarhus: Aarhus Universitetsforlag.
Albertsen, N. (2005), 'From Calvin to Spinoza. The New Spirit of Capitalism', *Distinktion* No. 11.
Albertsen, N. and Diken, B. (2004), 'Artworks' Networks: Field, System or Mediators?', *Theory, Culture and Society*, 21: 3.
Bauman, Z. (1993), *Postmodern Ethics*, Oxford: Blackwell.
Bauman, Z. (2000), *Liquid Modernity*, London: Polity.
Boltanski, L. and Chiapello, È. (1999), *Le Nouvel Esprit du capitalisme*, Paris: Gallimard.
Bourdieu, P. (1996), *The Rules of Art: Genesis and Structure of the Literary Field*, Cambridge: Polity Press.
Bourdieu, P. and Accardo, A. (eds) (1999), *The Weight of the World*, London: Polity.
Brown, G. S. (1969), *Laws of Form*, London: George Allen and Unwin.
Callinicos, A. (1982), *Is There a Future for Marxism?*, London: The Macmillan Press.
Castells, M. (1996), *The Information Age: Volume I: The Rise of Network Society*, Oxford: Blackwell.
Deleuze, G. (1988a), *Foucault*, trans. S. Hand, Minneapolis: University of Minnesota Press.
Deleuze, G. (1988b), *Spinoza: Practical Philosophy*, trans. R. Hurley, San Francisco: City Lights.
Deleuze, G. (1994), *Difference and Repetition*, trans. P. Patton, London: The Athlone Press.
Deleuze, G. (1995), *Negotiations*, trans. M. Joughin, New York: Columbia University Press.
Deleuze, G. and Guattari, F. (1983), *Anti-Oedipus: Capitalism and Schizophrenia*, trans. R. Hurley, M. Seem and H. R. Lane, Minneapolis: University of Minnesota Press.
Deleuze, G. and Guattari, F. (1987), *A Thousand Plateaus: Capitalism and Schizophrenia*, trans. B. Massumi, Minneapolis: University of Minnesota Press.
Deleuze, G. and Guattari, F. (1994), *What is Philosophy?*, trans. G. Burchell and H. Tomlinson, New York: Columbia University Press.
Foucault, M. (1991), *Discipline and Punish: The Birth of the Prison*, trans. A. Sheridan, England: Penguin Books.
Goodchild, P. (1996), *Deleuze and Guattari: An Introduction to the Politics of Desire*, London: Sage.
Guilhot, N. (2000), 'Review of Luc Boltanski and Eve Chiapello's *Le Nouvel Esprit du capitalisme*', *European Journal of Social Theory*, 3: 3.
Hardt, M. and Negri, A. (2000), *Empire*, London: Cambridge.
Holmes, B. (2004), 'Reverse Imagineering: Toward the New Urban Struggles', *NIFCA Info*, 1: 4.

Illuminati, A. (2003), 'Postfordisten Spinoza', *Agora*, 2: 3.

Kaplan, C. (1995), ' "A World Without Boundaries". The Body Shop's Trans/national Geographics', *Social Text*, 13: 2.

Latour, B. (1993), *We Have Never Been Modern*, Hertfordshire: Harvester Wheatsheaf.

Latour, B. (1999), 'On recalling ANT', in J. Law and J. Hassard (eds), *Actor Network Theory and After*, Oxford: Blackwell.

Lingis, A. (1994), 'The Society of Dismembered Body Parts', in C. V. Boundas and D. Olkowski (eds), *Gilles Deleuze and the Theatre of Philosophy*, London: Routledge.

Luhmann, N. (1990), 'Weltkunst', in N. Luhmann, F. D. Bunsen and D. Baecker (eds), *Unbeobachtbare Welt: über Kunst und Architektur*, Bielefeld: Verlag Cordula Haux.

Luhmann, N. (1993), 'Die Evolution das Kunstsystems', *Kunstforum International*, 24: November–December.

Luhmann, N. (2000), *Art as a Social System*, Stanford: Stanford University Press.

Mol, A. and Law, J. (1994), 'Regions, Networks and Fluids: Anaemia and Social Topology', *Social Studies of Science*, 24: 4.

Patton, P. (2000), *Deleuze and the Political*, London: Routledge.

Sennett, R. (1998), *The Corrosion of Character*, New York: W. W. Norton.

Serres, M. (1982), *The Parasite*, trans. L. R. Schehr, Baltimore: Johns Hopkins University Press.

Spinoza, B. (1994), *A Spinoza Reader: The Ethics and Other Works*, ed. and trans. E. Curley, Princeton: Princeton University Press.

Thévenot, L. (2001), 'Pragmatic Regimes Governing the Engagement with the World', in T. R. Schatzki, K. K. Cetina and E. von Savigny (eds), *The Practice Turn in Contemporary Theory*, London: Routledge.

Thrift, N. (1997), 'The Rise of Soft Capitalism', *Cultual Values*, 1: 1.

Tilghman, B. R. (1991), *Wittgenstein, Ethics and Aesthetics: The View from Eternity*, London: Macmillan.

Virilio, P. and Lotringer, S. W. (1997), *Pure War*, Semiotext(e), New York: Columbia University Press.

Williams, R. (1989), *Resources of Hope*, London: Verso.

Žižek, S. (1989), *The Sublime Object of Ideology*, London: Verso.

Chapter 13

Deleuzian Social Ontology and Assemblage Theory

Manuel DeLanda

The most critical question which a philosophical analysis of social ontology must answer is the linkage between the micro and the macro. Whether one conceives of these levels as 'the individual and society' or as 'agency and structure' or even as 'choice and order', an answer to the question of their mutual relations basically determines the kinds of social entities whose existence one is committed to believe. One family of solutions to the micro–macro problem relies on a reductionist strategy, either reducing the macro to the micro (microreductionism) or vice versa, reducing the micro to the macro (macroreductionism). The first strategy is often illustrated with classical or neo-classical microeconomics in which the key social entities are rational decision-makers making optimising choices constrained only by their budgets and ranked preferences. But the branches of microsociology born in the 1960s (ethnomethodology and social constructivism) are also microreductionist even if their conception of agency is quite different, based on phenomenology and stressing routine behaviour rather than rational choice (Garfinkel 2002; Berger and Luckmann 1967). Microreductionism does not imply disbelief in the existence of society as a whole, only a conception of it that makes it into an epiphenomenon: society is simply an aggregate or sum of either many rational agents or many phenomenological experiences shaped by daily routine. In other words, this macro entity does not have emergent properties of its own.

The opposite ontological strategy consists in asserting that society makes the individual, that what really exists is the world of enduring social structures. The older Marx, as well as the main representatives of classical sociology (Durkheim and Parsons), subscribed to this belief. To say that this is a macroreductionist strategy is not to say that in these theories individual persons do not exist but, again, that they are mere epiphenomena: persons are socialised as they grow up in families and attend schools, and after they have internalised the values of their societies their obedience to traditional regulations and cultural values can be taken for granted. The two forms of microsociology mentioned above emerged as a rebellion against this idea of a once-and-for-all socialisation, emphasising that it is only through the exercise of day-to-day routines that obedience can be guaranteed. Hence the emphasis on the phenomenological aspects of experience, or more exactly, on those aspects of experience which routine makes us take for granted. These two ontological strategies, however, do not exhaust all the possibilities. There is, in fact, a third strategy: one can reduce both agency and structure to some intermediate level, asserting, for example, that both are mutually constituted in practice, then making social practices the ultimate reality. This seems to be the position taken by some contemporary sociologists such as Anthony Giddens (1986) (and his theory of structuration) as well as Pierre Bourdieu (1999) (and his theory of the habitus). We may refer to this third possibility as the 'meso-reductionist' solution to the micro–macro problem.[1]

What I want to sketch here is a new solution to this problem, a solution that avoids each one of these three forms of reductionism using concepts created by the philosopher Gilles Deleuze. The basic strategy will be to abandon the idea that there are only two (or three) levels between which one has to make a choice, and to bridge the level of persons and that of the largest entities (territorial states like empires, kingdoms or nation-states) with many intermediate levels, each operating at its own spatial scale and having its own relative autonomy. Roughly, at the bottom scale we have a population of interacting individual persons; from those interactions (in recurring conversations, for example) a new scale emerges, that of interpersonal networks; from interactions among these networks (and persons) the scale of institutional organisations emerges; from interactions among organisations (and networks), the scale of urban centres emerges; and from the interactions among cities (and organisations), larger territorial entities emerge. This way of characterising a multi-scaled social reality needs many qualifications, but for the time being it can serve as a rough guide. The main four features of this simplified scheme I want to call attention to are:

1. That each differently scaled individual entity (individual persons, individual organisations, individual cities and so on) is made out of entities at the immediate lower scale, that is, that the relations among scales is one of *parts to whole*.
2. That at any level of scale were are dealing with populations of interacting entities (populations of persons, of organisations, of cities) and

that it is within these populations, and the processes generated by their interactions, that larger entities emerge as a kind of *statistical result*, or as collective unintended consequences of intentional action.

3.   That once a larger-scale entity emerges it immediately starts acting as a source of limitations and resources for its components. In other words, even though the arrow of causality in this scheme is bottom–up, it also has a top–down aspect: the whole both *constrains and enables* the parts.

4.   And, finally, that at the very top we do not get 'society as a whole', that is, a vague, general entity or category, but simply another concrete, *singular* entity (an individual nation-state, for instance, part of a population of such territorial states).

One immediate consequence of this ontological strategy is that the terms 'micro' and 'macro' cease to have absolute referents ('the individual' and 'society') and become relative to a given spatial scale, so that organisations, for example, are macro if we are considering persons, but micro if we are considering cities. Although Deleuze does not use the terms 'micro' and 'macro' he does refer to levels distinguished by order of magnitude, which he calls 'the molecular' and 'the molar', and the term 'molecular' is clearly not intended to refer only to the world of chemical molecules. Rather, what is molecular at any one scale is that which plays the role of component or part, while the molar is the statistical result of molecular populations at any given level of scale (Deleuze and Guattari 1987: Chapter 3). Moreover, the molar aggregate that results from the molecular interactions does not have a different ontological status than its components. Both are historically produced entities, hence singular or unique individuals, whose only difference being that they operate at different spatial scales. Despite the fact that one could legitimately ascribe to Deleuze this view about the micro and the macro in the human sciences, however, other aspects of his social philosophy confront us with a difficulty. Deleuze remained until the end of his life a committed Marxist and, as I just mentioned, Marxism tends to favour a form of macroreductionism. While in the social ontology I will be sketching there is no such thing as 'society as a whole', it is not clear that Deleuze rejected that notion. So if Deleuze himself did not subscribe to this multi-scale model, in what sense is the social ontology I am presenting 'Deleuzian'? The answer is that each of the singular, individual entities that make up each scale may be considered an *assemblage*, and Deleuze's theory of assemblages is exactly the kind of theory we need to conceptualise correctly each entity without any essentialist presuppositions.

What is an assemblage? The key idea in Deleuze's theory is the *exteriority of relations*. This implies not only that relations are external to their terms, but also that 'a relation may change without the terms changing' (Deleuze and Parnet 2002: 55). In other words, assemblages are not Hegelian totalities in which the parts are mutually constituted and fused into a seamless whole. In an assemblage components have a certain autonomy from the whole they compose, that is, they may be detached from it and plugged into another assemblage. On the other hand, assemblages must be defined not only negatively, by opposing them to organic totalities, but also by their positive characteristics. Deleuze and Guattari characterise assemblages along two dimensions: on one axis or dimension, they distinguish the role which the different components of an assemblage may play, a role which can be either *material or expressive*; on the other axis, they distinguishes processes which stabilise the emergent identity of the assemblage (by sharpening its borders, for example, or homogenising its composition) from those which tend to destabilise this identity, hence opening the assemblage to change. These are processes of *territorialisation and deterritorialisation*, respectively (Deleuze and Guattari 1987: 88).[2] In addition, Deleuze and Guattari make an important distinction among the expressive components, between those which are directly expressive and those which rely on a specialised vehicle for expression, such as human language or the genetic code. In the case of social assemblages, there are many aspects of both experience and behaviour which are directly expressive but which in today's analyses are all lumped together under the label 'symbolic'. In an assemblage approach it is crucial that those expressive components be given their own separate status and that linguistic components be considered a separate, specialised assemblage.[3]

In the limited space of this chapter all I can do is give a sketchy description of the material and expressive components of each entity, and of the processes which stabilise or destabilise their identities. The smallest scale comprises a population of individual persons, but the subjectivity of each of these persons must itself be conceived as an assemblage of sub-personal components. From the empiricist philosopher David Hume, Deleuze derives a conception of the subject or person as an entity that emerges out of a heterogeneous collection of sense impressions and of ideas, which are low-intensity replicas of those impressions. These sub-personal components are assembled through the habitual application of certain operators to the ideas. More specifically, a subject crystallises as an assemblage through the habitual grouping of ideas via relations of contiguity, their habitual comparison through relations of resemblance, and the habitual perception of constant conjunction in the case of linear causality which allows one idea (that of the cause) to always evoke another (the effect). Perceived contiguity, causality and resemblance, as relations of exteriority, constitute the three principles of association which transform a mind into a subject (Deleuze 1991: 98–101).

Deleuze never gave a full assemblage analysis of subjectivity, but it is possible to derive one from his work on Hume. The expressive components of the assemblage would comprise both those that are directly expressive (as in sense impressions of varying vividness) and those dependent on the specialised line of expression formed by language (such as beliefs). Material components would include the labour performed to assemble ideas into a whole, as well as the biological machinery of sensory organs needed for the production of impressions. Habit itself would constitute the main process of territorialisation, that is, the process which gives a subject its defining boundaries and maintains these boundaries through time. Habit performs a *synthesis of the present and the past* in view of a possible future (Deleuze 1994: 70–4). This yields a determinate duration for the lived present of the subject, a fusion of immediately past and present moments, and generates a sense of anticipation, so that habitual repetition of an action can be counted on to yield similar results in the future. A process of deterritorialisation, on the other hand, would be any process which takes the subject back to the state it had prior to the creation of fixed associations between ideas, that is, the state in which ideas are connected as in a delirium. Madness, fever, intoxication, sensory deprivation and a variety of other processes can all cause a loss or destabilisation of subjective identity.

To move to the next scale I will first describe the assemblages which lead to the formation of friendship networks (social encounters such as conversations) and then give an assemblage analysis of the networks themselves. The author who has done the most valuable research on conversations is without doubt the sociologist Erving Goffman, who defines the subject matter of this research as

> the class of events which occurs during co-presence and by virtue of co-presence. The ultimate behavioral material are the glances, gestures, positionings, and verbal statements that people continuously feed into the situation, whether intended or not. These are the *external signs of orientation and involvement* – states of mind and body not ordinarily examined with respect to their social organisation. (Goffman 1967: 1)

The emphasis on the external signs exchanged during social encounters makes this research ripe for a treatment in terms of assemblage theory, that is, in terms of emergent wholes in which components are joined by relations of exteriority.

While the most obvious expressive component of this assemblage may be the flow of words itself, there is another one which is not directly linked to language. Every participant in a conversation is also expressing his or her public identity through every facial gesture, dress, choice of subject matter, the deployment of (or failure to deploy) poise and tact and so on. These and other components express in a direct way the image which every participant wants to project to others, that is, they are *claims to a certain public persona*. The expression of these claims must be done carefully: one must choose an image that cannot be easily discredited by others. Any conversation will then be filled with objective opportunities to express favourable information about oneself, as well as objective risks to unwittingly express unfavourable facts. The material components of the assemblage are more straightforward, consisting both of the physical bodies assembled in space, close enough to hear each other and correctly oriented towards one another, as well as the attention needed to maintain the conversation going and the labour involved in repairing breaches of etiquette or to recover from embarrassment (ibid.: 19). Of course, some technological inventions, such as the telephone, can change the requirement of co-presence, eliminating some of the material components (spatial proximity) but adding others (the technological device itself, as well as the infrastructure needed to link many such devices).

Processes of territorialisation giving a conversation well-defined borders in space and in time are exemplified by behaviour guided by conventions. As assemblages, conversations have a well-defined temporal order, in which ways of initiating and terminating an encounter, as well as turn-taking during the encounter, are normatively enforced by the participants. The spatial boundaries of these units are also clearly defined, because of the physical requirements of co-presence but also because the participants themselves ratify each other as legitimate interactors and exclude nearby persons from intruding into the conversation (ibid.: 34). Embarrassment, damaging as it is to the public personas projected during the encounter, may be viewed as the main destabilising factor. Goffman, in fact, discusses critical points of embarrassment after which regaining composure becomes impossible to achieve and the conversation falls apart (ibid.: 103). But other critical events may take place which may transform a conversation into a heated discussion or an intense argument into a fist fight. These should also be considered deterritorialising factors, as should technological inventions which allow the conversation to take place at a distance, that is, blurring its spatial boundaries.

When many conversations among the same groups of participants, or among different but overlapping groups, have taken place a new social entity may emerge: an interpersonal network. To analyse this larger assemblage we can use the resources offered by network theory, the only part of theoretical sociology which has been successfully formalised. In the theory of networks the recurring patterns of links between nodes are often more important than the defining properties of the nodes themselves, a fact that orients the theory towards relations of exteriority. The links in a network may be characterised in a variety of ways: by their presence or absence (the absences indicating the borders separating one network from another, or defining a clique within a given network); by their strength, that is, by the frequency of interaction among the persons occupying the nodes, as well as by the emotional content of the relation; and by their reciprocity, that is, by the mutuality of obligations entailed by the link. One of the most important properties of a network is its *density*, a measure of the degree of connectivity among its indirect links (Scott 2000: 70–3). Roughly, if the friends of my friends (that is, my indirect links) know the friends of your friends, and they know the friends of everybody else's friends in a given community, the network is said to have a high density. A dense network is, among other things, capable of acting as an enforcement mechanism for local norms because its high degree of connectivity implies word of mouth travels fast through its links. In other words, information about transgressions of a norm (unfulfilled promises, unpaid debts, unreciprocated favours) becomes known to all nodes rapidly, so that the network becomes capable not only of storing local reputations but also (via ostracism and other penalties) of deterring cheaters.

The links in these assemblages must be constantly maintained and the labour involved constitutes one of the material components. This labour goes beyond the task of staying in touch with others via frequent routine conversations. It may also involve listening to problems and giving advice in difficult situations as well as giving a variety of forms of physical help, such as taking care of other people's children. In many communities there exists a division of labour when it comes to the maintenance of relations, with women performing a disproportionate amount of it, particularly those who, by obligation or choice, are involved in full-time domestic activities (Crow 2002: 52–3). The main expressive component is exemplified by the variety of expressions of *solidarity and trust* which emerge from, and then shape, interaction. These range from routine acts, such as having dinner together or going to church, to the sharing of adversity, or the displayed willingness to make sacrifices for the community (ibid.: 119–20). Expressions of solidarity may, of course, involve language, but in this case (as in many others) actions speak louder than words.

As in the case of conversations, territorialisation in interpersonal networks is closely related to physical proximity. Much as conversations, in the absence of technology, involve face-to-face interaction, communities structured by dense networks have historically tended to inhabit the same small town, or the same suburb or neighbourhood in a large city. These bounded geographical areas are literally a community's territory and they may be marked, and distinguished from others, by special expressive signs. Another important territorialising process in these assemblages is the presence of *conflict* with members of other interpersonal networks. Conflict tends to sharpen boundaries between insiders and outsiders, between 'us' and 'them', increasing the degree to which a community polices its borders (that is, the degree to which it controls its members' behaviour and promotes internal homogeneity) and the degree to which it represents outsiders as holding an inferior set of values. Thus, while solidarity viewed in the abstract may always seem like a desirable property, it may also have undesirable effects in terms of social exclusion, as well as in the way it constrains its members' autonomy and their scope to be different (ibid.: 128–9).

Deterritorialising processes in these assemblages include any factor which decreases density, promotes geographical dispersion, or eliminates some of the rituals which, like churchgoing, are key to the maintenance of traditional solidarity. Social mobility and secularisation are among these processes. The former weakens links by making people less interdependent, by increasing geographical mobility, and by promoting a greater acceptance of difference through less local and more cosmopolitan attitudes. For the same reason, the resulting networks require their members to be more active in the maintenance of links and to invent new forms of participation given that connections will tend to be wider and weaker and that ready-made rituals for the expression of solidarity may not be available (Scott 2000: 12). The same kind of resourcefulness in the means to maintain linkages may be needed in technologically mediated, deterritorialised interpersonal networks. In the early 'virtual communities' that emerged in the internet (such as the Well), for example, the members were aware of the loss which a lack of co-presence involved and special meetings or parties were regularly scheduled to compensate for this (Rheingold 1994).

While in a friendship network a particular node may become dominant by being more highly connected, directly and indirectly, to other nodes, this centrality or popularity seldom gives the person occupying that position the capacity to issue commands to those located in less centrally located nodes. This capacity implies the existence of an authority structure, and this, in turn, means that we are dealing with a different assemblage: an institutional organisation. Organisations come in a wide range of scales, with nuclear families at the low end and government bureaucracies and commercial, industrial or financial corporations at the other end. This wide range makes it hard to conceive of the relations between networks and organisations as one of parts to whole, since individual families are often the components of a community network. On the other hand, big organisations do comprise a large number of persons as well as the friendship and occupational networks that form within the organisation. A modern hierarchical organisation may be studied as an assemblage given that the relations between its components are relations of exteriority, that is, what holds the whole together are relatively impermanent contractual relations through which some persons transfer rights of control over a subset of their actions to other persons. This voluntary submission breaks the symmetry of the relations among persons in an interpersonal network where a high degree of reciprocity is common (Coleman 2000: 66). For this reason, the most important property of an organisation is the *legitimacy* of its authority structure.

The sociologist Max Weber, who can be considered the founder of organisation theory, distinguished three different sources of legitimacy: traditional, charismatic and rational-legal. Strictly speaking, contractual relations exist only in the latter type, exemplified by a bureaucracy (governmental or economic) in which a complete separation of role or office from the person occupying that role or office has been achieved. The resources under the command of an incumbent, for example, must be connected to the role itself not to the person who happens to occupy it. In addition, the definition of rights and obligations associated with a role must be specified in writing and must have a technical basis. When these requirements are met, obedience is owed to the impersonal order itself, that is, legitimacy rests on a belief of both the legality and technical competence of claims to authority (Weber 1964: 328ff.). But the existence of such a sharp separation between role and incumbent is a contingent historical fact, one which took centuries to be achieved in the west. So other forms of legitimacy co-existed with this one in the past and continue to co-exist with it today. In traditional authority structures, obedience is owed to the person occupying a role by virtue of sheer past precedent, that is, justified in terms of inherited rules and ceremonies which are assumed to have always existed and to have a sacred status (ibid.: 348). Finally, in the charismatic type of authority, obedience is owed to a leader but in terms of his or her own personal characteristics without either abstract legality or sacred precedent.

Regardless of the form of authority, a variety of *expressions of legitimacy* form a crucial component of these assemblages. In the rational-legal and traditional types, these expressive components are tightly linked to language, whether in the form of sacred texts or oral histories about origins, which must be constantly interpreted and reinterpreted by the incumbents of certain roles (such as priests), or the written constitution which gives a bureaucracy its legal rationale and which, in the case of conflict of interests, must also be interpreted by specialised functionaries, such as judges. In the charismatic form of authority, language plays a secondary role and the expressivity of certain actions, in which the leader displays his or her courage or wisdom, is what matters. But behavioural expression is important in all three forms in a different way: automatic obedience to commands on a day-to-day basis constitutes an expression of legitimacy. For the same reason any act of disobedience, particularly when it goes unpunished, will threaten this expression and may damage the morale of those who obey. Hence, the expressive role of some forms of punishment designed to make an example of transgressors.

Punishment, on the other hand, also has a physical aspect, and this points to the material components of the assemblage, related not so much to practices of legitimisation as to *practices of enforcement*. In the bureaucracies that developed in seventeenth- and eighteenth-century Europe, as Michel Foucault has carefully documented, these practices went beyond mere punishment and involved three components: a specific use of space, in which dangerous groupings were broken up and individual persons were assigned a relatively fixed place; a much more regular form of inspection and monitoring of activity than was customary before, a practice that shaped and was shaped by the analytical use of space; and finally, a constant use of logistical writing, like the careful keeping of medical or school performance records, but also inventories of all organisational resources, to store permanently the product of monitoring practices. In short, *spatial partitioning, ceaseless inspection and continuous registration* are the material components of rational-legal organisations, the components that go beyond the problematic of legitimacy (Foucault 1979: 195–6).

As with interpersonal networks, territoriality in the case of organisations has a strong spatial aspect. On the one hand, most organisations possess physical premises in which to carry out their activities. In the case of rational-legal authority (bureaucratic office buildings, but also hospitals, schools, prisons, factories) the architecture of the building itself is what enables the spatial partitioning and monitoring of activity. On the

other hand, and regardless of the form of authority, all hierarchical organisations possess a spatial territory defined by the extent of their *jurisdiction*. This territory is defined both formally, by the legitimate jurisdictional
area, as well as materially, by the area in which authority can actually be
enforced. But just as in networks, processes of territorialisation go beyond
the strictly spatial. A good illustration here are the processes that transform a small sect ruled by a charismatic leader into one of the other two
forms of authority. Weber argues that a sect will always be in danger of
being destabilised by a *crisis of succession*. Given that personal qualities
are so important in this form of authority, finding a successor after the
death of a leader may be problematic. The solution is to *routinise* the succession process, either by making charisma hereditary (causing the organisation to become traditional) or by writing technical qualifications which
a leader must meet (thus, becoming rational-legal) (Weber 1964: 363).

Thus, routinisation of the process of succession (as well as of everyday
activities) is an important territorialising factor, that is, a factor stabilising the identity of an organisation. Innovation, on the other hand,
whether organisational or technological, can destabilise this identity and
open the assemblage to other possibilities. Technological innovations (in
both transportation and communication) have deterritorialising effects
on organisations similar to those in face-to-face interaction, that is, they
allow organisations to break from the limitations of spatial location.
Weber argues, for example, that the rational-legal form emerged in part
thanks to the precision with which the dispersed activities of many
branches of an organisation could be coordinated via the railroads and
the telegraph (ibid.: 339). And a similar point could be made about the
transformation which large commercial or industrial corporations
underwent in the nineteenth century, as they became nationwide corporations, as well as in the twentieth when they became international.

Individual organisations may form larger social entities, such as sup-
plier and distribution networks, or hierarchies of governmental agencies
operating within smaller or larger jurisdictions depending on their rank.
The limits of this chapter prevent me from tackling these larger entities
but, as I attempt to show elsewhere, they can also be subjected to an
assemblage treatment (DeLanda, forthcoming). On the other hand, it is
important to briefly consider here social entities such as cities or nation-
states. Neither urban centres nor territorial states should be confused
with the organisations that make up their government, even if the jurisdictional boundaries of the latter coincide with the geographical boundaries of the former. Cities and nation-states must be viewed as physical
locales in which a variety of differently scaled social actors (from

individual persons to organisational hierarchies) carry on their day-to-day activities. A city, for example, possesses not only a physical infrastructure and a given geographical setting, but it also houses a diverse population of persons; a population of interpersonal networks, some dense and well localised, others dispersed and even shared with other cities; a population of organisations of different sizes and functions, some of which make up larger entities such as industries or sectors. In short, a city assembles the activities of these populations in a concrete physical locale. This happens similarly for territorial states, from empires and kingdoms to nation-states.

Cities possess a variety of material and expressive components. On the material side, we must list for each neighbourhood the different buildings in which the daily activities and rituals of the residents are performed and staged (the pub and the church, the shops and the local square) as well as the streets connecting these places. In the nineteenth century new material components were added, water and sewage pipes, conduits for the gas that powered early street lighting, and later on electricity cables and telephone wires. Some of these neighbourhood components simply add up to a larger whole but city-wide systems of mechanical transportation and communication can form very complex networks with properties of their own, some of which affect the material form of an urban centre and its surroundings. A good example is locomotives (and their rail networks) which possess such a large mass that they are hard to stop and accelerate again, determining an interval of two or three miles between stops. This, in turn, can influence the spatial distribution of the suburbs which grow around train stations, giving them their characteristic bead-like shape (Vance 1990: 373).

On the expressive side, a good example is a city's skyline, that is, the silhouette cut against the sky by the mass of its buildings and the decorated tops of its churches and public buildings. For centuries these skylines were the first image visitors saw as they approached a city, a recognisable expression of a town's identity, an effect lost later on as suburbs and industrial hinterlands blurred city boundaries. In some cases, the physical skyline of a town is simply a sum of its parts but the rhythmic repetition of architectural motifs – minarets, domes and spires, belfries and steeples – and the counterpoint these motifs create with the surrounding landscape, may produce emergent expressive effects.[4] In the twentieth century skyscrapers and other signature buildings were added to the skyline as a means to make it unique and instantly recognisable, a clear sign that the expressivity of skylines had become the object of deliberate planning.

A variety of territorialising and deterritorialising processes may affect the state of a city's boundaries, making them either more permeable or more rigid, affecting the sense of geographical identity of its inhabitants. Two extreme forms of these boundaries stand out in western history. In ancient Greek towns a large part of the population lived in their rural homes during the summer months. This double residence and the lack of clearly defined city boundaries affected their sense of identity, as shown by the fact that a town's residents congregated into neighbourhoods by their rural place of origin, that is, they maintained their original geographical loyalties (ibid.: 56). European medieval towns, on the other hand, were surrounded by stone walls, giving not only a definite spatial boundary to a town government's jurisdiction but also a very clear sense of geographical identity to its inhabitants. As the historian Fernand Braudel puts it, these rigidly bounded cities 'were the West's first focus of patriotism – and the patriotism they inspired was long to be more coherent and much more conscious than the territorial kind, which emerged only slowly in the first states' (Braudel 1992: 512). The development of suburbs and industrial hinterlands, starting in the nineteenth century, blurred the boundaries of urban centres. For a while cities managed to hang on to their old identities by retaining their centre (which became home for train stations and, later on, large department stores) but the further extension of suburbs after the Second World War and the differentiation of their land uses (retail, wholesale, manufacturing, office space) re-created the complex combinations that used to characterise the old city's central business district. This process, in effect, created brand-new centres in the suburban band further deterritorialising the identity of cities (Vance 1990: 502–4).

But centuries before residential suburbs replaced city walls another process was militating against the strong identity of urban centres: a loss of autonomy relative to the emerging territorial states. Once cities were absorbed, mostly through military force, the local patriotism of their citizens was largely diminished. Indeed, strong urban identities were obstacles to the creation of nationwide loyalties. For this reason, the first European territorial states (France, England, Spain) were born in those areas which had remained poorly urbanised as Europe emerged from the shadow of the collapse of the Roman Empire. The regions that witnessed an intense urbanisation between the years 1000 and 1300 (northern Italy, northern Germany, Flanders and the Netherlands) delayed the formation of larger entities for centuries. But between the year 1494, when a French army invaded the Italian city-states for the first time, and 1648, the end of the Thirty Years War fought mostly in German territory, most autonomous cities were brought under control. Indeed, the peace treaty that ended that long war, the treaty of Westphalia, is considered the event that gave birth to international law, that is, the legal system in which territorial states were explicitly recognised as actors (Barker 2000: 5–8). Despite the fact that cities resisted being incorporated into larger assemblages they eventually became component parts of them.

As assemblages, territorial states possess a variety of material components. These range from the natural resources contained within their frontiers (mineral deposits like coal, oil, precious metals, agricultural land of varying fertility) to their human populations (a potential source of taxpayers and of army and navy recruits). The frontiers (and natural boundaries) defining these social entities play a material role in relation to other such large entities. That is, each kingdom, empire or nation-state has a given geostrategic position relative to other territorial entities with which it shares frontiers, as well as material advantages deriving from some natural boundaries such as coastlines (which may or may not give it access to important sea routes). After the treaty of Westphalia was signed, future wars tended to involve several national actors. This implies that, as the historian Paul Kennedy has argued, geography affected the fate of a nation not merely through

> such elements as a country's climate, raw materials, fertility of agriculture, and access to trade routes – important though they all were to its overall prosperity – but rather [via] the critical issue of strategical *location* during these multilateral wars. Was a particular nation able to concentrate its energies upon one front, or did it have to fight on several? Did it share common borders with weak states, or powerful ones? Was it chiefly a land power, a sea power, or a hybrid, and what advantages and disadvantages did that bring? Could it easily pull out of a great war in Central Europe if it wished to? Could it secure additional resources from overseas? (Kennedy 1987: 86)

There is also a wide range of expressive components of these larger assemblages, from the natural expressivity of their landscapes to the ways in which they express their military might and political sovereignty. The hierarchies of government organisations, operating at national, provincial and local scales, played a key role in determining how nationalist allegiances would be expressed in nation-states through flags and anthems, parades and celebrations. Cities also played an important expressive role, the best example of which is the style of urban design that became fashionable in Europe from the seventeenth century on. This style, referred to as the 'Grand Manner', transformed the new national capitals into Baroque displays of the power of their centralised governments: wide avenues were built and lined with trees; sweeping vistas were created, framed by long rows of uniform façades and punctuated by visual markers, such as obelisks, triumphal arches, or statues; and all the different design elements, including the existing or modified topography, were joined in ambitious, overall geometric patterns (Kostoff 1991: 211–15).

National capitals also played a territorialising role, homogenising and exporting to the provinces a variety of cultural materials from a standard language and currency, to legal codes, and medical and educational systems. Territorialisation also had a directly spatial manifestation: the controllability of the movement of immigrants, goods, money and, more importantly, foreign troops, across a nation's borders. While the peace treaty of Westphalia gave frontiers a legitimate legal status, the decades that followed its signing witnessed the most intense effort to rigidify these legal borders through the systematic construction of fortress towns, perimeter walls and citadels. In the hands of the brilliant military engineer Sebastian Le Prestre de Vauban, for example, France's borders became nearly impregnable, maintaining their defensive value until the French revolution. Vauban built double rows of fortresses in the northern and south-eastern frontiers, so systematically related to each other that one 'would be within earshot of French fortress guns all the way from the Swiss border to the Channel' (Duffy 1985: 87).

The main deterritorialising processes were those that affected the integrity of these borders. These could be spatial processes such as the secession of a province, or the loss of a piece of territory to another country. But they could also be border-defying economic processes. As the frontiers of territorial states were becoming solidified after the Thirty Years War, some maritime cities that had resisted integration were creating commercial and financial networks that were truly international. Such a city was Amsterdam, the seventeenth-century core of what is today called a *world-economy*: a large geographical area displaying a high degree of economic coherence and an international division of labour (Braudel 1992: 21). A world-economy, in fact, has existed in the west since the fourteenth century, with Venice as its core, but when it acquired global proportions in the seventeenth it became a powerful deterritorialising process for nation-states, governing economic flows that, to this day, easily cross political frontiers.

Having reached the largest dimensions that social assemblages can take (or have historically taken, since there is no a priori reason why there could not be larger ones) we have finished bridging the micro and macro scales with entities with a definite identity and yet not defined by an essence but by a process of emergence. There is no implication that the list of entities presented here is an exhaustive one. This ontology is capable of being expanded as long as any additions are also defined in a non-essentialist way and as long as whatever novel entities are introduced maintain relations of exteriority with those already included. While the solution to the micro–macro problem presented here may be incomplete, the problem itself has been posed in a novel way which escapes any of the different forms of reductionism mentioned at the outset. Ontologically speaking, framing the right question may be as important as answering it.

References

Archer, M. (1995), *Realist Social Theory: The Morphogenetic Approach*, Cambridge: Cambridge University Press.

Barker, J. C. (2000), *International Law and International Relations*, London: Continuum.

Berger, P. L. and Luckmann, T. (1967), *The Social Construction of Reality*, New York: Anchor Books.

Bourdieu, P. (1999), *The Logic of Practice*, trans. R. Nice, Cambridge: Polity Press.

Braudel, F. (1992), *The Structures of Everyday Life*, Berkeley: University of California Press.

Coleman, J. S. (2000), *Foundations of Social Theory*, Cambridge: Belknap Press.

Crow, G. (2002), *Social Solidarities*, Buckingham: Open University Press.

DeLanda, M. (forthcoming), *Assemblage Theory and Social Complexity*.

Deleuze, G. (1991), *Empiricism and Subjectivity*, trans. C. Boundas, New York: Columbia Univerity Press.

Deleuze, G. (1994), *Difference and Repetition*, trans. P. Patton, New York: Columbia University Press.

Deleuze, G. and Guattari, F. (1987), *A Thousand Plateaus: Capitalism and Schizophrenia*, trans. B. Massumi, Minneapolis: University of Minnesota Press.

Deleuze, G. and Parnet, C. (2002), *Dialogues II*, trans. H. Tomlinson and B. Habberjam, New York: Columbia University Press.

Duffy, C. (1985), *The Fortress in the Age of Vauban and Frederick the Great*, London: Routledge and Kegan.

Foucault, M. (1979), *Discipline and Punish: The Birth of the Prison*, New York: Vintage Books.

Garfinkel, H. (2002), *Studies in Ethnomethodology*, Cambridge: Polity Press.

Giddens, A. (1986), *The Constitution of Society*, Berkeley: University of California Press.

Goffman, E. (1967), *Interaction Ritual: Essays on Face-to-Face Behavior*, New York: Pantheon Books.

Kennedy, P. (1987), *The Rise and Fall of the Great Powers: Economic Change and Military Conflict from 1500 to 2000*, New York: Random House.

Kostoff, S. (1991), *The City Shaped: Urban Patterns and Meanings throughout History*, London: Bulfinch Press.

Rheingold, H. (1994), *The Virtual Community: Homesteading on the Electronic Frontier*, New York: Harper Perennial.

Scott, J. (2000), *Social Network Analysis*, London: Sage Publications.

Vance, J. E. (1990), *The Continuing City: Urban Morphology in Western Civilization*, Baltimore: The John Hopkins University Press.

Weber, M. (1964), *The Theory of Social and Economic Organization*, New York: Free Press of Glencoe.

Notes

1. Archer does a similar critique of sociological theories but speaks of 'conflation' rather than 'reduction'. My microreductionism, macroreductionism and meso-reductionism are labelled 'downward conflation', 'upward conflation' and 'central conflation' by her, see Archer 1995.

2. Deleuze and Guattari: 'We may draw some conclusions of the nature of Assemblages from this. On a first, horizontal axis, an assemblage comprises two segments, one of content, the other of expression. On the one hand it is a *machinic assemblage* of bodies, of actions and passions, and intermingling of bodies reacting to one another; on the other hand, it is a *collective assemblage of enunciation*, of acts and statements, of incorporeal transformations attributed to bodies. Then, on a vertical axis, the assemblage has both *territorial sides*, or reterritorialized sides, which stabilize it, and *cutting edges of deterritorialization*, which carry it away' (Deleuze and Guattari 1987: 88).

3. On the specialisation of language and DNA see Deleuze and Guattari: 1987: 59 and 62.

4. On skylines see Kostoff 1991. Deleuze and Guattari view rhythmically repeated motifs and the counterpoints they create with the external milieu as the two ways in which expressive components self-organise in territorial assemblages, including animal assemblages, transforming what was mere signature into a style. See Deleuze and Guattari 1987: 317.

Notes on contributors

Niels Albertsen

Niels Albertsen graduated in political science form Aarhus University. He is Research Professor, Head of Department at Department of Landscape and Urbanism, Aarhus School of Architecture, and Co-director of the Centre for Strategic Urban Research. His main research fields are social theory, urban theory, the sociology and philosophy of art and science, and the sociology of the architectural profession. From 1998 to 2000 he was the president of the Nordic Association for Architectural Research. Among his recent publications are 'Artworks' Networks. Field, System or Mediators?', *Theory, Culture and Society* (2004) and 'Welfare and the City', *Nordic Journal of Architectural Research* (2004, both with Bülent Diken).

Éric Alliez

Éric Alliez is a philosopher and former professor at the Akademie der Bildenden Kuenste (Vienna, 1997–2003). He is presently Senior Research Fellow at Middlesex University. Among his works are: *Les Temps capitaux* (preface by G. Deleuze); *Récits de la conquête du temps* (1991, English trans.: 1997); *La Signature du monde, ou qu'est-ce que la philosophie de Deleuze et Guattari?* (1993, English trans.: 2005); *Gilles Deleuze: une vie philosophique* (1998, editor); *La Pensée-Matisse* (2005, with Jean-Claude Bonne). He is the general editor of the book series *Œuvres de Gabriel Tarde*, and is currently a member of the editorial board of the journal *Multitudes*.

Thomas Bay

One query in particular possesses me: what is economy? Impossible question. Lifetime project. A question carrying failure within itself, as a creative prerequisite and constant residue. What more could a joyful writer possibly ask for? Only problems inseparable from the vitalities of life do I find worthy of attention: problematising the ways in which economy – whether as a discourse, an image of thought or a practice – arrests our feelings, actions and thoughts, economises our possibilities of life, pre-fixes every real encounter with this world as it is – preventing us thereby from creating events, unpredictable becomings setting our bodies and minds in motion. This, I believe, is where I have my capacities. Thomas Bay is Lecturer at Stockholm University School of Business.

Ian Buchanan

Ian Buchanan is Professor of Critical and Cultural Theory at Cardiff University. He is the author of *Deleuzism* (2000).

Manuel DeLanda

Manuel DeLanda is the author of four philosophy books, *War in the Age of Intelligent Machines* (1991), *A Thousand Years of Nonlinear History* (1997), *Intensive Science and Virtual Philosophy* (2002) and *Assemblage Theory and Social Complexity* (forthcoming), as well as of many philosophical essays published in various journals and collections. He teaches two seminars at Columbia University, School of Architecture: Philosophy of History: Theories of Self-Organization and Urban Dynamics, and Philosophy of Science: Thinking about Structures and Materials.

Bülent Diken

Bülent Diken graduated from and did his Ph.D. at Aarhus School of Architecture, Department of Town Planning. From 1998 to 1999 he held an assistant professorship at Roskilde University, Department of Geography. Since 1999 he has been teaching at Lancaster University, Department of Sociology. His research fields are social theory, poststructuralism, migration and urbanism. His publications include *Strangers, Ambivalence and Social Theory* (1998). Recently, he has co-authored *The Culture of Exception: Sociology facing the Camp* (2005).

Martin Fuglsang

Martin Fuglsang is Associate Professor in Organisational Philosophy at the Department of Management, Politics and Philosophy, Copenhagen

Business School. He has published *At være på grænsen* [Being on the Border] (1998); *Det nøgne liv – en poetik for det sociale* [The Naked Life – A Poetic for the Social] (2000, with Alexander Carnera). He follows the same problematics as discussed in *Deleuze and the Social* in a series of articles all entitled 'Beyond . . .'. He is at present engaged in the research project 'A social-philosophical investigation of the pathologies of contemporary work-life', focusing on the biopolitical production of subjectivity and its self-relation, especially expressed in the assemblage of modern technologies of management.

Eugene W. Holland

Eugene W. Holland is best known for his work on the writings of Deleuze and Guattari. He is the author of *Baudelaire and Schizoanalysis: The Socio-Poetics of Modernism* (1993) and *Deleuze and Guattari's 'Anti-Oedipus': Introduction to Schizoanalysis* (1999), and has published widely on Deleuze and Guattari and French poststructuralism in anthologies and journals such as *Angelaki*, *South Atlantic Quarterly* and *Substance*. He is currently completing a book of political philosophy on the concept of nomad citizenship, and is also working on a book on capitalist perversions. Dr Holland is Professor of French and Comparative Studies at the Ohio State University.

Martin Kornberger

Martin was born in a small little town in the west of Austria; after he moved a bit further east to Vienna to study philosophy, humanities and management, he decided to move even further east and came to Sydney and has practically stayed there ever since. Martin has had extensive experience of being managed, having worked for a rail cargo company, a hospital, a local council, a gas company, and as a social worker. These days, Martin works at the University of Technology in Sydney and on a research project with the University of Innsbruck. In order to conduct periodic reality checks, with two partners he founded a company called PLAY, which helps him to maintain a balance between writing and doing.

Chris Land

Chris Land is a freelance academic and bike mechanic. His research interests include millenarian topics such as subjective apocalypse and cyborganisation (which pretty firmly places his intellectual naissance in the late 1990s). More recently both his research and practice have become orientated towards the problematic of 'community' and he spends much of his time in anarchist communities working towards the overthrow of global capitalism . . . and fixing bikes.

Maurizio Lazzarato

Maurizio Lazzarato is a sociologist and philosopher, living and working in Paris. He is doing research on immaterial work, cognitive capitalism and post-socialist movements. He also writes on cinema, video and new technologies of image production. For the project *IO_dencies/ Lavoro immateriale* at the biennale in Venice he collaborated with the Group Knowbotic Research. Since 1990 he has written, in collaboration with Angela Melitopoulos, a number of texts for various exhibition catalogues. He is one of the founding members of the journal *Multitudes*, and is also a member of its editorial board.

Stephen Linstead

Stephen Linstead is Professor of Critical Management at the University of York, UK. He has edited special issues of *Organization* and *Culture and Organization* (with John Mullarkey) on aspects of the work of Henri Bergson, and *Thinking Organization* (2005, with Alison Linstead) is a collection of applications of philosophical thought to organisation studies. Other relevant publications include *The Aesthetics of Organization* (2000, with Heather Höpfl), *The Language of Organization* (2001, with Robert Westwood), *Organization Theory and Postmodern Thought* (2004), and *Casual Organization Theory* (forthcoming). He co-convenes a Standing Working Group of EGOS and co-edited the journal *Culture and Organization* from 2002 to 2005.

Peter Lohmann

Peter Lohmann is chief consultant in a large Danish company. He is working as an assistant to the board of directors. Among many different work projects he is taking part in all aspects of merger and acquisition. He received a Ph.D. in Business Economics from Copenhagen Business School. With the concept of 'change' as a focal point, his research centres around how an intermezzo of individuals, organisations and politics drives forward the human organising of everyday life.

Paul Patton

Paul Patton is Professor of Philosophy at The University of New South Wales in Sydney, Australia. He is the author of *Deleuze and the Political* (2000), editor of *Between Deleuze and Derrida* (with 2003 Protevi, John), *Deleuze: A Critical Reader* (1996) and translator of Deleuze's *Difference and Repetition* (1994). His current research interests are in political philosophy, especially at the borders of poststructuralist and contemporary liberal political theory. They include issues such as the nature and function of rights, concepts of power and freedom, democracy, sovereignty and justice in both domestic and international contexts.

Carl Rhodes

Carl Rhodes likes to write about organisations. His position as Associate Professor in the University of Technology Sydney's School of Management provides him with some space to do so. This pursuit of pleasure, variously achieved, has resulted in some books and articles.

Bent Meier Sørensen

Bent Meier Sørensen is Associate Professor in Management Philosophy at the Department of Management, Politics and Philosophy at Copenhagen Business School. He has worked with technology, art as critique, war and entrepreneurship, albeit in a 'biopolitical' version, and came out in 2004 with the book *Making Events Work: Or, How to Multiply Your Crisis*. Currently, he is a member of the editorial collective of the journal *ephemera. theory and politics in organization*. Furthermore, Dr Sørensen (the title adding some Strangelove-aura to his very common Scandinavian name) believes in the virtues of Japanese karate and Tango Argentino. And in the writings of St Paul.

Chris Steyaert

Chris Steyaert is Professor of Organisational Psychology at the University of St Gallen. After receiving his doctoral dissertation in psychology from the Katholieke Universiteit Leuven (Belgium), he was connected to the Institute of Organisation and Industrial Sociology, Copenhagen Business School, Denmark, and to the Entrepreneurship and Small Business Research Institute (ESBRI), Stockholm, Sweden. He has published in international journals and books in the area of entrepreneurship and organisational innovation. His research themes include organising creativity, diversity management and difference, language and translation, forms of performing/writing research and the politics of entrepreneurship and human organising.

René ten Bos

René ten Bos is a philosopher who works as a professor for Nijmegen School of Management, Radboud University Nijmegen and as a management teacher for a company called Schouten & Nelissen. He has published extensively about bicycles, football, wonders, bestiality, gestures, melancholy, hygiene, sex, cruelty, mafia, luck, water, rats and stupidity.

Torkild Thanem

Torkild Thanem received his Ph.D. from Warwick Business School, University of Warwick, UK, and now works as a research fellow in the School of Business, Stockholm University. He has been a visiting scholar at the University of Oregon and he is currently a visiting associate at the University of York, UK. Torkild's research interests are organisation theory and critical management studies, philosophy and embodiment, and he is currently undertaking a research project funded by the Swedish Research Council on the organisation and non-organisation of bodily aesthetics in public health and public space. He is also guest editor for a special issue of *Tamara* on 'Deleuze and Organization Theory'.

Jussi Vähämäki

Jussi Vähämäki teaches political philosophy at The University of Jyväskylä. He is currently working on a book entitled 'The Mimetic Tools' and among his recent publications are: *Elämä teoriassa. Tutkimus toimettomasta tiedosta kommunikaatioyhteiskunnassa* [Life in Theory: A Study on the Inoperative Knowledge in the Information Society] (1997); *Yhteisö ja politiikka* [Community and Politics] (1997); *Displacement of Politics* (2000, with Sakari Hänninen); *Kuhnurien kerho. Vanhan työn paheista uuden hyveiksi* [The Drones Club: From the Vices of the Old Work to the Virtues of the New] (2003); *Odotusila* [The Waiting Room] (2005, with Jakke Holvas).

Akseli Virtanen

Akseli Virtanen teaches at the Helsinki School of Economics. His recent works include: *Biopoliittisen talouden kritiikki. Modernin talouden loppu ja mielivallan synty* [A Critique of Biopolitical Economy: The End of Modern Economy and the Birth of Arbitrary Power] 2006; *Uuden työn sanakirja* [A Map to Precarious Life] (forthcoming, with J. Peltokoski and M. Jakonen); *Talous ja yhteiskuntateoria* [Economy and Social Theory], (2005, with Risto Heiskala); *Theory of the Multitude* (editor together with Jussi Vähämäki), special issue of *ephemera. theory and politics in organization* (2004) 4:3.

Index